CURRICULUM
The Teacher's Initiative

John McNeil

University of California at Los Angeles

Merrill,
an imprint of Prentice Hall

Englewood Cliffs, New Jersey   Columbus, Ohio

Library of Congress Cataloging-in-Publication Data

McNeil, John D.
    Curriculum: the teacher's initiative / John McNeil.
      p. cm.
    Includes bibliographical references and index.
    ISBN 0-02-379761-4
    1. Education—Curricula. 2. Curriculum planning. I. Title.
  LB1570.N36   1995
  375'.001—dc20
                                                        94-6194
                                                          CIP

Editor: Debra A. Stollenwerk
Production Editor: Louise N. Sette
Text and Cover Designer: Robert Vega
Production Buyer: Deidra Schwartz
Electronic Text Management: Marilyn Wilson Phelps, Matthew Williams, Jane Lopez,
  Karen L. Bretz

This book was set in Zapf Elliptical 711 by Prentice Hall and was printed and bound by
R.R. Donnelley & Sons Company. The cover was printed by Phoenix Color Corp.

© 1995 by Prentice-Hall, Inc.
A Simon & Schuster Company
Englewood Cliffs, New Jersey 07632

Printed in the United States of America

10 9 8 7 6 5 4 3 2 1

ISBN 0-02-379761-4

Prentice-Hall International (UK) Limited, *London*
Prentice-Hall of Australia Pty. Limited, *Sydney*
Prentice-Hall Canada Inc., *Toronto*
Prentice-Hall Hispanoamericana, S. A., *Mexico*
Prentice-Hall of India Private Limited, *New Delhi*
Prentice-Hall of Japan, Inc., *Tokyo*
Simon & Schuster Asia Pte. Ltd., *Singapore*
Editora Prentice-Hall do Brasil, Ltda., *Rio de Janeiro*

PREFACE

This book is for teachers—beginning, experienced, and teachers of teachers. It is designed to engage readers in answering curriculum questions about:

▼ *Purpose.* What should my curriculum achieve? What content is of most worth? What counts as knowledge? On what grounds? How can I best justify my instructional intents? Who should determine what is learned?

▼ *Method.* How does learning best occur? What is appropriate instruction for particular purposes and given circumstances?

▼ *Organization.* How are ideas best related? Are there optimum sequences for ordering content? Are academic disciplines organized for effective learning or for advancing a special area of study?

Teachers who initiate curriculum answer these questions. The chapters in this book are designed to provide both background knowledge and exemplars to assist teachers in developing definable curriculum.

Part 1 focuses on learners as the most important source of information in deciding what should be taught as well as how learning best occurs. This part features teachers who aim at giving voice to students by putting students at the center of their curriculum.

Part 2 emphasizes the importance of relating curriculum to the present world and actions that are likely to bring about a better world. This part highlights teachers whose curriculums are relevant to improving the quality of life in different social contexts.

Part 3 gives a historical perspective on the subject matter taught in schools. This part is designed to stimulate readers' thinking about their beliefs regarding particular subjects, to identify what is central in a given field, and to recognize how knowledge is socially determined rather than externally fixed. Part 3 shows the many ways teachers have interpreted the academic fields and transformed them to meet changed social needs and influences.

Part 4 addresses questions about the selection and use of instructional materials in the curriculum. The content of Part 4 consists of information for teachers who will perform as autonomous consumers and developers of curriculum materials, adapting those materials to their particular teaching situations and enriching existing materials.

Part 5 provides information for teachers who will design plans for instruction in areas with no or few existing materials.

There are two worlds of curriculum. One is the rhetorical world in which members of commissions, boards of education, heads of government, and others give their answers to what should be taught and how. Curricular reform, policy statements, goals, frameworks, mandates, and other features of school restructuring are associated with this world. The other world is the experiential world in which the teacher and students enact curriculum and pursue their goals, constructing knowledge and meanings in the process. This book does not deal directly with the rhetorical world of curriculum; it focuses on how teachers and students create curriculum as they decide what to learn and how.

This book falls in the genre for texts of possibility. It describes the curriculum work of more than 50 teachers to illustrate what is possible when teachers undertake curricular initiatives in the interest of human betterment. Examples from both present and distant elementary and secondary school teachers and their curriculums are included, not as examples to be copied, but as sources for stimulating fresh thinking about the curriculum initiatives the reader may want to take. Throughout the text there are provisions for readers to act in response to the wide range of practical alternatives for developing curriculum and to the many historical, psychological, and philosophical perspectives introduced.

ACKNOWLEDGMENTS

I would like to express my appreciation to the reviewers of this book: Kenneth E. Cypert, Tarleton State University; Hugh J. Fant, Southeastern Oklahoma State University; Barbara M. Parramore, North Carolina State University; Kay W. Terry, Western Kentucky University; Guy O. Wall, Indiana University Southeast; and Leslie Owen Wilson, University of Wisconsin–Stevens Point.

BRIEF CONTENTS

CONTENTS

PART

Giving Voice to Students

Voice implies the right to have a say in policy. Giving voice to students involves putting students' own efforts to understand at the center of the curriculum.

Developing curriculum that follows from listening and responding to the concerns, ideas, and goals that students have for themselves is one approach in giving voice. Another is found in curriculum whereby students develop the powerful concepts, understandings, and sense of possibilities that will enable them to fulfill their potentials.

The first two chapters of *Curriculum: The Teachers' Initiative* present curriculums that do not separate the learner from content but that do focus on students attempting to understand subject matter. Chapter 1 features curriculum development from a constructivist view of learning, one that holds that the curriculum is not a prior body of knowledge to be transmitted but rather the knowledge and meanings students construct as they form goals and act upon materials and other aspects of the classroom environment, exploring with others a matrix of ideas. Chapter 1 also introduces the context of an ideal activity curriculum, one that links the real-world activities of learners to subject matter that will be functional for them and that may transform their cultural contexts.

Chapter 2 presents alternatives to the question of how curriculum can best harmonize with the psychological needs of students. The curricula featured in this chapter are not naive in assuming that development from within is enough or that engagement necessarily leads to growth. In addition to showing how curriculum can contribute to personal development, Chapter 2 emphasizes the importance of relating the developmental concerns of students to the construction of knowledge in subject matter areas.

CONSTRUCTIVIST AND ACTIVITY CURRICULUMS

This chapter deals with two, related curriculum trends—constructivist and activity curriculums. It introduces the concept of the constructivist approach to curriculum development and illustrates curriculums that follow from this approach. Comparisons are made between traditional and constructivist approaches.

The historical antecedents of constructivist and activity curricula, particularly the work of Pestalozzi and Froebel, are presented along with modern parallels. The chapter draws contrasts between school tasks that do not uncover the goals of students or lead to significant learning, and ideal activities that both relate to students' conceptions of their world and extend student knowledge in fruitful ways.

The chapter concludes with examples of teachers who are aiming at ideal activity curriculums that make and transform the cultural contexts of learners.

CONSTRUCTIVIST CURRICULUM DEVELOPMENT

The constructivist approach to curriculum development is an alternative to preplanning, needed because preplanning often limits students to imitating surface structures of organized knowledge. This orientation has as its focus activities that will encourage students to construct solutions and form knowledge (beliefs) rather than repeat ready-made solutions to problems and verbalize particular constructs without understanding or accepting them.

It is not possible to reduce constructivist curriculum development to a set of rules. Unlike development of traditional curriculum, where the teacher begins with a formal structure or logic of the subject matter, the development of constructivist curriculum begins with whatever students understand about a particular phenomenon or life situation. Nevertheless, implicit in this student-centered curriculum are the familiar curriculum elements of purpose, content, activities, materials, and evaluation.

Purpose

Most teachers of the constructivist persuasion have as a purpose students constructing increasingly abstract concepts and procedures and reorganizing their current beliefs in the interest of resolving student problems and attaining personal and group goals.

Content

Although teachers help structure a learning environment that is likely to promote constructing of meanings and understandings for particular subject matter, moral areas, and social areas, there is no particular understanding to be acquired by students. Subject matter topics are not something to be covered by the teachers and passed on to students but areas of experience and ideas to which students relate their own associations and concepts for these topics.

Activities, Materials, and Methods

No specific activities determine a constructivist environment. However, some qualities are common to constructivist curriculums. One commonality, particularly in math and science classrooms, is the introduction of manipulatives for students to act upon and for constructing ideas. However, only when students have the intent to make sense of their experiences with manipulatives do those manipulatives serve constructivist purposes. For example, young children using blocks to calculate 34 take away 18 might only be routinizing a primitive method of counting; while other children who have been encouraged to devise their own methods for engaging in the activity may extend their initial primitive methods by constructing other mathematical relationships. In brief, it is not the manipulatives themselves that are important, but the students' reflections on their physical and mental actions with the manipulatives.

The introduction of resource materials that might have learning potential and be problematic for students is a second common quality. Materials and tasks are selected on the basis of the students' current knowledge rather than on the basis of their match to a fixed curriculum—text, syllabus, or framework. A constructivist second-grade teacher, for instance, would not introduce tasks involving the subtraction of two-digit numbers if the students have not yet constructed ten as an abstract unit. Materials and tasks are presented with a minimum of teacher talk, and students work on them in pairs. The pairs attempt to reach consensus on their solutions, and subsequently the entire class discusses the different methods and answers created by students. The class has the obligation to try to understand all student explanations. Assignment of ill-defined problems that are open to a variety of different solutions (depending on the assumptions made) is sometimes given to help students explore how concepts are constructed and to weaken their authoritarian view of knowledge; for example, "In a certain population, two thirds of men are married, but only three fifths of all the women are married. What fraction of the population is single?" (Whimbey, 1984).

Most problems in the constructivist curriculum arise from students as they attempt to achieve their goals while interacting with others. Conflicting points of view are especially useful in helping individual students reconstruct and verbalize their ideas and solutions.

Teacher Strategies that Foster Active Learning

Basic to many constructivist curriculum in mathematics, social science, science, reading, and writing are teaching strategies that foster active learning. These strategies follow three phases: a preparation for learning phase, a presentation phase, an application and integrative phase. In the *preparation phase*, students think about the phenomena or topic to be studied. Often this entails giving their present knowledge of and prior experience with the topic and sensing what they do not know about a situation but would like to find out. Observation of discrepant events, provocative questions, the making of predictions, and dialogue and debate about the phenomenon are used. Contrary concepts and student preconceptions become the starting point for inquiry.

In the *presentation phase*, students attempt to confirm their predictions and to clarify their views. The sources of new information—texts, films, interview, computer programs, as well as experiments and manipulatives—are introduced, and students select from these sources' relevant ideas, comparing the new ideas with previously held concepts. Students and teacher process the information and attempt to understand its meaning.

The *application and integrative phase* is characterized by judging whether the goal of learning has been met and, if not, what further activity is appropriate. The new information is summarized and critiqued, a problem is solved, and old ideas are contrasted with the new. The newly generated knowledge is applied in other situations, especially to tasks in everyday contexts and to other tasks in the same subject field.

Active learning in the science curriculum usually begins with observation, such as where to stand in order to see someone else in a mirror, what a pencil looks like in a glass of water, or which direction light is traveling when one "looks out" of a window. Dialogue and debate among students helps them become aware of other ways than their own to think about the observed objects and events. Although students can discover on their own many interesting things about plants, light, and other phenomena, constructivist teachers introduce scientific concepts related to the problem at hand, not as facts or definitions to be learned but as alternative conceptions for the students to evaluate.

Active learning in the reading of literature means encouraging students to connect their prior experiences to those portrayed in the text while keeping themselves open to new social, cultural, and economic perspectives. Although learning to interpret text may still call for learning about the rhetorical strategies for reading different genres and understanding the symbolic meaning of acts, author's intentions, and perspectives, the newer practice of giving students opportunities to write their own opinions rather than repeat correct answers about a text increases the level of interpretation. Participation with others in judging the sufficiency, relevancy, validity, and insightfulness of student interpretations helps students assess their own performance and create meaning from the text.

Application of the active learning strategies in the teaching in other content areas may include the same three phases. Most important is that at the closing of lessons, students share what they have learned and how they might use their knowledge. They may say why they find something difficult as well as tell what helps them most with their problems.

ILLUSTRATIONS OF CONSTRUCTIVIST CURRICULUMS

Constructivist Early Childhood Curriculum

Rheta DeVries has described how curriculum has been derived from constructivist goals (DeVries and Kohlberg, 1990). In the interest of helping children construct knowledge of objects that move but do not change, and knowledge of objects that do change, one preschool teacher planned a blowing activity whereby four- and five-year-olds could act on objects to produce a desired effect. She reasoned that merely acting on objects and seeing how they react would not have the same appeal as an activity where children blew on things for a clear purpose. This teacher selected a variety of objects on the basis of their potential for reacting in different ways—straws, ping-pong balls, cotton balls, spoons of various sizes, rubber bands, plastic tops, paper cups, scissors, soap, wadded paper towels, and so on.

The teacher planned to give a straw to each child and to suggest that the children find the object that would get across a water table the fastest. She also introduced activities such as games in which two children on opposite sides of the water table blew on a ping-pong ball, each trying to make it touch the other side. Such activities are flexible enough for the teacher to respond to children's inventions and questions and to interact in ways that will encourage experimentation.

Children were invited "to see what you can do with these things," and "Can you ____?" Each child had his or her own materials and engaged first in parallel and later in cooperative play. Figuring out what the child was thinking was the greatest challenge for the teacher. Questions such as these were helpful in revealing children's thoughts about ways to act on objects:

▼ Predicting: "What do you think will happen if you do X?"

▼ Determining cause and effect: "How did you do X?"

▼ Explaining: "Why does X happen?"

Although new ideas are introduced when children's play becomes repetitive, a child should not have his or her train of thought interrupted. After an activity, it is desirable for children to reflect on what they did, what they found out, and how they produced a desired effect—"What happened when you blew through two straws instead of one?" "What did you have to do to make the straw go straight?" "What happened when the string of a pendulum broke?" "What do you want to try next time?"

Unlike traditional primary science activities, those of the constructivist are not aimed at having children learn to recognize and define some phenomena or object; instead, the objective is for children to pursue the question(s) they come up with, to stimulate various ideas, to encourage decentering of ideas through the exchange of ideas, and to make and check out predictions.

Reflections in Elementary Math

Constructivist teachers hold that reflective abstractions play a critically important role in the mathematics learning of elementary school students and that just completing tasks is insufficient. In mathematics, reflection is characterized by distancing oneself from the actions of doing mathematics. In the process of reflecting, students think about what they are doing and become aware of their methods and options and often modify their actions. Grayson Wheatley (1992) provides an example of an instructional setting with math curriculum at Florida State Lab School that fosters reflection. A complex geometric figure is briefly shown to students, and they are asked to draw what they see (see Figure 1–1). Then they are asked, "What did you see and how did you draw it?" In this way, the students' mathematics is acknowledged in contrast to traditional questions that demand a single correct answer: "Did your drawing match what I showed you?" "Did you get it right?"

Students are encouraged to give meaning to their experience in ways that make sense to them. A variety of interpretations are presented by the students. When some fourth-grade students were shown the shape in Figure 1–1, they reported seeing several things:

▼   A cube

▼   A hexagon with a *y* in it

▼   Two diamonds and two triangles

FIGURE 1–1
Quick-draw shape

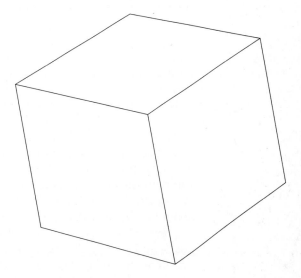

As students presented alternative interpretations, the element of surprise at another's conclusion led to reflection, and students reported still other ways of seeing the figure. When the teacher responded nonjudgmentally, the students were free to construct their own mathematics.

In addition to selecting tasks, the constructivist teacher negotiates the social norms that encourage students to talk mathematics and learn to listen. Students assume the obligation of trying to make sense of the explanations of others. Those presenting a solution or explanation must present a self-generated solution, and explanations can be challenged. The purpose of classroom discussion and dialogue is not to be right but to make sense, and questions raised by members of the class should be sincere and for the purpose of giving meaning to the explanation (Wheatley, 1992).

CONSTRUCTIVIST CURRICULUM WITH ADOLESCENTS

Increasingly, teachers of English in the middle schools are designing interpretive curriculum that focus on the interaction between adolescent personal concerns, the social concerns of the world at large, and the language arts. One seventh-grade teacher began her experience with constructivist curriculum using literature-based materials thought to address the personal and social needs of students (Smith and Johnson, 1993). The teacher surveyed her class a month before the thematic unit was to start, asking "What is your greatest concern for the world?" and "What is your greatest fear?" Responses ranged from "failing at school," "dying of AIDS," to "going to Hell," with the majority revolving around their own death. Global concerns included, "war," "pollution," and "the environment." The overlap of personal and social concerns about death suggested the tentative theme.

In her preplanning, the teacher decided she would negotiate the parameters of the study, allowing students to make choices about what to read and assume responsibility for their learning within a structure that included journal writing, whole-class discussions stemming from journal entries, and small literature study groups. At the center of the studies, however, was a desire to hear student voices. The selected literature presented the topics of death in a multitude of settings and from various perspectives. Novels such as *Sheila's Dying*, *Park's Quest*, and *Z for Zachariah* were introduced.

Enactment of the plan began with students constructing the topical framework for the unit—stating what they were going to study, how they would approach it, what materials they would use, and what their responsibilities would be. Students gave their ideas of what death and environmental problems meant to them. They raised questions about the topic. They wanted to know about spirits and who believed in ghosts; they wanted to know what happened to us as we die and after we die. The conversation gradually shifted to talking about the death of the planet.

Figure 1–2 shows the semantic map created by students for their study of death and dying. The students chose the books that different groups would read and decided on group projects, individual papers, or persuasive pieces. They also accepted responsibility for studying a specific aspect of the topic—the death of a place, crime, euthanasia, rain forests, endangered animals, AIDS, and the like.

Journal writing began in response to the prompt, "What do you expect to learn in the next six weeks?" During group sessions, students made decisions about how to work together, kinds of activities, problem identification, and solutions. Typically, class members were given tasks that would contribute to a common goal. Individual journal entries often revealed problems in the group activity—particularly those associated with group dynamics. During the last week of the study, groups presented their projects, showing what is possible when students are given responsibility for their own learning. The presentations showed a diversity in designs—original information pamphlets about the ozone and the dangers of its extinction, dramatic skits about hate crimes and their impact on America, persuasive posters for saving the rain forests, a seminar about AIDS and its prevention, and a panorama of types of pollution. The studies allowed students to use their own knowledge in addressing their own questions and concerns. Although discussions were prompted by individual journal writing, they led to group participation in clarifying and understanding why certain problems exist. The selected books served many purposes—as

FIGURE 1–2
Semantic map of students' ideas about death and dying

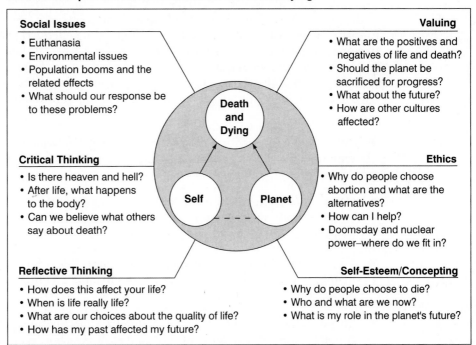

tools for reflection, bases for exploring ideas and feelings, and sources for stimulating intellectual curiosity.

Not all constructivists believe it wise to extend each and every child's constructions. In her Algebra 1 constructivist curriculum, Susan Magidson limited the constructions addressed (Magidson, 1992). She believes that because of the sheer number of students and the fact that some constructions are not fruitful, the teacher must strike a balance by creating situations that encourage student constructions yet limit those selected for full-class discussion. Discussion validates student constructions and allows different levels of construction and understandings within shared core ideas. Her curriculum unit "Functions and Graphs," for instance, had as its centerpiece the computer program *Grapher*, which allowed students to manipulate the parameters in equations and observe the graphical entailments of the manipulations. The curriculum involved two types of activities:

1. Computer labs and other activities where students worked in small groups to explore, extend, and apply ideas.
2. Whole-class discussions where the results of the lab explorations were probed.

In an effort to limit the direction of individual experiments in the interest of some common knowledge about slope, Magidson restricted the computer lab activity to the challenge of finding an equation that produces a line that is part of a starburst (a problem that invokes the ratio of directed line segments) and cautioned students to use equations that begin with the form y = (which deals with slope and not the reciprocal of slopes). Students still invented alternative forms of the equation, which multiplied the task of generalizing about the effect of slope numbers on the resulting lines. Magidson learned that the diversity of mathematical knowledge of students generated a variety of approaches to a problem and that the sharing of small-group discoveries led to both new knowledge and new questions far beyond the realm of the traditional algebra course:

▼ "Why isn't a line with a slope twice as steep?" (Twice the angle of a line with a slope of 2—the student is attempting to reconcile previous knowledge of angles with new knowledge of slope.)

▼ "Does the origin of the Cartesian plane signify the exact middle of the whole plane?" (The student is exploring the ramifications of the standard definition.)

▼ "Where does the name Y-intercept come from?" "Why isn't it the X-intercept instead?" (The student is trying to understand a connection that doesn't appear to make sense.)

▼ "What is the difference between fractions and equations?" "If you have a run and a run of 2/4, can you reduce it so it is easier to find the slope?" (Is the slope just a regular fraction or does it have a different entailment?)

Some students' constructions are variations on a theme—larger numbers produce steeper lines—others address distinct aspects of a slope's behavior; and some combine subjects in different ways.

The need for clarifying and relating fragmented ideas was met through whole-class discussions where ideas were pooled, strengthened, eliminated, and lined to an underlying structure. (In the starburst activity, student ideas were integrated by the concept of slope as a circular continuum from −00 to 00.) The selection of a large structure to which individual constructions can be connected precludes attending to and refining some individual constructions. Also, although the class construction is in the direction of creating public knowledge, individual constructions for the domain remain.

COMPARISON OF TRADITIONAL AND CONSTRUCTIVIST APPROACHES IN CURRICULUM DEVELOPMENT

Traditional approaches to curriculum are based on different views of knowledge and learning than the approaches of constructivists. Traditionalists assume that knowledge results from information coming from outside the learner to the inside through the senses, with what is learned depending on the external stimulus presented by the text and the teacher. In contrast, constructivists believe that knowledge is created through the learner's interaction with a social and physical environment whereby the learner interprets the stimuli in light of his or her previous knowledge (prior experiences) and modifies current ideas that appear inconsistent or inadequate for dealing with new situations.

It follows that, unlike traditional curriculum planners, teachers with a constructivist framework must develop curriculum as it evolves within the classroom. Inasmuch as the teacher must work with the understanding the student is showing at the moment, the classroom environment must be continually recreated in light of both individual student constructions and those of the class as a whole.

A related tenet is that whereas the traditional curriculum is presented in a particular sequence that outlines a common path to prespecified understandings, constructivists expect different pathways to similar understandings and different kinds of understandings from the same subject matter task. In the constructivist's curriculum, more emphasis is given to having students justify what they say and do, so that they will reveal their theory and logic. Also, the great variation among students' understandings is used to enhance the richness of understanding that evolves through classroom negotiation of meanings. Hence, the constructivist teacher seeks to develop a classroom community in which students are helped to communicate their reflections on the meanings of events and ideas, to express feelings, to construct new meanings, and to resolve conflicting points of view as they interact with others in their attempts to construct a consensual domain of knowledge representative of the classroom and a larger community.

FIGURE 1–3
Traditional versus constructivist approaches to curriculum development

Traditional	Constructivist
Outcomes are thought to be attainable and predictable.	Unpredictable outcomes are highly valued.
Predetermined objectives are based on formal structures	The learners' current understandings of a topic are the starting point for curriculum development.
There is an optimum sequence of instruction, a continuum of skills or expected subject matter.	It is recognized that each student will have a different sequence for developing understanding of a topic.
	Allowances are made for different levels of understanding both between students and within the individual.
Specific activities are planned in advance.	The activity belongs to the individual learner. The teacher can only provide an environment that will support through interpersonal processes the learner's activity in pursuit of his/her goals and contribute to further learning.
Curriculum is developed from information *about* the learner.	Curriculum incorporates data *from* the learner.
Materials assume that all interested learners are at a given conceptual level.	The same materials can be used by those at different conceptual levels.
Problems are given by text and teacher.	Problems arise as students attempt to reach their own goals.
There is emphasis upon each student doing his/her own work.	Students are encouraged to interact with others in solving problems and in negotiating meanings.
Students are expected to accept official knowledge.	Students are expected to regard knowledge as interpretations of reality to which they can contribute.
Evaluation is based on the students' reproduction of official knowledge.	Evaluation is based on the students' growth in reconstructing personal knowledge.

Figure 1–3 presents a summary of the curriculum differences that follow from the traditional and constructivist beliefs.

ANTECEDENTS TO CONSTRUCTIVIST AND ACTIVITY CURRICULUMS

Most of us are surprised at the similarities between contemporary American curriculum and the practices and insights of early teachers. Some would point to Comenius for his use of manipulatives and other teaching aids in developing sensory experiences before verbalization; others would tell how Herbart stressed the linking of the child's previous knowledge and interest to whatever newer content is introduced; and, of course, many would refer to Montessori's curriculum where children were free to learn at their own pace and to discover by themselves using self-teaching aids.

▼ ─── ▼

ACTIVITY 1–1   NEGOTIATING MEANING
FROM LITERARY TEXTS

Where does meaning lie? Of course, some believe that meanings of text
are those intended by the author and that these meanings can be deci-
phered by learning the syntax and other communication symbols and
structures of the text or by becoming acquainted with the backgrounds of
authors and their times. Others know that the text carries meanings that
were unrecognized by the author and that what is *not* said is often significant. Still others believe that meanings are constructed through the
interaction of readers who bring their past experiences and cognitive
frameworks to the text and others know that texts are forever new as
changing circumstances give rise to fresh meanings.

Test for yourself the range of interpretations a selection generates, and
explore techniques to help students or peers gain more powerful ways for
constructing meanings.

1. Choose a literary text—short story, play, or film.
2. Have students read or view the selection.
3. Initiate discussion of the text with a series of sentences to complete.
   The sentences should draw out individual feelings about the human
   relations issues provoked by the selection.
4. Encourage students to share their ideas with others in the class,
   pointing out how the full range of ideas expands the knowledge of
   everyone.
5. Encourage students to support their ideas with evidence from the
   text, to go beyond their own sense of the characters, and to see how
   characters fit in the context of the text.
6. Feel free to introduce any aspects about the text (important details or
   historical background) that you think are important for understanding
   the text.
7. Together, try to effect a consensus on meanings that will link individual interpretation.
8. At the conclusion of the activity, discuss whether or not the understanding channeled the beliefs of students into visions of new possibilities.

▲ ─── ▲

Two teachers from the past, however, are closely associated with the
antecedents of important trends in learner-centered curriculum—constructivism and activity theory. In addition to considering these early trends as a way
to better understand contemporary trends, the work of these two teachers may
encourage us to find better ways for helping students expand their lives.

Teachers who place their learners at the center of curriculum planning have
ties to two early nineteenth-century teachers—Henry Pestalozzi and Friedrich

▼ ───────────────────────────────── ▼

**ACTIVITY 1–2   PLANNING LESSONS FROM
AN ACTIVE LEARNING PERSPECTIVE**

1. Select a subject matter topic of interest to you.
2. Describe a sequence of activities related to the topic that follows the active learning phase of preparation for learning, presentation of content, and application and integration.
3. You may wish to consider under the preparation phase such activities as previewing, activating prior knowledge, setting of purposes, forming hypotheses, and making predictions.
4. Under presenting, you may wish to illustrate how you might encourage clarification, elicit preconceptions or contradictions, and further a classroom community of discourse.
5. Under applying and integrating, show how the new experience relates to prior views of the learners and how the new learning can be extended.

▲ ───────────────────────────────── ▲

Froebel. The sections that follow emphasize Pestalozzi's concern for initial concrete experiences (as opposed to verbal abstraction in learning to learn) and Froebel's efforts at connecting the learner's developmental stage, inner potential, and desire for expression to the learning of important subject matter, symbolic thought, and educational goals.

Learning By Doing: The Broad Curriculum of Henry Pestalozzi

In about 1776, Pestalozzi began his teaching by bringing 37 abandoned children of different ages to his Swiss farm where he clothed, fed, and treated them as his own children. They were always with him, sharing work in the garden and the field, domestic duties, weaving, spinning cotton, and learning music, French, arithmetic, reading, and writing. His act was in response to the prevailing misery of the day; poor children then were exploited by the selfishness of the villagers and left without spirit or energy, giving up their feeling and power for a useful life, on the grounds that such children were by nature vicious and depraved. Pestalozzi attempted to regenerate children who would otherwise have been lost as vagabonds or criminals through a new, broadly based curriculum entailing hand, heart, and head. Under his curriculum, children learned to work with their hands to make a living; they experienced gentleness, kindness, and trustful behavior; and they acquired basic subject matter as tools for independent use.

One of the first of Pestalozzi's curriculum plans called for students to cultivate small plots of land. Students were to learn how to lay down pasture, understand the uses of manure, recognize the different sorts of grasses and the importance of mixing them, the nature and use of marl, the effects (disputed at the time) of the repeated application of lime, and the management of fruit trees and some forest trees.

ACTIVITY 1–3   EXPERIMENTING WITH KNOWLEDGE ABOUT SOLUTIONS AND DENSITY

Judith Johnson Richards (1991) uses the following set of four experiments to help fourth-grade students generate knowledge about solutions and density. You may wish to try the experiments with your learners and to note how students learn by explaining their theories and listening to conflicting views.

Experiment 1

Sand and water.   Students are shown a 100 ml cup filled with sand and a 250 ml cup filled with water. "If I pour this amount of sand into one liter of water, will the water level (a) rise, (b) fall, or (c) stay the same?"

A vote is taken. Students try to persuade one another, giving reasons and prior experiences with sand and water.

A second vote is taken. Students see the demonstration and are then asked to write about the empirical evidence, their explanations, and the names of any children who persuaded them to change their thinking or whose arguments made sense.

Experiment 2

Salt and water.   Students review the previous experiment and then are shown the materials for the new experiment. They are asked: "If I pour the same amount of salt into one liter of water, will the water level (a) rise, (b) fall, or (c) stay the same?"

A vote is taken. Students try to persuade each other, giving their reasons and prior experiences with salt and water.

A second vote is taken. Students see the demonstration and are then asked to write about the empirical evidence, their explanations, and the names and arguments of children who persuaded them to change their opinions.

The students might want to double the solute experiment by finding out what would happen if they continue to pour salt into the water. The terms *dissolve*, *solution*, and *saturated solution* may be introduced.

Experiment 3

Water, salt, and sand.   Students review the previous experiments. The teacher points out that the contents of the presented container look like plain water and asks the students how they can be sure the container holds saline solution. Discussion follows.

Students are shown the materials and asked, "Will the saline solution for Experiment 2 weigh (a) more than plain water, (b) less than plain water, or (c) the same as plain water?"

A vote is taken. Students try to persuade each other with their reasoning and prior experiences.

▼ ─── ▼

ACTIVITY 1–3   *continued*

Experiment 3, *continued*

A second vote is taken. Students see the demonstration and then write about the empirical evidence, explanations, and what changed their thinking. The concept of *density* (mass and volume) may be discussed.

Experiment 4

Water, salt, and ball.   Students are shown the materials and asked, "Will the ball float (a) higher in the saline solution than in plain water, (b) lower in the saline solution than in plain water, or (c) the same in the saline solution as in plain water?"

A vote is taken. Students try to persuade each other by reasoning and prior experiences.

A second vote is taken. Students see the demonstration and write about the empirical evidence, explanations, and arguments that changed their thinking.

▲ ─── ▲

Pestalozzi's view of instruction began by exposing the learner to an environment that would make a personal impression, whether physical or moral, and then supporting the development of these impressions through other activity. Thus, Pestalozzi emphasized doing and talking before reading, precepts before concepts, first-hand experience before confirming generalizations. Nature study and activities that required the manipulation of objects and materials were used to form the sense data (observation of color, structure, number from other characteristics) necessary for understanding objects and their uses.

Pestalozzi spent the next 50 years in different schools with different kinds of students designing programs that would help children be the agents of their own knowledge. The study of geography, for instance, was sometimes introduced with a trip to the valley where the children first gained a general view and then examined the exact idea of the valley. They took some clay that lay in beds on one side of the valley. On their return to the school, the students reproduced in relief the valley they had studied. Over the course of the next few days, the students made more explorations and further extension of their work. Only when the relief was finished were they shown a map; they would not see the map until they were able to understand it. Also, from the first day, students sought connections between geography and instances from other studies, such as natural history, agriculture, and geology.

Similarly, the children were to discover the truths of geometry for themselves. After given problem situations and a clear picture of the end to be reached, students were left to work alone. They first distinguished among vertical, horizontal, oblique, and parallel lines; right, acute, and obtuse angles; different kinds of triangles, quadrilaterals, and so on; and they tried to find out how many points a given number of straight lines would be made to cut one another, or how many angles, triangles, or quadrilaterals could be formed from them, leading to the first problems of theoretical geometry.

Pestalozzi's concern for self-directed learning relegated the teacher's role to evoking purposes and to supplying appropriate resources for the child to pursue these purposes.

City Building: A Current Pestalozzian-Type Curriculum

Similarities are found between Pestalozzi's curriculum and Doreen Nelson's celebrated city building curriculum (1985). Modern City Building classrooms emphasize self-directed learning through a scale model of the students' own city or community projected into the future and constructed in the classroom as an ongoing classroom activity. In an introductory phase of the activity, students explore what they know of their environment, draw maps of the major features of their community—landmarks, streets, significant buildings, vegetation, and so on. Individual maps are combined to form a large common map. In one classroom, students walk around their community observing geographical features and then learn to convert their community to scale, making a relief map with styrofoam depicting the natural landscape of mountains, valleys, lakes, and open land. The map becomes the basis for other city building activities. The students create a list of what they want and what they don't want in their city. This list of criteria is used to guide decision making and to evaluate transformations of "the city." The site is divided into governmental districts, and students serve as representatives on a city council and commissions. Students develop housing, transportation, and other services and facilities to keep up with growing population and environmental concerns.

Early in the project, students explore the world of objects. Each student selects and builds a model of an object—a toothpaste tube; a film reel at actual, decreased, and increased scale, and at the scale of the student's own body. Thus students become familiar with the concepts of structure, scale, ratio, proportion, and geometry. They become inventors and begin to see that buildings and cities are merely spaces fitted with objects that have grown vertically (like a skyscraper) or horizontally (like tract homes).

Concepts of community, structure, and transportation are related to questions of organization. Construction of a three-dimensional model of the classroom interior is thus an empowerment tool, giving students the opportunity to experiment with change before committing to it. Students learn that there are many ways to arrange classrooms depending on the immediate needs of the classroom community.

The students research the basic forces acting on their community, theories of land division, and actual forms of government. They decide on their own governing structure and begin the planning, design, and construction of their own city. Professionals from the community—architects, city planners, environmentalists, lawyers—serve as consultants and resource people for the students, contributing information the students use as they design and construct a model of their community projected into the future. A large flow chart serves as a visual and organizing aid for the entire year, and events are documented on a "history wall."

The "city," like the work of Pestalozzi, helps students recognize that they live in a world of objects that affect them and that, if they desire to affect that world, they must know the nature and essence of other aspects. For example, a student may learn to find the radius and circumference of a circle in order to construct models of a film reel. Ultimately, any subject can be revealed through city building—movement, mathematics, science, ecology, verbal and visual skills.

Froebel and the Inner World of the Child

Frederick Froebel had experience with Pestalozzi as a teacher of drawing and as his assistant. Early in his career, Froebel taught students of various ages in his elementary school at Keilham, Germany, and in schools in Switzerland. Later, he became preoccupied with early childhood education and opened the first kindergarten. Excerpts from a state evaluation of the school at Keilham reveal Froebel's emphasis on the personal construction of knowledge:

> What the pupils know is not a shapeless mass, but has form and life, and is, if at all possible, immediately applied in life . . . There is not a trace of thoughtless repetition of the words of others, not of captive knowledge among any of the pupils. What they express they have inwardly seen. Even the objections of the teachers cannot change their opinions until they have clearly seen their error. Whatever they take up, they must be able to use, and what they cannot think, they do not take up. Even dull grammar begins to live with them, inasmuch as they are taught to study each language with reference to the history, habits, and character of the respective people. (Hailman, 1887, pp. 86–87)

Froebel capitalized upon the inner, active forces of learners and gave them encouragement and direction. He regarded them somewhat as plants that need cultivation and protection in order to realize their potentials, yet he believed that, unlike plants, children through conscious perception and reason can direct the process of their own growth.

In his kindergarten, Froebel sought to understand the child's inner life, not merely attend to external behavior:

> For the child that seems good outwardly is not necessarily good inwardly, i.e., does not desire the good spontaneously or from love, respect, and affection. Similarly, the outwardly rough, stubborn, self-willed child that seems outwardly not good, frequently is filled with the liveliest, most eager, strongest drive for spontaneous goodness in his actions; and the apparently inattentive boy frequently follows a fixed line of thought that withholds his attention from all external things. (Hailman, 1887, pp. 86–87)

Froebel's kindergarten curriculum was an activity curriculum that gave opportunity for the self-expression that would draw children out and reveal their potentialities. He regarded language as a fundamental way to encourage expression and to reveal inner needs. Hence, he encouraged young children to engage spontaneously in pictorial writing, to invent their own alphabets, and to seek assistance with squibble writing in their attempts at expression (Hailman, 1887, pp. 86–87).

Similarly, the love of story, story drawing, and rhythms was seen as manifesting inner development. These activities, as well as nature study, handwork, and physical activity, were part of Froebel's curriculum. Activities were also intended to help children free themselves, to differentiate self from external things, and these things from one another.

Play was central to Froebel's curriculum. The play activities were organized systematically to correspond with developmental needs of children of a given age and to point to larger symbolic meanings. His curriculum included many types of cooperative play and group games, physical activities that aimed at strength and dexterity, games that initiated joy and imagination, and intellectual games that demanded reflection and judgment. Some activities, "gifts," entailed the manipulation of balls, blocks, and other materials in a sequential order and were introduced to help children discover universal or conceptual ideas thought to correspond to an external world—colors, shapes, number (divisibility), proportion, and the like. (Of course, today the idea of universal concepts is regarded by many as an illusion, just as the notion of an external world where students can "discover" through observation is challenged by the view that any "real" world is in one's mind and that any common view of reality must be constructed in given social situations). Other activities, "occupations," promoted invention and furnished material for practice. In playing with occupational activities, such as those involving clay, wood carving, and painting, children used the concepts discovered through the "gifts" to apply, modify, and create something new.

The importance of relating the "inner" world of the child with powerful principles or concepts for dealing with the universe is illustrated in Froebel's view of the ball as an educational device. He recommended giving one to the child at the age of three months, believing that the play it stimulates trains the senses, muscles, and power of attention, while at the same time building the child's confidence in his or her abilities. The moving ball, now held, now lost, teaches the meaning of such key concepts as *space* and *time* (past, present, and future). A caretaker singing a description of the motion of the ball helps a child learn the meaning of such significant readiness concepts as *up, down, out, around, middle, first*.

Froebel introduced nature study and manual construction for older children. Accordingly, children took trips through neighborhood fields and along lake shores, making observations, drawing, connecting their work in science with their studies in language and art. Mathematics was frequently introduced in connection with laboratory work as well as with the occupations found in the manual training room where students made the equipment for their studies of nature and other activities (Cremin, 1961, p. 133).

THE ACTIVITY CURRICULUM: AN AMERICAN RESPONSE TO FROEBEL

By 1900, Froebel's ideas had become a basis for elementary school practice in the United States. School gardens formed an organic part of schoolwork. The care and observation of living things, plants and animals, occupied a place in the curriculum. Storytelling and recognition of the importance of having children love stories was common. Activities involving music, art, and physical education reflected a change from viewing subject matter as something set out to be learned, to an emphasis on activity and appeal to the developmental needs of children.

The practice of offering manual training at all grade levels, not for vocational purposes but for mental and cultural value, was introduced. Manual training reflected Froebel's belief that it would advance creativity and help children express their own ideas by developing dexterity in the use of tools. As will be described in Chapter 3, nature study became the basis for the teaching of science in American schools. Children carried out investigations in the field and in the classroom where they were introduced to biology and physics.

Mathematics was frequently presented in connection with laboratory work, as well as with the occupation in the manual training room. Students often made the equipment they needed for their study of science, nature, and drawing, along with other products. The range of subjects that were introduced through nature study—music, drawing, hygiene, geography, history, economics—was considerable, but all were seen as vehicles for child expression. All began with what had meaning for the children themselves. The job of the teacher was to start where the children were and lead them into the several fields of knowledge, extending meaning and sensitivities along the way (Cremin, 1961, p. 133).

J. L. Meriam's Activity Curriculum

In 1904, Junius Meriam developed an activity curriculum based on four categories—observation, play, stories, and handwork (Meriam, 1920). This curriculum is noteworthy for its consistency with Froebel's belief that concrete objects could be used to connect the inner world of the child to powerful ideas related to the external world.

The following list of play activities taken from Meriam's curriculum illustrates the potential of play for developing concepts of science:

▼ *Water.*   Playing with water, pouring, wading, splashing, watching objects in water, throwing objects into water, building dams and water wheels, watching the actions of water on land, "erosion models," and so on, which develop problems in fluids.

▼ *Air.*   Playing with air, sailboats, kites, windmills, airplanes, which develop problems in air pressure, air currents, wind, temperature, humidity, rainfall, and so on. Watching fire, making fires, observing friction and heat, playing with toy steam engines and thermometers, which develop problems in heat, combustion, expansion, contraction and the effects of heat.

▼ *Mechanical devices.*   Playing with hoops, tops, pulleys, wheels, toy machines, gyroscopes, pendulums, levers, watching thrown objects, balancing objects, and so on, which develop problems in motor dynamics.

▼ *Sound.*   Vocalization; beating and drumming; blowing on toy instruments; "listening to shells"; speaking through tubes and telephones; experimenting with conduction through air, water, timbers; and experimenting with vibrating bodies, echoes, and so on; which develop problems in vibration, noises, tones, music, and so on.

▼ *Light.*   Playing with reflectors, mirrors, prisms, lenses, water refraction, glasses, and telescopes, which develop problems in light, color, optics, time, and so on.

▼ *Electricity.*   Experimenting and playing with magnets, induction coils, telephones, telegraph instruments, dynamos, electric motors, electric lights, and so on, which present problems in electrodynamics.

In playing with such phenomena, students shared their experiences with others, used their imaginations and constructed useful objects, investigated and experimented, and acquired knowledge of materials and processes. Incentives to learn reading, writing, and arithmetical processes arose from the activities involved with the materials. The teacher's role was to help students plan what they wanted to do, how they would do it, and how they would evaluate their undertakings. The teacher's role was also to help students pursue purposes that would offer the greatest possibility for further learning.

The entire class seldom worked on the same materials at any one time. While some were constructing objects, others used books and reference materials dealing with the problems growing from the activity, and still others were preparing their reports or displays.

Difficulties and Promise of the Activity Curriculum

Two kinds of related difficulties confront the activity curriculum. One difficulty centers on the selection of content: the failure to develop powerful ideas or content that could enhance the efforts of learners as they pursue their goals. In part, this is a problem of stimulating or knowing the goals of students and helping them extend their existing perspectives, procedures, and solutions in creating more fruitful methods and tools. A second difficulty is one of context: the failure to consider the cultural context in which learners live so that content of the curriculum can become functional in the lives of the learners and help them transform these contexts.

The promise of an activity curriculum rests on two things:

1. Constructivism and its contributions in suggesting ways to arrange classroom conditions for extending the knowledge of students.
2. Situated learning where subject matter is related to the everyday activities of learners so they can be more inventive and forceful in their real life.

In the past, many teachers found it difficult to place control of learning in the hands of students. Often nature study became object study with formal and analytical questions posed by the teacher to shape children's thinking. Ellwood Cubberly (1934) tells how if common salt was the "object" of the lesson, the class would be expected to learn of its chemical structure, its uses, how and where it is found in nature, how it is mined and refined, that its crystalline form is cubical, that it varies in color from white to bluish and reddish, that it is transformed to translucent, that it is soluble in water and saline in taste, and that it imparts a yellow color to flame (p. 353).

The principle of self-activity was often corrupted to "busy work." Inasmuch as the child's active nature called for a busy life, teachers found many devices to keep students employed—activities like designing words with beans and clipping and folding paper. Instead of constructing their own knowledge, children were expected to meet organizational demands, obeying authority, behaving uniformly, and acquiring information in common.

Meriam himself catalogued 15,000 activity units from different school systems in the United States and found that more than 50 percent of the activities were assigned by school officials, 31 percent by teachers, and only 18 percent generated by students. Many of the activities were misplaced, with serious and advanced topics in the lower grades and trivial topics in the upper grades. Meriam faulted the imposing of activity topics that appealed to children's interests but were unrelated to daily living and the continuity of teaching experience. One teacher chose the topic of a music band on the grounds that noise appeals to children; another chose the topic "candles" because messy handwork attracts children; and another the topic "Eskimos" because the study of such people provides the spectacular. In general, activities were formed more from what teachers wanted students to be interested in than from information about the interests of students. Also, teachers had concern about the transcendency of student interests—"fads"—and how these interests could promote progress toward significant educational goals.

A recent analysis of elementary curriculum materials found that many of the problems identified by Meriam persist in many of today's learning tasks and school activities (Brophy and Alleman, 1991). These problems include the following:

▼   Activities that do not contribute to significant learning because they are built around peripheral content rather than key ideas (e.g., identify clothes that would be worn to a birthday party) or are busy work (e.g., word searches, memorizing names of state capitals and state symbols, cutting and pasting, coloring, connecting dots).

▼   Activities that will induce misconceptions instead of accurate understanding (e.g., forced categorizations, such as exercises in distinguishing foods eaten today from foods eaten long ago, classifying foods as breakfast, lunch or dinner foods).

▼   Activities that do not justify the trouble it takes to implement them (e.g., pageants, culminating activities, complicated simulations, and collage and scrapbook activities that call for a lot of cutting and pasting of pictures but not thinking or writing about ideas linked to major goals).

▼ Activities that are not matched to students' readiness levels (e.g., students already know what the activities are intended to teach and other activities that embody prior knowledge assumptions or procedural complexities that make them too difficult for students to understand).

TOWARD AN IDEAL ACTIVITY CURRICULUM

It's easy for a teacher to present educational tasks, but ideal learning activities belong to the corresponding goals, decisions, projects, and actions of the student. Stories of student alienation and resistance to school tasks are legion. "Would you like to get out your green math books?" Peter springs upright in his seat. "Do we have to? You said, 'Do we want to?'" Sue grins with a wry twinkle. "Well, I guess I just meant to ask you nicely to get out your books." She pauses; then, nodding to Peter but addressing the class, says, "*Please* get out your green books and get ready."

Teachers often assign tasks or arrange situations in hopes of initiating educative activity—exploratory or problem solving on the part of students. Ideally, the tasks prompt activity that links subject matter (content or thinking skills) to the students' own motivations for various kinds of knowledge. The ideal activity curriculum requires tasks that both relate to the students' conceptions of their world and offer the possibility of transforming their world.

Prior discussion in this chapter about constructivism highlighted the importance of uncovering the motive, goal, question, and perspective of students as they act on materials and other aspects of the classroom environment. These passages also encouraged the social creation of knowledge and collective learning through group and classroom discussion and projects. However, the ideal activity curriculum requires the teacher to gain broader insights into the real world activities of learners, as well as insights into the thinking and behavior of students as they undertake classroom tasks. The additional challenge for teachers is to understand the life situations of students so that school tasks involve subject matter that will be functional for students.

Approaches to this challenge are found in Part 5, which presents extensive accounts of teachers and students creating curriculum, particularly with respect to long-term units of instruction. For this chapter, however, the concept of designing educational activities that are in harmony with students' historical and social contexts is illustrated by excerpts of the work of Stieg Mellin-Olsen, a Norwegian teacher of mathematics who has aimed at an ideal activity curriculum which matches and transforms the cultural contexts of learners (Mellin-Olsen, 1987).

Deriving School Tasks from Life in the Community

Four six-year-olds were brought to the roadside and for five minutes were asked to do three things: count the number of cars driving toward the town, count those coming from the town, and write down their counting. The children were organized into pairs, with one to do the counting and reporting to the other who was to write the information down. The problem of how to write was solved as 1111 or xxxx, and the like. Upon returning to the classroom, the results were written on the chalkboard for interpretation, counting, and discussion.

Subsequently, groups recorded other results and the variations in the figures were discussed: When did the most cars pass? In the morning? Afternoon? What about the ceremony near the church? Later, questions were asked and answered about how many people a car can seat. (Unexpectedly, the children's mode number was 7, which probably reflects their experience rather than the experience of the teacher who wanted 5.) Then the children were grouped in fives, and each group took a place near the wall to do some driving—two children in front, three in the rear. The 24 members of the class were transformed to full cars and one with an empty seat. The children found themselves counting cars with just one person, changing their statistics into a statistic of fives. Their graphs were impressive, showing from 1 to 30 cars with 1 occupant, to 6 cars with 5 occupants. The children counted and reported the number of buses seen and estimated how many people the buses could seat.

These children used their own inventions of symbols which they compared and discussed. Spoken mathematics was encouraged: How many are absent today? Yesterday? The day before? Is a flu epidemic around? Is it mostly children from one specific area who are absent? How many pages are left? You will have to go four by four to the nurse. Eight minutes per group. Will we make it before lunch? How many minutes will each group have then? Could you show us your method? So you drew the clock and counted like that? Very clever. Does anyone else have a method they would like to show?

As indicated, this activity curriculum connected to the lives of beginners and involved powerful math content—counting, graphing, classification and grouping, variation in data in a function of time, and the function of mathematical symbols—all in the context of using mathematics as a tool to solve problems.

Relating Popular Knowledge to School Knowledge

Mellin-Olsen (1987) knows that knitting and carpentry have deep roots in Norwegian culture. Hence, he connected the folk mathematics of these activities to the learning of formal mathematics. Knitting involved wool left over—blue and red in two balls. Decisions about what to make—socks, mittens, scarf—depended on the quantity and quality of the wool, time of year, and other factors. If the decision is socks, the student knows that 100 grams are needed for a pair, which corresponds to a ball of a given size. But there are two colors, so a pattern must be designed—visualized, but not drawn—and one must take into account the ratio of colors compared with the ratio of the two sorts of wool. The wool must be divided into halves (two equal socks are required), but how? One way is to weigh the wool: one sock is 100 grams. Another way is to wind the ball into unit balls (but there is a problem of ratios: 150 grams of blue and 250 grams of red). Where is the textbook problem or symmetry that asks about the ratio of colors involved? If 150 grams is slightly more than half of 250, every row of blue should perhaps have two rows of red—or is this too much red? What about the idea of *proportion*?

Similarly, carpentry involves materials and an intended end product. As with knitting (planning, matching materials and experience to goals), it involves considerations about design and visual imagery. The design will change as the building continues and probably involve the participation of others.

Mellin-Olsen (1987) relates his formal math curriculum to the visual imagery, language, and activities of the local culture. The geometry of knitting and carpentry differ from textbook geometry in asking "How much do I need?" instead of asking "How can I use what I have in the best way?" The relation between available materials and the possible end result dominates most practical situations. In Euclidean geometry, the result is reached by a minimum of information and operation, but craftspeople can't afford the risk this may imply. Therefore, in the case of young builders, Mellin-Olsen introduces Euclid with such problems as these:

> You have these materials for the frame of the floor of a hut (7.5 cm, 9 cm, 10 cm, 6 cm). Don't think about what else you will need for the hut. How will you make the frame, and how would you check that it is OK? Draw what you would like it to look like and write the measures on the drawing. (Mellin-Olsen, 1987, p. 62)

Whereas in traditional Euclidean geometry, two triangles and the congruents of their corresponding sides are equal in length, carpentry geometry says that when one builds a rectangular frame, a diagonal bar is needed to prevent the frame from collapsing. In traditional Euclidean geometry, a quadrilateral is a parallelogram if and only if both opposite pairs of sides are equal; carpentry geometry says if you have a given frame and want a particular result, you measure 60 cm (or less) at a time along both sides, using the theorem that a parallelogram in which the diagonals are equal is a rectangle.

Using School Knowledge in Activities for Transforming Aspects of Daily Life

In contrast with the traditional elementary school math task that requires students to quantify their day and night activities so they can have experience with data and some analysis of the distribution, the ideal activity curriculum features projects in which students address problems in their neighborhood and use math investigations as part of a plan for approaching the adult world with the idea of improving the neighborhood. In one instance, a new housing project failed to provide recreational areas for children, so teachers of three elementary classrooms involved their students in a project whereby students generated possible recreational suggestions and then interviewed other students about their preferences. Data collection, statistics and data analysis, and other mathematical tools were important in documenting the situation and possible

▼ ————————————————————————————— ▼

ACTIVITY 1–4   ASSESSING ACTIVITIES IN A
TEXTBOOK OR TEACHER GUIDE

1. Select a textbook of interest to you.
2. Sample the activities suggested in this textbook or the accompanying teacher's guide.
3. What percentage of the sampled activities can be faulted using Brophy and Alleman's negative criteria (1991)?
   a. Peripheral content
   b. Likelihood of inducing misconceptions
   c. Uneconomical use of students' time
   d. Too easy or too difficult for the intended learners

▲ ————————————————————————————— ▲

▼ ————————————————————————————— ▼

ACTIVITY 1–5   IDENTIFYING BELIEVABLE
PROBLEMS FOR LEARNERS IN YOUR
COMMUNITY

Examine an end-of-course test for a subject you might teach. The test specifications or curriculum objectives and sample test items might suffice.

What percentage of the test items would you consider to be practical for your students? For this exercise, define *practicality* as "problems and tasks the learner will probably face in daily life and which he or she will want to solve." (In one study, students evaluated 34 percent of a sample of problems as practical, while their teachers regarded 57 percent of the sample as practical.)

▲ ————————————————————————————— ▲

solutions. Subsequently, students prepared and carried out a plan of action whereby they presented their justified claims to various boards and councils that might support their demands for change. An ideal activity emerged as analysis and discussion developed into action for transforming an aspect of the students' daily life.

SUMMARY

The trend toward constructivist and activity curriculums is giving students more responsibility for their own learning. Sense making and understanding is prized over the production of "right answers" to contrived and limited questions. Preparation for uncertainty and change is a dominant factor in these trends. Although variability in outlooks is recognized and appreciated in the new curriculums, teachers make a conscious effort to help students extend their outlooks in the direction of more encompassing, mature, and public

▼ ———————————————————————————————— ▼

ACTIVITY 1–6   GENERATING AN IDEA FOR A POSSIBLE LEARNING OPPORTUNITY

1. You may find it useful to think of a particular book, resource person, record, experiment, excursion site, film, newspaper, musical selection, dance, sport, community problem, controversial issue, or other aspect of daily life that could serve as a bridge between certain students and content area(s).

2. Next, consider the learner(s) who would be expected to participate in the teaching opportunity—their interests, prior experiences, future goals, and the activities they are presently enjoying in both in and out of school.

3. How do you visualize the opportunity being carried out? Is your visualization likely to be consistent with these three purposes?

   a. *Satisfaction for learners.*   Why do you think this opportunity could be satisfying? What is its appeal to students (provides opportunity to interact with significant others; is challenging; combines thinking, feeling, and moving; offers the learner choice and control in planning and carrying out the opportunity)? What else?

   b. *Likelihood that learners will be successful in the situation.*   What resources will be necessary to increase the probability of learner success? Peer support? Ways to get help and clarification? Rehearsal on key tasks and lower risk tryouts before "real" high-stake requirements?

   c. *Contribution to multiple outcomes.*   What educational value might your visualized opportunity have for your learners? What aesthetic, moral, intellectual, social, psychological or other dimensions of students' development will be served?

▲ ———————————————————————————————— ▲

views. The classroom as a community and the negotiation of meaning are characteristic of this effort.

Meaning-based approaches to curriculum development reflect a paradigm shift from the traditional model of planning that has dominated schools. Instead of the organized subject matter of the adult and the prespecification of instructional objectives as the starting points for curriculum design, constructivist teachers begin with the multiple goals and backgrounds of their students. The tentative plans of teachers give way to an enacted curriculum whereby teacher and students determine the validity of goals and content as they reconstruct their experiences through instructional activity.

This chapter has shown that student-centered curriculum does not imply that scientific and other meaning systems are expelled. On the contrary, powerful content is introduced when it is likely to serve student purposes and address their concerns about issues and problems.

The contributions of Pestalozzi and Froebel to constructivist and activity curriculums, and their viable alternatives to formalizing have been described. Implicit in the work of those early teachers is the point that teachers have initiated mighty winds of curriculum change. The accounts in this chapter of modern teachers who follow their examples may also inspire.

This chapter has acknowledged the difficulties of placing control of learning in the hands of students and drawn contrasts between sterile school tasks and ideal learning activities. It has featured examples of teachers who are relating the real-world activities of students to the classroom and provoking activities whereby students construct knowledge by reorganizing their thinking and beliefs and, in some instances, transform the social contexts in which they live.

QUESTIONS FOR DISCUSSION

1. How does the teacher's view of human nature affect classroom practice? Do some teachers believe children must be controlled and shaped? Do others believe that students have predispositions to goodness and should be given new freedom to pursue their own inclinations and goals?
2. What are some curriculum implications for believing that students are individual learners who bring their own resources to the learning context and construct their own meanings from it?
3. Indicate how curriculum materials might best reconcile two sometimes conflicting concerns:
    a. Encouraging individual thinking and creating strategies for solving problems.
    b. Learning rules and procedures established by the wider society.
4. What are some reasons that teachers might have for not implementing a constructivist curriculum? How might such constraints best be overcome or circumvented?
5. In what way does constructivist curriculum address problems associated with increasingly diverse student populations and the conflicts and contradictions between popular culture and academic knowledge?
6. Ask any two or three people to talk about and explain something they "know" in common—the concept of an atom, electricity, poetry, prime numbers, multiplication of fractions, the Bill of Rights, the Federal Reserve system, use of geometry in solving real-world problems, origin of the self, time, respiratory system, or any other topic. Have them avoid textbook generalizations in form or content but instead give their own understanding of the topic. What are the gaps and uncertainties in their explanations? What are the conflicting views on the topic? Relate the inquiry to constructivist curriculum.
7. Is it the unpredictable rather than the predictable outcomes from student actions that make education worthwhile? If so, how should we develop curriculum?

REFERENCES

Brophy, J., & Alleman, J. (1991). Activities as instructional tools: A framework for analysis and education. *Educational Researcher, 20*(4), 24–30.

Cremin, L. A. (1961). *Progression in the transformation of the school: American education 1876–1957.* New York: Alfred A. Knopf.

Cubberly, E. D. (1934). *Public education in the United States.* Boston: Houghton Mifflin.

DeVries, R., & Kohlberg, L. (1990). *Constructivist early education: Overview and comparison with other programs.* Washington, D.C: National Association for Education of Young Children.

Hailman, W. H. (1887). Superintendent Zechs' report of his visit to the Educational Institute at Keilham, 1826. *The Education of Man.* New York: D. Appleton & Co.

Magidson, S. (1992). From the laboratory to the classroom: A technology intensive curriculum for functions and graphs. *Journal of Mathematical Behavior, 11*(4), 361–377.

Meriam, J. (1920). *Child life and the curriculum.* Yonkers, NY: World Book Co.

Mellin-Olsen, S. (1987). *The politics of mathematics education.* Norwell, MA: Kluwer Academic Publishers.

Nelson, D. (1985). *City building education.* Los Angeles, CA: Center for City Building Education Programs.

Richards, J. J. (1991, April). The implementation of a Japanese science education method in the United States. Paper presented at American Educational Research Association Annual Meeting. Chicago, IL.

Smith, J. L., & Johnson, H. A. (1993). Content in the classroom: Listening to adolescent voices. *Language Arts, 70*, 18–30.

Wheatley, G. H. (1992). The role of reflection in mathematics learning. *Educational Studies in Mathematics, 25*(5), 29–54.

Whimbey, A., & Lockhead, J. (1984). *Beyond problem solving and comprehension.* Hillsdale, NJ: Lawrence Erlbaum.

PERSONAL DEVELOPMENT IN THE ACADEMIC CONTEXT

This chapter defines *personal development* as a curricular aim and shows the difficulty of trying to justify the selection of content on the basis of psychological and biological needs. Knowledge that contributes to meeting these needs in one situation is inadequate in another.

The chapter illustrates procedures for deriving curriculum goals from studies of individual learners and draws contrasts between (1) teachers who attempt to address psychological needs and problems of learners by introducing wide sources of knowledge and (2) teachers who focus on needs or concerns as the springboard to academic study. Ways to create curriculum that are responsive to fundamental concerns, such as those identified by Erikson, are presented. Additionally, illustrations of newer curriculum support Piaget's views of how students construct knowledge.

CURRICULUM FOR PERSONAL DEVELOPMENT

Personal development is generally viewed in terms of autonomy, self-knowledge, or the formation of personal values. Abraham Maslow proposed a hierarchy of universal needs that must be met for optimum personal development—physiological needs, safety needs, belongingness and esteem needs, the need to develop one's potential talent and capabilities (self-actualization), and the need to understand and appreciate aesthetically. Although personal development and the meeting of human needs can serve as a broad aim, no one-to-one correspondence exists between such aims and the answer to the teacher's question, "What should I teach?" Specific situations determine how universal needs can best be met. The eloquent reply in 1744 of Indian leaders of the Six Nations to an invitation from commissioners of Virginia to send Indian boys to the College of William and Mary illustrates how responses to universal needs are shaped by culture.

> WE KNOW THAT YOU HIGHLY ESTEEM THE KIND OF LEARNING taught in those colleges, and that the Maintenance of our young Men, while with you would be very expensive to you. We are convinced, that you mean to do us Good by your Proposal; and we thank you heartily. But you, who are wise must know that different Nations have different Conceptions of things and you will therefore not take it

▼ ━━ ▼

**ACTIVITY 2–1   DETERMINING
DEVELOPMENTAL GOALS FROM
INFORMATION ABOUT THE LEARNER(S)**

Any instructional program should be responsive in part to the individual
learner's nature and needs. This activity offers you the opportunity to
explore different ways of gathering pertinent information about a learner
population, to reveal your own interpretation of what this information
means—what you consider to be positive or negative—and, finally, to
state what educational responses would be appropriate to your findings
and interpretation (individual goal, content, or activity).

1. Select the learner(s) for whom you might actually develop a curriculum or at least consider for the purposes of this exercise.
2. State the area or areas in which you will seek information about the
   learner—health, interests, activities, peer relations, attitude toward
   school and learning expectations, and so on.
3. Conduct an interview, survey, or observe your learners in specific situations or examine readily available school records about the learners.
4. Record a summary of the information collected, the generalizations or
   interpretations you drew from the information, and state what implications you see for either *what* should be taught the learners or *how*
   something should be taught the learners in light of your study.

Figure 2–1 shows a suggestion form for your report.

▲ ━━ ▲

amiss, if our ideas of this kind of Education happen not to be the same as yours. We
have had some experience of it. Several of our young People were formerly brought
up at the Colleges of the Northern Provinces: they were instructed in all your Sciences; but, when they came back to us, they were bad Runners, ignorant of every
means of living in the woods . . . neither fit for Hunters, Warriors, nor Counsellors,
they were totally good for nothing.
     We are, however, not the less oblig'd by your kind Offer, tho' we decline accept-
ing it; and, to show our grateful Sense of it, if the Gentlemen of Virginia will send us
a Dozen of their Sons, we will take Care of their Education, instruct them in all we
know, and make Men of them. (McLuhan, 1971, p. 57)

Universal Needs

The idea of universal needs is useful to curriculum makers in several ways.
First, the concept suggests content for human nature. Edward Decci and others
(1991) postulate that three needs are innate and inherent in human life:

FIGURE 2–1
Curriculum implications from studies of the learner

Summary of Findings	Generalizations and Interpretations of the Findings	Curriculum Implications (a logical answer to what you have uncovered—the action, content, or goal you would introduce to help the learner)
Health		
Interests		
Peer relations		
Attitude toward learning		
Other		

1. *Competence:* understanding how to attain various outcomes and be able to perform the requisite actions.
2. *Relatedness:* developing secure and satisfying connections with others in one's social milieu.
3. *Autonomy:* self-initiating and self-regulating of one's own actions.

A curriculum can be justified to the extent that it is shown to help learners fulfill one or more of their needs.

Second, the teacher's theory of universal human needs serves to help the teachers make sense of a multitude of student behaviors. Many observations and facts regarding a student's participation in activities, academic performance, attitudes toward school, plans for the future, peer and parent relations, and the like can be connected through an interpretation that explains the observations, actions, and facts from a human needs perspective. On the basis of this interpretation, the teacher conceives and implements a curriculum plan of action regarding the learner.

Third, the concept of need allows one to specify the contextual conditions that will facilitate academic performance and development. This point has special relevance for those who want to see students achieve in particular subject areas. Accomplishment in a field requires conceptual understanding and the flexible use of knowledge. Curriculum contexts that support student competency, social relations, and learner autonomy are linked to these prerequisites. A central theme of this chapter is that unless a curriculum contributes to the basic psychological needs of learners, that curriculum will diminish motivation, impair the developmental process, and lead to poorer academic performance.

ACADEMIC APPROACHES TO PERSONAL NEEDS

It is assumed that among those who completed Activity 2–1, some drew curriculum implications that called for helping the learner(s) increase their motivation, find new interests, enhance self-concept; recognize sources of help or recognize one's own talents and become aware of how one is inhibiting or facilitating decisions of personal consequence; or learn to get more realistic standards, to engage in multiple ways to express oneself, or to consider alternative conceptions to one's intuitive beliefs. The possibilities are numerous.

Immediately, however, some teachers will question the extent to which such goals should be pursued in the classroom, where they believe that academic subject matter should be the focus. Other teachers believe that personal development is the function of other people and agencies—parents, medical specialists, psychologists, and social workers, for example. Most teachers, however, understand that they have a unique contribution to make to the personal development of their students through knowledge, social interventions, and learning activities. These teachers divide in their approach, with some giving priority to the developmental problem and introducing a wide variety of resources for resolving it, while others capitalize on student psychological and social concerns, using them as a means to activate the learning of academic subjects. The following sections illustrate curriculum from the two perspectives.

A Curriculum that Prioritizes Personal Concern

Jesse Goodman (1991) has described how Ursina, a teacher in an Indiana middle school, has responded to the growing sexual maturity of early adolescents by designing a curriculum that breaks out of the subject matter mold in addressing student concern. Although biological information regarding adolescent development and reproduction was introduced in her science class, Ursina ensured that the social and psychological context within which adolescents become sexual beings also received attention. Among the themes of Ursina's human sexuality curriculum were these:

▼ *Communication*: the ability to discuss openly sexual feelings and behavior in mixed-gender groups and with adults. Communication was necessary to avoid the mistrust and fear associated with gender separatism. Students were expected to respect the information that others gave, right to privacy, and student-generated questions. A communicative climate was established as students discussed topics that were formerly taboo—anal sex, transvestites, incest, birth control methods, and others. All materials for the course (films, guest speakers, books) were available for both girls and boys. Boys role-played fathers, explaining physiological and emotional aspects of development to the girls as if the girls were their ten-year-old daughters. In turn, girls explained the same information to their "sons".

▼ *Appreciating one's own body*: examining attitudes toward students' own bodies through such activities as viewing themselves in front of a mirror.

They critically analyzed the images of "beauty" conveyed in advertising, films, and television. They viewed photographs of external and internal sexual organs, and discussed the "beauty" of human sexuality and the wonder of conception. Students discussed the implications of taking full responsibility for the health of their bodies.

▼ *Dynamics of sexual development*: considering cultural consequences of living in a society that follows a patriarchal rationality, how the "negative" characteristics of being a girl could be a positive given a different cultural world view. In response to the statement that "anything that two consenting people do (sexually) is OK," content emerged regarding government's role, sexual exploitation, subtle forms of coercion, and the concept of informed judgments. The issues of date rape and the evaluation of intimate relationships were treated. In pursuing their concern about homosexuality, students interviewed male and female members of the Gay Alliance. Throughout their study, students gained understanding of the responsibilities and caring necessary for a healthy love relationship.

▼ *Teenage pregnancy*: demystifying teen pregnancy. Students interpreted facts about social, economic, and health costs of teenage pregnancy. They discussed reasons so many teenagers in the U.S. became pregnant. They sought answers to the questions of who are responsible for this situation and how can it be avoided. Issues of adoption, abortion, birth control, and ethical dimensions were considered by students and guest speakers.

A Curriculum of Concern that Prizes Biology

H. Craig Heller's Human Biology Curriculum (Hum Bio) is also a response to the negative aspects of adolescent lifestyle—drugs, violence, and unplanned pregnancy (Heller, 1993). However, Heller is as much troubled by student disaffection and alienation from science. He focuses on human and adolescent concerns in the belief that in doing so more science will be taught than in a standard curriculum.

In each unit of the Hum Bio curriculum, Heller emphasizes information from the behavioral sciences, biological sciences, and safety and health. When teaching about the heart and circulation, he provides information about the effects of fatty foods, cholesterol, and stress. The "Your Changing Body" unit describes what happens during puberty, the role of hormones, and the menstrual cycle. Discussion of feelings about body changes, gender, attractiveness, dieting, anoxia, and steroid abuse is generated. Active learning is promoted through such activities as students calculating how much blood their hearts pump per hour, finding the blind spots in their field of vision, and creating scenarios for an adolescent whose wish for independence conflicts with parental standards.

Hum Bio is primarily a life science curriculum. The conventional topics such as the nervous system and how it works together with scientific concepts are viewed as essential. Each topic is related to a personal concern of students. Study of the topic of the brain, for example, includes discussion about the effect of drugs on the brain.

The underlying assumption of this curriculum is that if the teacher can capture student interest with topics that adolescents find relevant, students will learn and retain more. Instead of starting with Mendel's pea plant, Hum Bio starts with human genetics, sex determinates, and genetic disease, capitalizing on adolescent concerns as the springboard to appreciation of science. In turn, a relevant information base should help students make wiser decisions about their lives.

CURRICULUM FROM THE INSIDE OUT: USING THE THEORIES OF ERIKSON AND PIAGET

Two intellectual sources that explain human development and influence the way teachers respond to learners are the writings of Erik Erikson (1968) and Jean Piaget (1991). Both of these theorists follow Froebel in adhering to the *epigenetic principle*, which holds that just as certain organs of the body appear at specified times and allow the individual to perform life sustaining functions, so, too, does the personality and intellect of an individual form through a series of interrelated stages.

Linking Curriculum to Erikson's Developmental Concerns

The idea of linking academic content to psychological needs is powerful. Unless curriculum is tied to basic needs, it is unlikely to lead to high academic performance. Erikson's states provide a vehicle for effecting such linkages (1968). To the extent that a teacher of mathematics, art, reading, or any other subject succeeds in addressing a developmental task through the subject matter, that content will be valued. A teacher of history, for example, became aware how her adolescent students' concern for identity (an Erikson concept) was reflected in their conflict between parental and peer expectations for a certain social behavior. Responding to this, she encouraged a project in which students conducted a historical study related to the social practice in question. The students used primary and secondary sources in their investigation into the origins of the practice. Subsequently, the students evaluated the current social context that was responsible for changed beliefs regarding the practice. The research resulted in great gains in student interest in history, historical information, methodology, and interpretation. It led to better student–parent understanding.

A further example of how academic goals in conventional subject matter— reading, writing, and arithmetic—can be related to psychological needs is found in Terry Borton's "Curriculum of Concern." Borton selected the concern of self-identity and encouraged students to explore the disparity between what they thought about in school, what they were concerned about in their own lives, and the ways they acted. The curriculum outline consisted of a series of questions designed to lead the students to a personal sense of identity and finally to an examination of actions that would express that sense of self. Some of the questions were these: "What is human about humans?"

"Who am I?" "How can we find activities to express our thoughts and feelings?" Additionally, students engaged in many activities, such as a trip to the zoo to contrast humans with animals, improvised drama to imitate the movement of animals, and discussions of animal metaphors in the characterizations of humans. All activities reflected the teacher's commitment to the three Rs. In addition, students drew generalizations about identity, such as, "If a consciousness of self is one of the major differences between animal and human, then one of the most effective ways to make people more human or more humane, would be to help them explore the significance of their own diversity."

Erikson's Developmental Stages

Erikson has proposed eight stages, each of which poses a critical task of development and consists of positive and negative qualities (1968). Individuals adapt to the world best when they successfully possess more of the positive quality of a given stage than the negative quality. The following outlines the tasks, qualities, typical age ranges, and characteristics of the stages:

Trust vs. Mistrust (birth to one year). The basic task to be learned by infants is that they can trust their world. Trust is acquired by consistency, continuity, and sameness of experience in satisfying the infant's basic needs by the caretaker. If the care they receive is inadequate, inconsistent, or negative, children will approach the world with fear and suspicion.

Autonomy vs. Shame and Doubt (two to three years) A sense of autonomy develops when toddlers are permitted and encouraged to do what they are capable of doing at their own pace and in their own way. If caretakers are impatient and do too many things for young children, then the children may doubt their ability. Also, adults should not shame young children for unacceptable behavior for this will contribute to feelings of self doubt.

Initiative vs. Guilt (four to five years). Four- and five-year-olds want to be active. If given freedom to explore and experiment (and if caregivers take time to answer their questions), the inner drive of these children toward initiative will be encouraged. If these children are restricted and made to feel that their activities and questions are bothersome, they will feel guilt about doing things on their own. Froebel's words are appropriate here:

> Show no impatience about their ever-recurring questions. Every repelling word crushes a bud on a shoot of their tree of life. Do not, however, tell them in words much more than they can find themselves without your words. . . . [I]t is, of course, easier to hear the answer from another, perhaps to only half hear and understand it, then to seek and discover for oneself. Do not, therefore, always answer your children's questions at once and directly, but as *soon* as they have gathered sufficient strength and experience furnish them with the means to find the answers in the sphere of their own knowledge. (Hailman, 1887, p. xiv)

Industry vs. Inferiority (six to eleven years). Upon entering school, children are dominated by curiosity and desire for performance. They are ready to learn by producing things, developing a sense of industry. The danger at this stage is that they may feel inadequate or inferior. If the child is encouraged to make and do things well, to persevere, and to finish tasks and is praised for trying, industry results. If the child is unsuccessful, derided, or treated as bothersome, a feeling of inferiority results. Children who feel inferior may never enjoy intellectual work and take pride in doing things well. Worse, they may feel that they will never excel in anything.

Identity vs. Role Confusion (twelve to eighteen years). At this stage, adolescents are concerned about the kind of person they are becoming. The goal at this stage is "the accrued confidence of sameness and continuity." The danger at this stage is role confusion, such as doubt about sexual and occupational identity. If teenagers succeed, as reflected by the reaction of significant others (parents, teachers, peers), in integrating roles in different situations so they experience continuity in their perception of self, identity develops. If they are unable to establish a sense of stability in other aspects of their lives, role confusion results.

Intimacy vs. Isolation (young adulthood). The goal at this stage is to establish an intimate relationship with another person. A willingness to be truthful about oneself and the other contributes to this goal. Failure to achieve the goal will lead to a sense of isolation.

Generativity vs. Stagnation (middle age). **Generativity** refers to productive and creative efforts that will have a positive effect on younger generations. Teaching, research, curriculum development, and political and social action that benefit children and youth are cases in point. The negative qualities of this stage are stagnation and self-absorption.

Integrity vs. Despair (old age). Integrity is the acceptance of one's life as something that had to be and that by necessity permitted no substitutions. Despair is the feeling that time is too short to take alternative roads to integrity.

In planning curriculum, one should identify the development stage of the learners to be served and attempt to shape learning opportunities so they contribute to the positive qualities of the tasks at hand. Examples of curriculum that assist students with their needs for *industry*—the feeling of competence—are found in many Montessori schools. The "practical life" area of many Montessori programs includes a large set of activities that prepare young children for success in tasks of daily life, such as personal hygiene, cleaning, care of the environment, courtesy, repair of machines, and nutrition and food preparation. Prerequisite skills for these real life tasks, including pouring, spooning, and use of tools are taught to enhance success and a sense of competence.

In the academic area, also, many children in Montessori schools have success because they are presented with materials that interest them, offer a clear

▼ _____ ▼

ACTIVITY 2–2   GENERATING ACADEMIC ACTIVITIES THAT ARE ALSO RESPONSIVE TO DEVELOPMENTAL CONCERNS

1. Identify a developmental concern—trust, initiative, industry, identity, or other—for a learner or learners with whom you are familiar.
2. Sketch an idea for a learning activity whereby the above concern can be related to the learner's progress in a subject matter of importance to you.

▲ _____ ▲

task that can be independently undertaken, and have a built-in feature whereby the child can tell whether his or her actions have been appropriate (for example, in constructing a tower, a cube placed out of order will result in an unstable structure).

Two illustrations of curricula that advance subject matter by meeting developmental needs are "Working from the Inside Out" and "Teaching the Holocaust," which follow.

Working from the Inside Out

The "Working from the Inside Out" curriculum for the elementary school encourages the persistency and success necessary for achieving the task of industry. Although learning arises when children seek means to resolve dilemmas, it is important that the curriculum provide a supportive environment that will structure how the dilemmas are resolved. In her elementary curriculum in art, Margot Grallert (1991) stimulates the individual to find his or her personal direction and expression but at the same time gives guidance in the use of tools so that there is experimentation and discovery. Accordingly, there are graphic observation centers in the classroom where students can illustrate either something they are looking at or ideas that have no concrete form. Sometimes students are asked to create a picture of an object, and sometimes they are asked to share the abstract quality of a condition, such as weather or motion.

In this curriculum, there is a balance between *craftsmanship*—the skill to use the tools necessary if the child is to have a sense of industry—and *expression*—the ability to "say" something. Discussion about the nature of materials that make it difficult to outline, confirm, or correct gives students access to the artistic process. Students draw in color and not just line. They learn terms such as *texture* and *form* because they see how these concepts contribute to expression.

> "It's different discovering techniques for yourself because you experiment as opposed to learning that there are tricks."

> "Students learn from each other. They see how others are trying things, coming up with ideas, making breakthroughs."

As an example of how color is used, when students work on colored paper or work with colored materials, they consider the space they are working on as important as what they compose on that space. They analyze the color, form, shape, and texture of the artifacts; the colors chosen are specific to what is observed; and the color of the paper shows through when it contributes to the color of the texture of the object.

Instruction and materials in the centers are structured to focus student observations. A study of shells at the first-grade level might involve only two or three media, and the student might draw only the different kinds of lines there are in a clam, a scallop, and a mussel. However, in order to capture the myriad and iridescent colors of the interior of an abalone shell, students combine colored sticks and watercolor. They start their work in the middle and discover how to show not only the colors, but also the hand-swirling texture.

Exercises with different media accompany observation of an artifact. The value of these exercises is less in the expression than in the confidence to express individual perceptions.

Art exercises start simply. In a study of Japanese art, first graders use watercolors to discover how brush, black paint, and water work together. They may spend two or three days producing dark and light, and two more days producing different kinds of strokes. Later, in a study of the desert, they use a combination of watercolor, chalk, and collage to illustrate their own ideas of what a nighttime or daytime desert environment might be like.

Tempera paint is used as a means of self-expression. In kindergarten, students paint only with shades of red for one week, then only with blue for another. When they mix paint to make the color of a fall leaf, they work only on the leaf color, not its shape. In third grade, they may paint the sky every day, morning and afternoon, for months. This enables them to discover color and atmosphere, literally and expressively. From their work, students learn to see the moods paint can create and to understand expression.

Teaching the Holocaust

Arye Carmon (1980) has developed a reproducible curriculum "Teaching the Holocaust" that places the adolescent and the problem of identity at the focal point in the presentation of history. This curriculum is based on Erikson's belief that people are confirmed by their identities and that society is regenerated by their lifestyles. To enter history, students must be able to relate their childhoods to the childhood experiences of former generations. They must be able to identify with the ideals conveyed in the history of their culture. According to Erikson, in youth, childhood dependence gives way; no longer is it the old teaching the young the meaning of life, it is the young who by their actions tell the old whether life as represented to them has some vital promise.

The major objective of the Holocaust curriculum developed by Arye Carmon is to heighten the student's awareness of the critical question of adult responsibility. This objective is achieved by fostering awareness of their human tendency toward stereotyping, prejudice, ethnocentrism, obeying authority, and thus escaping responsibilities. The subject matter is organized into units: the socialization of a German adolescent in Nazi Germany, the socialization of a Gestapo man, the moral dilemma of individuals and groups during the Holocaust, and the meaning of life in the post-Holocaust era. In each unit, students are given documents from the historical period. These documents provide historical background and serve as a basis for discussion of the moral dilemmas.

There are opportunities for both individual inquiry and group integration. Each person deals with a specific document; students form small groups to exchange feelings and opinions regarding the topics and their individual studies; then the entire class completes the discussion of the topic at hand. The content is not alien to the students, and they cannot remain apathetic to it. Students face questions that are relevant to their own lives: Why sanctification of life rather than martyrdom? What are the dilemmas that confronted the individual and the dilemmas that confronted Jews as members of a community? Which of these dilemmas touches you personally? Why? What is the common denominator of the dilemmas? Discussion manifests a dialogue between the student and his or her conscience and among student and peers.

During the first phase of this curriculum, resistance toward the subject matter increases; students tend to resist giving up their stereotypical attitudes and other protective mechanisms. Gradually, this resistance fades, only to be replaced by a feeling of helplessness. At this point, the study has opened students to the possibility of critical thinking and moral judgment. Students then begin to formulate the universal questions for confronting moral dilemmas: How would I have behaved if I had been in this situation? How should I have behaved? Thus the curriculum helps each student formulate a set of moral rules for self (Carmon, 1980).

Applying Piaget's Theories

From his investigations, Piaget concluded that cognitive development occurred in stages with the infant (birth to 2 years) acquiring understanding of the world primarily through sensory impressions and motor activities; the young child (2 to 7 years) learning to think with symbols such as words; the preadolescent (7 to 11 years) generalizing from concrete experiences and arriving at an understanding of logic-based tasks such as conservation (matter is not created or destroyed when it changes shape or form) and classification of items by constructing hierarchial relations and arranging them in particular order; and older students (11 years and older) acquiring mental structure and ways of learning that allows them to deal with abstractions, form hypotheses, and conceive of possibilities and ideals that conflict with existing reality (1991).

Piaget viewed mental structure as a product of both biological systems and learning from interaction with the world. Central to his theory is that learners must construct their own knowledge and assimilate new experiences in ways that make sense to them. Children create new knowledge by reflecting on their physical and mental actions. Telling students what they are to know does not work (Piaget, 1991).

Initially, teachers used Piaget's theory as a *screen*, a basis for deciding what *can* be taught effectively to students of specified age. For instance, activities involving cause–effect relations or inductive and deductive reasoning were postponed until the intermediate grades. Unfortunately, the use of Piaget's theory as a screen conflicted with the Piagetian value of freedom, expansion, and optimum development. The screen led to a restricted view of what students are ready for and limited the methods and content that might be introduced. Further, the practical problems of matching learning opportunities to assumed mental ages is immense. Students are likely to have a high level of ability in an area where they have much experience and are likely to conduct themselves at lower levels in unfamiliar areas.

Today, teachers are giving more attention to Piaget's interest in how outside stimulation affects individual initiative in pursuing relations among ideas. Curriculum developers are giving more attention to Piaget's views that children are like scientists who are attempting to make sense of their reality and that cognitive conflicts are generated when one's present ideas are not compatible with the logic of others and the attainment of a desired goal. Eleanor Duckworth (1987) is an example of those who have been influenced by Piaget and are now providing curriculum that takes children's knowledge and feelings into account as the starting points for learning.

Duckworth's Having Wonderful Ideas

Duckworth's curriculum first puts students in touch with concrete instances related to the area to be studied—math, science, art. Students are encouraged to notice what is interesting in the phenomenon and challenged to think and wonder about what they have observed. Next students are asked to share what sense they are making, and the teacher and peers try to understand the meanings students are creating from the situation. Students are helped to examine conflicting notions and to recognize inadequate explanations, modifying their views as they resolve the conflicts. Duckworth's curriculum offers situations in which learners at various cognitive levels come to know parts of the world in new ways, using multiple routes to knowledge—perception, action, and theory.

In a curriculum for teachers, Duckworth introduces a unit on "Moon Watching," an aspect of astronomy. This unit is a vehicle for helping teachers better understand teaching and learning. The study of the moon by teachers who have had little scientific background is analogous to the school curriculum where students have as yet little interest and few ideas of their own. "Moon Watching" begins with a discussion of when the students (teachers) last saw the moon, what it looked like then, when they think they'll see it next, and what it will look like then. This preliminary discussion gives rise to conflicting ideas and some involvement on the topic, although some of the students think a study of the moon is a waste of time.

Students are asked to keep and bring to class a notebook in which they make an entry every time they see the moon—when and where and what it looks like. After the first week's reporting, some students have something specific they want to look for, and little by little the task changes from one that is arbitrary and trivial to one that is absorbing and serious.

Excepts of accounts from students illustrate the responses:

> I keep my notebook on my bedside table, and every night it's there to remind me to look out the window. It takes only two to three minutes to write down my observations and draw my pictures, but later when I sit down and read several weeks' notes all together, I can spend fifteen to twenty minutes just generating questions and checking answers. I get excited when the moon moves across the sky just the way I thought it would, and I'm so disbelieving when it does something unexpected that I check my notes again and again.

> My questions caused my observations to change. I'm now concentrating on the path of the moon each night, not on its color or shape, although I'm still shaky enough to always note those, too . . . everything is expanding—my questions and observations are getting broader.

> My biggest problem in this class is forgetting about being a teacher and relearning how to be a learner. The notebook is a big help. I can make hypotheses and they can be wrong and that's OK. I can share observations and theories and be proud when someone says, "Ah, that's good." I can move at my own pace and ask my own questions. I like it.

> I felt I knew a great deal about the moon. (I'd thought about the moon as part of a unit on astronomy with sixth graders). I knew things about orbits and distance and reflected light. The first class discussion clued me in to the fact that my knowledge of the moon falls short of an understanding. My knowledge was only from a perspective of out in space looking in. It was always easy to think about those three objects in space and their interaction (sun, moon, earth). With this new perspective, I had many questions without answers, not knowing can be much more fun than knowing. It has opened my eyes to look for understanding.

After observing and engaging with real phenomena and fellow learners, students are encouraged to reveal the meanings they are generating and to make their thoughts clear for others.

> Class discussions have helped a lot. Often people have seen the moon at different times than I did, and they tentatively fill in some of my gaps in knowledge. (The gaps won't really be filled in until I see things for myself.) I also like to hear other people's hypotheses because they give me other avenues and ideas to check out. I especially like it when I can't believe what someone else has seen. It makes me slow down and reevaluate my own notes and theories.

Duckworth's students come to recognize knowledge as a human construction. As teacher of the course, she centers her efforts on helping students to see that their own ideas are reasonable and the best starting points. She does, however, offer ideas for consideration when she has a point of view that no one else has mentioned, not as the "right" idea, but simply as an alternative to consider (Duckworth, 1987).

▼ ————————————————————————————————— ▼

ACTIVITY 2–3   SETTING THE STATE FOR
COGNITIVE DISSONANCE AND
DEVELOPMENTAL GROWTH

Inquire with others (class members, peers, family) regarding their exposure to music: what type of music they prefer, how music affects their moods and behavior, and how they interpret its messages. If possible, conduct a "conversation" with your respondents to further their intellectual and emotional development.

▲ ————————————————————————————————— ▲

SUMMARY

This chapter began with traditional approaches to developing curriculum on the basis of psychological needs and interests. The possibility of a universal values direction in keeping with the biological nature of human life was examined. Particular curriculum aims for personal development were proposed.

The chapter included an extensive treatment of the issue of whether curriculum should aim at personal growth and at the same time educate for competency in academically valued fields. The methods of teachers who departed from strict domains of knowledge in addressing student concerns were discussed, as well as those of teachers who used the concerns of learners as a way to enlighten them about a particular academic subject and its relevance. Attention was given to modern theorists and teachers who follow the tradition of Froebel in giving voice to students by involving them wholly—mind, body, spirit—as they explore aspects of nature and culture. Exemplars of curriculum derived from the theories of Erikson and Piaget were presented to show how students can be helped to connect their own experiences and inner world to the interests and ideas of others. The importance of considering Erikson's concepts of *industry* and *identity* in elementary and secondary school curriculum was emphasized. Finally, the chapter provided illustrations of curriculum practices that used Piaget's views regarding the active construction of knowledge and the importance of cognitive dissonance for knowing the world in new ways.

QUESTIONS FOR DISCUSSION

1. How might the following assumption be used in setting priorities in curriculum planning?

   "If intrigued by the opportunities of a domain of knowledge, most students will make sure to develop the skills they need to operate with it."

2. In planning curriculum, should children of all ages have the right to be heard and have their views taken into account?
3. Regardless of student ability, performance is best in classes that are enjoyable. Why don't we, then, stop worrying about the presentation and coverage of content and concentrate on how to make learning enjoyable?

4. What is the best "test" to show that a particular program, learning opportunity, text, or content is developmentally appropriate for a student of a given age?

5. "Tagging"—the painting of symbols for personal and group identity (graffiti) on freeway signs, ramps, and walls—is a problem in many cities. What are the reasons for this activity? What needs are taggers trying to fulfill that might be addressed through the curriculum?

6. How can a teacher best resolve the dilemma of balancing (a) student's need for choices and control in selecting problem questions and approaches with (b) curriculum mandates and requirements set by those outside the classroom?

7. Piaget has suggested that development can be encouraged by inducing cognitive conflict—confronting children with evidence contrary to their beliefs. If true, are mixed-age groups and variability among learners better for development than homogeneous settings?

8. The lives of geniuses and profound scholars are associated with three factors:

   a. Capacity to concentrate on central questions of personal concern.

   b. Assistance of a model or mentor (including distant teachers of a previous generation).

   c. Openness to collaborating together with the ability to go it alone.

   What are the curricular implications of this finding?

9. What gender differences should be taken into account in developing your curriculum? Which of these differences are wittingly and unwittingly fostered by culture? Which ones are innate?

10. Is there a danger that if students are encouraged to be attentive to their own well-being, they will turn out to be egoists? Or does an enlarged conception of well-being include care for others?

REFERENCES

Carmon, A. (1980, July). Problems in coping with the Holocaust: Experiences with students in a multinational program. *American Academy of Political and Social Services Annals*, 450.

Decci, E., et al. (1991.) Motivation and education: The self determinist perspective. *Educational Psychologist*, *26*(3 and 6), 25–347.

Duckworth, E. (1987). *The having of wonderful ideas*. New York: Teachers College Press.

Erikson, E. (1968). *Identity, youth, and crisis*. New York: W. W. Norton.

Goodman, J. (1991). Redirecting sexuality: Education for young adolescents. *Curriculum and Teaching*, *6*(1), 12–22.

Grallert, M. (1991, August). Working from the inside out: A practical approach to expression. *Harvard Educational Review*, *61*(3), 260–269.

Hailman, W. H. (1887). Superintendent Zechs' report of his visit to the educational institute at Keilham, 1826. *The Education of Man*. New York: D. Appleton & Co.

Heller, H. C. (1993). The need for a core interdisciplinary life science curriculum in the middle grades. *Teachers College Record*, *94*(3), 644–652.

McLuhan, T. C. (1971). *Touch the earth: A self-portrait of Indian existence*. New York: Simon & Schuster.

Piaget, J. (1991). Adaptation and intelligence. *Organic Selection and Phenocopy*. Chicago: IL.

PART

Labyrinth of Curriculum Relevance

Few problems in the curriculum field are more difficult than those of deciding on relevant purpose and content. To what should the curriculum be relevant—to the individual, the world, the nation, or the local community? to a past, present or future life?

Part 2 provides an opportunity for you to evaluate your own views about whether curriculum should adjust to present and likely future social conditions, transcend negative features of society, or encourage social change by fostering skepticism about social practices and institutions and engaging in critical inquiries and political action. The curricula, including those of past generations, presented in these chapters show the range of options available in answering the question: In postindustrial society, what knowledge is of most worth?

▼ ——————————————————————————————— ▼

ADAPTING TO SOCIAL CHANGE

This chapter explores facets of curriculum relevancy, beginning with the early American colonists' concerns that the curriculum prepare one for life after death as well as ensure conformity to local standards of conduct. Following that, the chapter presents an account of a curriculum designed to prepare students for "the great end and real business of living" in the face of expanding social needs.

Later, the chapter examines a curriculum that is less focused on preparation for adulthood and more centered on the immediate quality of the student's experiences in the classroom. Initial curricular responses to an industrialized society, characterized by social disorganization and the fragmentation of knowledge and work, are illustrated by the curricula as introduced in progressive schools, community schools, and active citizenship programs in the first half of the twentieth century.

Finally, the chapter describes curricula responses to the postindustrial society, including both those that attempt to prepare students for a changing world and those that aim at transcending negative features of that world.

TRADITIONAL CURRICULUM VERSUS REALITIES OF EARLY AMERICA

A Native American Curriculum for Survival

The Native Americans offered the most important curriculum to the early American colonists. For example, consider the account of how Squanto, upon his release from being kidnapped by the English, became the pilot, interpreter, and teacher of early settlers until he died in 1622. Squanto's students recalled how he taught them, among other things, "how to set their corn, where to take fish, and how to procure other commodities" (Axtell, 1974, p. 248). He was only the first of many Native Americans who shared agricultural and other knowledge. As the English acknowledged, "Our first instructors for the planting were the Indians who taught us to cull out the finest seeds, to observe the fittest season, to keep distance for holes, and fit measure for hills, to worme it and

▲ ——————————————————————————————— ▲

weede it, to prune it, and dress it as occasion shall require" (Axtell, 1974, p. 248). The Native Americans' generosity in teaching what they knew about the natural life of their woods and fields gave the English a chance at survival rather than starvation in the new environment.

Reading and Latin Grammar

Squanto's curriculum contrasts with the one that was soon established in the early American colonial schools. The new settlers brought with them educational traditions and concern that students read and interpret the scripture correctly. Pilgrims and later colonists in New England established schools for children to receive catechized instruction, to learn songs of worship, and to read the Bible. Instruction in reading began with the letters of the alphabet using the names of biblical characters ("A is for Adam"). Reading material consisted of Bible stories and moral lessons based on passages of scripture.

Although most formal schooling in colonial America ended with learning to read by spelling out words, church leaders received additional training in some of the languages in which the Bible had originally been written, especially Latin and Greek, as well as instruction in theology. Preparation for college training in theology was provided at the Latin Grammar School, which offered instruction in Latin and Greek. This school was established in 1636 and remained the formal instrument of secondary education for more than 100 years. The curriculum of this school emphasized memorization of the rules and paradigms of Latin grammar, first through the study of Cheever's accidence (Eziekel Cheever was a school teacher in this early period who had his own summary of Latin grammar) and then the study of Lily's grammar (with its 25 kinds of nouns, 7 genders, 15 pages of rules for genders, and 22 pages of declensions of nouns). Mastery of grammar was followed by reading Latin classics through the major works of Cicero and the Bible. The rudiments of Greek (declaration) nouns and conjugation of Greek verbs were also included as a requirement for college entrance.

Upon completing the Latin Grammar School, the future leader was eligible for college and the continued study of Greek grammar as well as study of the New Testament, Hebrew, and perhaps Sanskrit. Language study was supplemented by further literary and theological instruction. Such a curriculum was intended to prepare selected young men for leadership roles, guiding the daily lives of their fellow colonists according to the scriptures.

In colonial America, experience was the great teacher. Daily living on the farm taught one to make and repair wagons and harnesses, to build and repair buildings, to take care of animals, to sow and reap, to interpret the signs of weather, and to provide the food, clothing, and necessities for existence. The apprenticeship system, in which students received technical instruction from a master in a craft or trade in return for labor (and in some cases a premium of money), was common.

In the 1770s, the demands for a more practical curriculum than that offered by the Latin Grammar School was met by "Venture" schools and academies.

Teachers in these schools taught for a fee the subject matter of most use to those interested in trade and geographical expansion—modern language, geography, bookkeeping, navigation, and surveying.

Ben Franklin's Curriculum

The academy had been proposed by Benjamin Franklin in 1749 as an agency to prepare students for the duties of life. Franklin's proposal offered both classical language for those who wanted college preparation and utilitarian subjects that could be chosen in light of one's desired future occupation. Husbandry and science were offered through formal studies, together with practice in planting, grafting, inoculating, and preserving health. The curriculum called for teaching the history of commerce, including study of the invention of the arts and manufacturing, and instruction in the mechanics, commodities, and materials that would increase productivity.

Franklin wanted the academy to have a well-equipped library, a garden, orchard, meadow, and a field or two. Students were to be "frequently exercised in running, leaping, wrestling, and swimming" (Franklin, 1749, p. 389). He anticipated the modern literature-based curriculum and the writing process in his recommendations for teaching English through the study of the best writers and the practice of students writing to each other, making abstracts of what they read in their own words, and expressing themselves by writing their own stories.

A Modern Curriculum for Use

Some teachers today try to meet the ideals of Franklin. Steve McKay, a science teacher at Anderson Valley High School in California, is a case in point. When McKay accepted his position, he knew that the emphasis in the school was academics, not practical application. In his second year, McKay set about turning the curriculum around by incorporating advanced technology and the principles of science into projects related to the environmental context of Anderson Valley.

Students were given opportunities to experiment with a vineyard plot, tending dozens of colonies of bees, and rigging "trellis networks" where male kiwi fruit vines were placed slightly above female plants so that the bees would fly between the two, increasing pollination and fruit production. Students were also involved in money-making projects in areas of their own interests. In a greenhouse the students had planned and constructed, they grew tomatoes, bedding plants, and herbs to sell at local markets. Students kept a percentage of the profits, and the remainder went to the school.

To be sure that the curriculum addressed employers' realities, students studied the local labor market. They found that local wine and fruit producers needed workers with management skills and experience with intensive farming techniques, that highly trained people were needed in laboratories, that nurseries wanted greenhouse workers who could handle complex environmental controls and advanced propagation techniques, and that a developing tourist industry had created a demand for local produce to be sold in restaurants and stores. The need for a local site to model agricultural development and apply research in production management, energy conservation, and marketing was clear.

McKay applied for and received a specialized secondary school grant from the California Department of Education and, in 1987, started its Center for Studies in Horticulture, Science, and Technology. Currently, the center is an outdoor laboratory. Its experimental orchard permits intensive land use; vegetables, flowers, and berries are propagated in plots. Tracts are allocated for a vineyard and a start of Christmas trees. Inoculated versus noninoculated legumes are compared and various irrigation methods are tested. There are pens of turkeys, a confinement location for 380 laying hens, and a spot for 25 hives of bees.

In five state-of-the-art greenhouses, students control insects biologically, cultivate parasitic wasps, and practice methods of eradicating weeds. Heat sensors under plant beds are hooked up to classroom computers and to the computers that monitor and regulate the environment. In a culture laboratory, students clone plants for single cells and experiment with the propagation of pineapples, bananas, and gooseberry plants. In a nearby lab, students research alcohol as part of a plan to use apples to fuel the school's trucks. Students also help manage a 15-acre apple orchard in return for produce. Apple juice is bottled and sold as a class project. The label on the bottles is designed by fine arts students.

Students have conducted outreach symposiums discussing agricultural topics and formed partnerships with the local university and colleges to obtain mentors and share resources. A cannery and freezing laboratory have been developed on the high school campus. Jams, jellies, apple butter, and juice blends are produced there, using fruits and vegetables that might otherwise be wasted for lack of a market.

The Center has become a unifying entity for the school. The mathematics class makes measurements and records the information from the greenhouse research; the science and fine arts departments help interpret and portray the data. Evidence of student achievement is found in the winning of science awards for a project such as tissue culture research and the continuing studies and work of graduates. McKay himself values the way students take ownership of the projects and discover a purpose for being in school. He believes that in dealing with their own research and enterprise, they feel valuable: "They ask more questions. They want to know why things happen and how they work. They develop skills in problem solving and decision making" (Perry, 1989, p. 32).

SCIENCE VERSUS CLASSICS IN NINETEENTH-CENTURY CURRICULUM

By the nineteenth century, teachers in the primary school had broadened their curriculum from the teaching of the alphabetic principle and the memorization of biblical sources to a study of the 3 Rs. Although most primary teachers focused on reading as oral expression, a few wanted students to understand what they read. Arithmetic was taught with an emphasis on numeration, counting by groups, addition, multiplication, and division of integers. Writing was undervalued and taught chiefly as spelling and handwriting.

Near the end of the nineteenth century, the primary curriculum was extended by an elementary curriculum. This new eight-year elementary curriculum reflected both the disciplinary and scientific views' demands for preparing children for every area of life by teaching them to think through the study of mathematics and grammar. The practice of teaching arithmetic for its practical uses gave way to teaching mathematics for its disciplinary value. English grammar replaced Latin grammar and was taught for disciplinary aims and patterned after the divisions of Latin grammar—orthography, inflection, syntax, and prosody.

The scientific view was that content from the natural and social sources would be more useful than the classics in preparing students to adapt to a changing world and better prepare them for the new scientific studies that were being introduced in colleges (such as those of the various biological and physical sciences) and the expanded social sciences (such as history, geography, and political economy). The concept *elementary* school was derived from the idea that children should learn the *elements* of knowledge found in the new scientific fields. The teacher was expected to select from the sciences those facts, principles, and laws that would be most frequently found and used in daily life. Music, good manners, principles of morality, and physical education were also regarded as foundations for personal and social living.

The curriculum of the new public high school was broad, with courses for those preparing for college, those who wanted an academic program but who had no plan for college education, and those who wanted vocational preparation. The classical emphasis on Latin and Greek continued for college preparation. Both college and noncollege programs stressed algebra and geometry because those subjects were thought to be useful both in developing the mind and in dealing with the technical and scientific applications of the developing industrial society. Physics and chemistry gained entrance on the grounds that their disciplinary values were equal or superior to the classics. English was first introduced for those not going to college, but the disciplinary argument soon won its acceptance as suitable for preparing students for college. History and geography were at first in the inferior position of content for the noncollege-bound student, but gradually were offered as college preparation, even though their disciplinary claims could not be established. The vocational studies—industrial arts, home economics, commercial studies, and agriculture—remained without prestige, unsuitable for academic purposes but necessary for their vocational and practical purposes. The arts and physical education were included for their values in developing the individual.

Public support for high schools rested on the claim that these schools were beneficial to the community, but few attempts to buttress this claim were made. In 1881, David Hoyt assessed what high schools did for the city and state. He found that all classes of society attended the school but that the middle class was most fully represented. His follow-up study of graduates showed that most were in the mercantile business, manufacturing, and mechanical pursuits, employed as bookkeepers and accountants. Only 13 percent were in the learned professions—law, clergy, medicine. Hoyt recommended that the curriculum include manual training, mechanical drawing, and the studying of mechanical operations to help more graduates avoid becoming sales representatives and accountants. He believed that the community's need for people able to engage in the practical operation of manufacturing was paramount and that the school had not been responsive to this need. Hoyt anticipated what today is considered a problem in American productivity—the need for people with both the intellectual attainment and the practical skills required for planning and guiding manufacturing enterprises (Hoyt, 1986).

CURRICULUM RESPONSES TO THE INDUSTRIAL SOCIETY

Contextualization: John Dewey's Curriculum

In the early years of the twentieth century, John Dewey implemented a curriculum for young children that addressed the negative consequences brought by large-scale industry and the corporate form of a business organization—the loss of community as the interests of a working class conflicted with the interests of a business group, and specialization of functions which robbed activity of the social and economic meanings it had previously possessed. Dewey's curriculum focused on occupations that served social needs (Mayhew and Edwards, 1936).

Four- and five-year-olds studied the familiar occupations of the home; six-year-olds studied large social industries like farming, mining, lumbering, so they could see the complex and varied occupations on which life depends. For instance, in one study by six-year-olds, children found the connection between raw material and the manufacturing of a finished product as they removed seeds from cotton plants, baled the cotton, and went through other stages in the manufacture of cotton cloth.

Seven-year-olds experimented with raw materials and various metals, noting qualities and their uses. Older students studied the development of industry and invention, in order to understand the steps of progressing to gain insight into social life and to realize what enters into the makeup of society and how it came to be.

History was taught as a pageant of techniques and cooperation rather than a chronicle of violence and oppression. The land was the center for science study because all work related to it sooner or later. Also, children at all ages were expected to engage in experimental work as a way to awaken consciousness of the world, develop powers of observation, and acquire a sense of the method of inquiry. Teachers and subject-matter specialists cooperated so that intellectual resources necessary for solving problems initiated by students would be available.

Linkages in the Lincoln School Curriculum

Teachers at the Lincoln School of the Teachers' College, Columbia University, in the 1920s continued to develop curricula by which students could find connections between modern society and its antecedents (Triplell, 1927). These teachers also gave more emphasis to the immediate quality of life in the classroom than to preparing students for some prespecified future. Gaining a maximum meaning from the present was thought to be the best preparation for the future.

The Lincoln teachers followed a "unit of work" procedure in their curriculum development. A *unit* consisted of an extensive project that would make use of many subjects. The selection of a unit or project was guided by several criteria:

1. *Realness.* The unit must develop from a real-life situation. The topic for study may be an individual or group suggestion and represent a past experience or a present need. Resources for conducting the project should be available.
2. *Breadth of opportunity.* The topic or question should stimulate many kinds of activities and provide for individual contributions—constructing, dramatizing, exploring, and expressing creative energy. The activity of each child must contribute to the unit as a whole.
3. *Personal growth.* The study should allow each child to exert effort in improving higher skills, habits, and attitudes. The unit should be rich enough to lead students in the discovery of new interests and possibilities for further study.
4. *Cultural resources.* The social meanings found in art, history, geography, mathematics, science, literature, and the like should be brought to bear in the unit and serve as a springboard to future study.

One unit for sixth graders evolved from a student's concern about daylight saving time and the question of who had the right to determine the correct time. Early discussion centered around various clocks, the master clock at the Naval Observatory, and arguments for and against daylight savings. Among the questions that arose from this discussion were these:

1. What causes the midnight sun?
2. How did early people tell time?
3. How is the master clock regulated?

In order to answer such questions, the important observatories in the world were located, the contributions of Galileo were discussed, sphericity, rotation, revolution, and their consequences were studied. Daily observations of the sky were made and reported. These observations began with smoked glass, old films, and compasses. In order to express themselves, students formed concepts for such terms as *celestial sphere, zenith, horizon, altitude declination,* and *degrees*. The moon as a measure of time was also a focus for study. With the help of the monthly *Evening Skymap*, the class knew what to expect to see each night. Activities with compasses led to interest in terrestrial magnetism and magnetic poles. Investigation of how to determine direction at night, the North Star, and sidereal time followed. Observations of Mars led to a collection of newspaper and journal articles on the topic. Theories and facts were defined.

Some of the questions that led to instruction in science as well as work in literature and history were these:

▼   What is atmosphere? Where does it end?

▼   What causes wind?

▼   How did the planets and stars get their names?

Imagination was stirred by the natural causes discovered. Poems with titles such as "Night," "Snowflakes," "Spring," and "Mars" were written. Students were stimulated to compose original myths and adventure stories such as "My Adventure in Star-Catching," "Professor ZoDiak and Me," and "The Heavenly Twins." Questions arose about how early people told time. Students considered the notions of astronomy and time that existed in old Mesopotamia, Egypt, Greece, Rome, and western England. The astronomical discoveries of the Chinese and Native Americans were reviewed.

The activities of the unit were extensive, involving using of telescopes; making a Zodiac calendar; inventing time instruments; using principles of shadow sticks, sundials, clepsydras, and time candles; using a hectograph; dramatizing a play of "The First Water Clock"; making a time line of history; and visiting museums that featured relevant exhibits. Some students set poems to music; others created dances around their ideas of the revolutions of the planets and their satellites. Geometry was used in estimating light and position of stellar objects above the horizon and below the Zenith.

Curriculum of the Community School

The community school in the 1930s was locally centered and directed toward the health, recreational, vocational, and other needs of the community in which students were a part. The curriculum was seen as a means to improve living conditions and, at the same time, help students think more intelligently about how national and world affairs were affecting their lives. Engaging in some useful work was a key element in the program. Community needs were analyzed by students and programs of action developed. Students not only read about problems but worked out solutions. Parents participated and aided in addressing the problem selected.

One illustration of a community school's curriculum is found in the story of Holtsville, Alabama (NEA, 1940). The Holtsville school, grades 7-12, took as its ideal the creation of better living conditions for all. The teachers shifted their emphasis from teaching subjects as ends in themselves to a functional view with the question of how the subjects could enrich the life of the community. In their study and analysis of needs, students found that many of the commercially canned fruits and vegetables bought in the community could have been raised there as a source of income. They also discovered that the community's heavy meat spoilage could have been saved if refrigeration and canning facilities had been available. Teachers secured federal and state aid to construct and equip facilities for community improvement. The home economics department took charge of the cannery, and students were trained to maintain the refrigeration plant and cold storage room. A chick hatchery was installed under the management of students. A power spray machine was acquired so that students could spray orchards. Students also engaged in terracing, corridor plowing, and planting and pruning fruit trees as service to the community. Home economics students engaged in home redecoration projects, remaking clothing, and designing draperies for home use. Students edited the only weekly paper for the community and ran their own print shop; opened a cooperative store that sold many of their own products, such as toothpaste made in their chemistry department; showed films for the community; and maintained a game-loan library and a bowling alley. Students formed a home nursery for the care of babies and operated a dental clinic and a beauty parlor and barber shop as well as a building devoted to crafts.

Another teacher who created a community school is Marie Turner Harvey of Porter, Missouri. Harvey worked with a group of interested women in galvanizing the community to make the school the focal part of Porter's social life. She formed clubs and organizations to come to grips with Porter's economic and social problems (Dewey, 1919).

Other detailed accounts of the nature and funding of community school curricula have been given by Elsie Ripley. She described how teachers in Kentucky and West Virginia became intimate members of their communities and educated themselves about the needs and resources of these localities as bases for further education of the community (Ripley, 1939, p. 38). For instance, in response to health needs, teachers and parents raised funds for a trained pediatrician to examine children, provided midmorning meals for undernourished children, offered courses in budgeting, obtained the service of dentists who would visit the community monthly, operated a nursery school for parents to observe the right conditions for children's well-being, and organized a "sick committee" whose members volunteered to assist the doctor and help ailing neighbors. These and other activities changed poor habits of personal and family hygiene in the community.

Foxfire: A Modern Curriculum that Connects to the Community

For more than 20 years, Eliot Wigginton and his students have published Foxfire books and magazines, reporting their studies of the traditions and history of their community (Wigginton, 1985a). Wigginton has shared the curriculum philosophy from which the Foxfire experience evolved, including the following:

1. *Student choice and responsibility.*   The tasks flow from student desire. Students choose, design, revise, carry out, and evaluate the worth of the activity. Most problems that arise during the project must be solved by the students themselves.
2. *Local connection.*   Connections of the work to the surrounding community are clear. Whenever students study real-world problems, like changing climate patterns, acid rain, racism, or AIDS, they must "bring them home" by identifying local attitudes about them, as well as illustrating and stating the implications of these problems in their own environment. Also, members of the community serve as the resources from which the students draw.
3. *Challenge.*   Rather than the students doing what they already know how to do, all are continually led into new work and unfamiliar territory.
4. *Cooperation.*   There is emphasis on peer teaching, small group work, and team working. At the end of the project, each student can identify his/her specific contribution to the project.
5. *Teacher role.*   The teacher is not the repository of all knowledge but a collaborator and guide.
6. *Audience.*   There is an audience beyond the teacher for student work, an audience the students want to serve. The audience may be another individual, a small group, or the community at large. The audience, in turn, must affirm that the work is important, needed, and worth doing.
7. *Subject matter.*   The academic integrity of the work is clear. Although texts are regarded as reference works, not as content to be covered, content such as grammar and mechanics are blended into purposeful writing activity, not isolated drill.
8. *Evaluation.*   Evaluation follows the teacher's challenging, "In what ways will you prove to me at the end of this program that you have mastered the objectives it has been designed to serve?" Students are taught to monitor their own progress, to devise their own remediation, and to understand that the progress of each student is the concern of every student in the room.
9. *Continuity.*   New activities grow from the old. A finished product is not the conclusion of a series of activities, but the starting point for a new series.

Questions that characterize the moment of completion include these:

▼ "So what?"

▼ "What do we know now and know how to do that we didn't know how to do when we started together?"

▼ "How can we use the skills and knowledge in new and more complex and interesting ways?"

▼ "What is next?" (Wigginton, 1985b, p. 52)

Wigginton tells how two ninth graders researched and completed an article for publication about Dan Crane who for the article demonstrated the almost lost art of hewing railroad cross ties by hand. In the class introduction to the piece, the boys wrote:

> The second reason John and I wanted to interview Dan is because he is our grandfather. He has about every issue of the *Foxfire* magazine, and he knows many of the people who have been interviewed, but he has never been interviewed himself so John and I decided to get him into one of the magazines. We thought this might make his life a little brighter, so this is our gift to him. (Bedingfield, 1987, p. 6)

A network of teachers is now applying the Foxfire approach. Typical of their accounts is that given by Elain Briscoe's sixth graders who had a concern about the fact that a local child had been abducted and killed. At the students' request, community resource people were interviewed, and existing safety booklets were critiqued and found wanting. The students decided to produce their own booklet, and one student created the booklet's spokesperson—a dog named Fido—and illustrated the pages and cover. All conducted the research, wrote the text, created word games, and designed the pages. Toward the end of the school year, the completed 24-page booklet was given to every elementary school student in the school.

Citizenship Education

The most important citizenship education has always gone on outside of schools. Hence, the Citizenship Education Project launched a program in 1949 to encourage students to take action in the community by working in areas of public policy: elections, government agencies, courts, conservation, and voluntary groups (Citizenship Education Project, 1958). This project provided resources in citizenship that more than 1,200 teachers used in devising their own citizenship education curriculum. The resources included three things:

▼ Annotations of documents related to the premises of American liberty, such as the Bill of Rights, major court decisions and basic legislation

▼ The premises of American liberty

▼ Guidelines for developing action plans called "Laboratory Practices" (The community was regarded as a laboratory for student learning.)

The guidelines stipulated that each citizenship practice should do each of the following things:

▼ Require students to inform themselves fully about the issue with which they would deal.

▼ Involve students in taking action to improve, change, serve, or otherwise influence some public matter (a situation that is not imaginary or speculative but of significance to the students themselves).

▼ Illustrate and be consistent with democratic standards and values (as reflected in the "Premises of American Liberty") in everything the students do.

Some of the practices involved social service, such as conducting a tuberculosis prevention campaign and setting up a consumer protection clinic. Other practices centered on doing something about public opinion, conservation, legislation, transportation, and international relations. One example of the latter featured an exchange of national history textbooks with a Canadian class and study of those books for evidence of nationalism through a cooperative treatment of topics like the War of Independence, the War of 1812, Canadian-American migration, and past and present United States–Canadian trade. The students subsequently took action by making appropriate recommendations to textbook authors, publishers, and civic groups interested in the content of U.S. history courses.

Teachers of many subject areas developed and carried out laboratory practices: a music class promoted a music appreciation organization for the community; a science class worked for better health policies; an English class rephrased local ordinances in simple English and interpreted official reports and publications in the local newspaper. Under the direction of government teachers, students did projects that included making a tax map of the county, forming a student mutual investment fund, promoting informative labeling, improving local zoning, and informing the community about food inspection. Members of one history class undertook a practice entitled "Immigration and Social Change" as a way to see what the past can teach the present. Students observed social mobility as shown in history as a basis of forming a generalization to use in weighing current issues that are a consequence of immigration. Answers were sought to such questions as "What attempts were made to integrate these people into the community?" and "What effect did their arrival or departure have on the community?" Students took action by establishing a speakers' bureau to send members who spoke the language of the immigrants to explain community resources available for helping them meet their needs.

CURRICULUM RESPONSES TO POSTINDUSTRIAL SOCIETY

Just as early twentieth century teachers helped formerly agrarian populations adapt to the requirements of the industrialized world, some teachers today are developing curriculum which they believe to be appropriate for the postindustrial world.

World View of Postindustrial Society

Although there is no single world view of postindustrial society, many recognize that such a society is characterized by its challenging of ideas from the Enlightenment such as the scientific method (the "objectivity" of science), faith in universal reason, and the belief that the natural and social world can be controlled so that human life can have higher levels of material comfort.

Technological and economic developments have created new industries and social realities. New technologies such as information systems, mass media, and computers that produce images and information rather than products are associated with many social consequences. Television determines what is real and brings loss of a sense of one's own perceptions and emotions. Personal dissatisfaction is associated with anything that isn't reinforced by a consumer ethic.

Globalization is occurring and blurring the meaning of the nation-state. We are seeing the rise of extraterritorial companies, the free flow of capital, regional organizations (created as the European Community, North American Free Trade Agreement, Association of South East Asian Nations), and the need for international cooperation in dealing with problems of place and the environment. Conversely, the fading of the superpowers is associated with growing popularist nationalism, which on the positive side offers more local determinism and political democracy, and seems to satisfy people's needs for connectedness, honor, and loyalty; and on the negative side gives rise to suspicion of others within the same nation who do not seem to agree with the dominant ideology and endangers the lives of those termed "minority" through discriminating practices.

Workers in the United States have been affected by these world events—the rise of consumerism and service industries, decline in manufacturing, and relocation of jobs and workers have widened the gap between the haves and the have-nots. Within the manufacturing plant, assembly lines with their emphasis on routine, accuracy, speed, and close supervision have given way to the team concept and its value of flexibility, cooperation, problem solving, and decision making by workers.

Postindustrial society is associated with a litany of gloom and doom—overpopulation; pressure on the land; pollution of the air; depletion of water, forests, and natural resources; problems in social relations; loss of community; personal isolation; detachment from suffering; and a sense of one's own mortality.

CURRICULUM ALTERNATIVES

Teachers respond to postindustrial society by centering on the local manifestations of the world conditions. They try to answer the question of how their curriculum can best prepare students for dealing with local problems of the environment—jobs, health, recreation, safety, immigration, and the like. Their answers fall into three categories:

▼ *Social adaption* attempts to help students fit into the society as it is.

▼ *Social revisionism* aims to help students transcend excessive individualism, consumerism, and materialism by encouraging local self-sufficiency and mutual aid, and focusing on relationships rather than the pursuit of material wealth.

▼ ─── ▼

ACTIVITY 3–1   DETERMINING CURRICULAR
IMPLICATIONS FROM DATA ABOUT
POSTINDUSTRIAL SOCIETY

Below is a sample of facts and generalizations about the postindustrial society. Check those that you accept as valid, and then indicate the kind of content—values, concepts, skills—you believe should be taught in response to the stated conditions:

1. There is a prevailing attitude that society can collapse around our lives and we will not be affected.
2. The security of the privileged will be jeopardized by global warming, ozone depletion, and contamination.
3. The knowledge now propagated by schools will not be appropriate for the experience children will face in the twenty-first century when economic contraction rather than expansion may be the norm.
4. What counts as knowledge is not found in reason but determined by the judgment and values of a social consensus.
5. How to learn is more important than specific knowledge and skills.
6. The loss of species and energy resources indicate that we are eroding the life system that supports us.
7. The exportation of firms to locations where labor is less costly reduces individual opportunities.
8. Among all social classes, there is a decline in mortality but an increase in suicide, drug abuse, family breakdown, and child abuse.
9. Population pressures produce different outcomes in different settings.
10. The Soviet lesson is that to rely on defense for securing goals is not effective in the postindustrial world.
11. Mass migration across national boundaries is associated with social–racial tensions.
12. The global village is becoming more fragmented even as it becomes more unified by systems of communication.

▲ ─── ▲

▼   *Social criticism* is the development of knowledge and critical perspectives on society, its practices, and its institutions, raising the consciousness of the uses and abuses of power in our lives.

Social Adaption

Illustrations of curriculum adaption at different periods of history are given in Part 3. Adaptation occurs through the introduction of new content, new ways to present content, and relations with students. The most obvious example of curriculum adaptation during the past decade is associated with the computer and its uses. Teachers at all levels and fields have adapted their curriculum to the computer and its capabilities. Writing using word processing in language arts and increased attention to estimation, discrete mathematics, graphing, simulations in mathematics are cases in point. Other adaptions reflect the needs of a changing work force. Curriculums that impart both vocational and academic skills, such as Nursing Mathematics, attempt to meet the demand for better educated workers. Similarly, classroom trends featuring student investigations over extended time durations, multiple solutions to problems, cooperative teaching, and delegation of the text and teacher's authority to the classroom community match the changed workplace of the postindustrial society.

Social Revisionism

Concern about AIDS, parenting, alienation, discrimination, and other social problems have prompted teachers to develop units of instruction and full courses on those topics. Sometimes the topics are included within a traditional academic subject as an added topic or as an application. Other times, the topics are regarded as important in their own right, and a range of subject matters are brought to bear on the study. Social revisionism can occur in the contexts of both disciplinary and community problem-solving approaches. Illustrating social revisioning in the disciplines, a teacher of literature who was concerned about the psychic consequences of prefabricated reading materials, especially the loss of a sense of self and the primacy of one's perceptions and emotions of a postmodern world, selected novels whose authors offered strategies for coping with the current condition. Her curriculum included works of Saul Bellow, who helps readers contemplate their own special resources; Joan Didion, who depicts the tragedies of postmodern life; Don DeLillo, who offers possibilities of self in a repressive world; and Thomas Pynchon, whose options range from the avoidance of commitment to acceptance of the multiple contradictions of life today.

Other social revisionists follow the tradition of the old community school, with its primary aim of sustaining a community that nurtures interdependency, achievement for the well being of the group, and a sense of moral responsibility to both the natural environment and to one another. One can point to The Media Academy, a supportive school community with the Fremont High School in a ghetto area of Oakland, California. Four teachers initiated a program for the school's predominately African-American, Latino, and Asian students, linking the curriculum to possible future vocational opportunities and to more appealing communities than in their own (Wehlage, 1987). The students issue a Spanish-language community paper as well as other publications, and they air their words on radio and television. Field trips and internships at telecommunication and other media centers offer experience in the media profession. Advisors from the media assist with curriculum support. For example, a reporter may help students follow leads and develop a story. Students are responsible for developing topics for articles and are encouraged to write about issues of immediate concern to themselves and the broader community—date rape, reverse discrimination, abortion. An unresolved question for the Academy is whether the cooperative skills and talents students develop under the curriculum should be viewed as a means for the students to escape from their ghetto neighborhood into lucrative employment opportunities or to regenerate their own neighborhood and deal with the larger political and economic practices that have contributed to their poverty.

To clarify the differences between social revisioning and social criticism— the theme of concern in most revisionist curriculums promotes a caring, cooperative environment; the theme of social criticism brings to question existing social structures. Consider a few curricula that deal with environmental issues. The garden ethic is popular among revisionists as a way to help students and community become creative caretakers of the land, working with nature rather than against her. Judy Karasky's National Service Program, in which young men and women create a garden curriculum for an early childhood development center, is a case in point. The curriculum begins with team members talking with the children about the soil and about how life comes from the earth. The children look at pictures of fruits and vegetables, decide what to plant, and then draw the many shapes and colors of leaves and flowers. The garden is used to teach nutrition, as well as ecology, botany, art, writing, and thinking. The goal is for children to feel that the garden is theirs and that when the plants come up, they made it happen. All are mindful of the danger of building something that would be abandoned, a garden gone to seed, and of the need for children to accept responsibility for the watering and weeding.

Another illustration of a revisionist curriculum in environmental studies is found in a text written by the people of Rock Point Community School on a Navajo reservation. *Between Sacred Mountain: Navajo Stories and Lessons from the Land* (Rock Point Community School, 1984) functions as a curriculum in history, science, and social studies. The text describes the relationships of the Navajo to their land. An overriding theme of the text is that the survival of all people depends on our abilities to keep peace with the land that sustains us. The book grew out of the need to teach about Navajo life and the concern of the community that teaching conform to the Navajos' view of themselves. Parents wanted their children to understand the ecology of the land and to comprehend their relationship to both the land and the animals that support their way of life.

David Orr's Meadow Creek Project is a third example of a revisioning response to the urgency for ecology literacy, an earth-centered curriculum. In an effort to learn to live by the garden ethic, faculty and students represent different fields of study and work together to transform the ecologically unstable culture of their "nice" campus.

Social Criticism

Chapter 4 presents social criticism in detail; the concept of this alternative is introduced here with an example of a critical curriculum developed by staff

▼ _____ ▼

ACTIVITY 3–2   DEVELOPING CURRICULUM PURPOSES IN RESPONSE TO LOCAL SOCIAL NEEDS

Consider a local community with which you are familiar.

1. List some of the most important trends or social facts about this community, considering health, recreation, environment, employment, social relations, and family life.
2. Form one or more generalizations stating the most pressing community needs as indicated by the trends and facts listed in step 1.
3. State what you want students to learn so that they will understand the community needs or prepare them for adapting to the situation (your curricular purposes, for example). Your statement of purpose may be within your field of expertise (math, language, science, or some other area) in which the subject matter is adapted to community needs, or the statement may call for students' learning something not now in the curriculum.

▲ _____ ▲

and students at Queenscliff High School in Australia. The curriculum was part of a larger network of schools engaged in water quality studies which were linked by the use of a computer network. Students at Queenscliff broadened their focus from a study of fresh water quality to a critical study of sewage pollution at local beaches. Their investigation showed bacteria counts far in excess of acceptable guidelines for safety.

After being rebuffed in their efforts to discuss their findings with the local Water Board and to obtain the Board's own record of bacteria count, students invoked a Freedom of Information Act to gain access to the Water Board's data. Students then published an account of their findings in the local press triggering a powerful community response, including the local health center's recording of complaints about infections possibly associated with the bacteria in the sea water and the State government's requiring the Water Board to justify its action and ultimately to improve at great expense their sewage treatment facility.

Not all went smoothly in the project. Although the media initially accelerated the controversy initiated by the students, it later reinforced the Water Board's power and brought forth the financial implications of the proposed remedy. Nevertheless, by taking social action, the students effected an environmental curriculum that did more than impart environmental content. Students developed working knowledge about the power relationships among agencies and about their own capacity to influence the issues through the media and reports. Rather than helping students adapt to society as it exists, the Queenscliff curriculum encouraged students to question the governmental agency's authority for water management and promoted social change.

SUMMARY

This chapter showed competing ideas about curriculum relevancy by providing a look at how teachers of the past adapted their curriculum to changing circumstances or tried to overcome social inequalities. The conservative teachers of the Latin Grammar School believed that studies of the scripture and the cultural literature of the past would reveal the principles and values behind the flux and flow of social change. Later, other conservatives justified the teaching of the classics and mathematics as the most effective way to develop the intellect. Paradoxically, they believed that training the mind while defiling practice and useful knowledge was the best preparation for solving problems of practical conduct and experience. Teachers who wanted to break the domination of cultural studies and introduce the new subject matters of English, modern languages, and the sciences (which they believed were more useful) first had to claim that these subjects were equal to the classics in their power to develop the mind.

Although a curriculum for use was found in the apprentice system, venture schools, and the new public high schools, it wasn't until the twentieth century that the major activities of life—those related to health, family, vocation, citizenship, and the like—became the basis for selecting the content for the formal curriculum replacing separate subjects set out to be learned. The curriculum developed by teachers in the community schools, vocational programs, and citizenship education projects are cases in point.

The curriculum in the Dewey School and the curricula of other progressive teachers of the early twentieth century also had a focus on life itself, particularly in the study of those occupations that served social needs. These curricula were a direct response to the fragmentation and loss of personal and local meaning brought by industrialization.

This chapter concluded with a review of curricular adaption to world views of the present postindustrial society, including those that introduce new content thought to prepare students for present living and those aimed at helping students to transcend the dangers of contemporary society and to create a saner future.

QUESTIONS FOR DISCUSSION

1. Give your opinion of the growing practice of moving an array of social services (such as a program for babies and their teenage mothers, health care, family counseling, or substance abuse) into the schools.
2. Mandatory service programs as a way to instill citizenship values and to make students take responsibility for others have become controversial. The controversy arises particularly when the service becomes a requirement for a high school diploma. What are the assumptions about the functions of schooling, the nature of a valid learning experience, and the role of the teacher held by those in favor and those opposed to mandatory service?

3. Public support for schools has always rested on demonstrating that schools are beneficial to the local community. In what ways does the curriculum in a school familiar to you contribute to life in the community? If this curriculum were eliminated, what difference would it make?

4. Joseph Pichler, chair of the "National Alliance of Business" is a hard-shell believer in the liberal arts as the best training for life at work—two years of Latin, two years of Greek. On the other hand, Robert Bjork, chair of a national research committee on training, says that excellent performance in the classroom does not necessarily predict good performance on the battlefield, on the shop floor, or in the sports arenas. What is the validity of these two viewpoints and what are the curricular implications of the two views?

5. The official educational hierarchy at national, state, and district levels is said to impede efforts of teachers to address the needs of their immediate communities. What are some of the ways teachers can subvert or ignore the hierarchy and link curriculum to the local situation? Should teachers be responsive to both the hierarchy and the local community? If so, how?

REFERENCES

Axtell, J. (1974). *The school upon a hill*. New Haven: Yale University Press.

Bedingfield, C., & Crane, J. (1987). From daylight to dark: hewing a cross tie. *Foxfire, 21,* 6.

Building better programs in citizenship. (1958). New York: Citizenship Education Project, Teachers College, Columbia University.

Dewey, E. (1919). *New schools for old*. New York: Dutton.

Franklin, B. (1907). Proposals relating to the education of youth Pennsylvania, 1749. In A. H. Smyth (Ed.), *The writings of Benjamin Franklin* (pp. 388–396). New York: Macmillan.

Hoyt, D. (March 1881). Relation of the high school to the community. *Education, 6*(5), 429–441.

Mayhew, K. C., & Edwards, A. C. (1936). The Dewey School. New York: D. Appleton-Century Company.

NEA Education Policies Commission. (1940). *Learning the ways of democracy*. Washington: NEA.

Perry, S. (January/February 1989). One part that's prologue. *Vocational Education Journal, 64*(1), 31–34.

Ripley, E. (1939). *Community schools in action*. New York: Viking Press.

Rock Point Community School. (1984). *Between sacred mountain: Navajo stories and lessons from the land*. Tucson, AZ: University of Arizona Press.

Triplell, J. (1927). *Curriculum making in the elementary school*. Boston: Ginn and Company.

Wehlage, G. G. (1987). *Dropout prevention and recovery: Fourteen case studies*. Madison, WI: National Center on Effective Secondary Schools.

Wigginton, E. (1985a). Foxfire grows up. *Harvard Educational Review, 59*(1), 24–50.

Wigginton, E. (1985b). *Sometimes a shining moment: The Foxfire experience*. New York: Doubleday.

FOMENTING SOCIAL CHANGE

Chapter 4 addresses the innovation of critical curriculum by first reviewing some of its history and then describing how radical teachers attempt to demythologize social institutions and foster critical attitudes toward such institutions and practices through academic subject matter. Additionally, the chapter describes the efforts of teachers and students in changing a social condition, along with a discussion of the conditions that sustain them, dealing with controversial social issues and projects. The chapter concludes with a view of critical pedagogy and popular culture—curricula that focus on cultural forms of everyday life and aim at developing the capacities of students to reshape the influences of popular culture that oppresses them and others.

BACKGROUND FOR CRITICAL CURRICULUM

For many years, some teachers have sought to develop curriculum that would bring greater equity and justice. They feared that too often the traditional curriculum contributed to structured inequality, environmental pollution, gender, and racial disharmonies. The following section describes curriculum efforts of radical teachers in the past.

Antebellum America and the Slavery Question

Most teachers in antebellum America played little part in the slavery question. Most of them in both the North and the South accepted slavery and drifted along with the sentiment of their community. Teachers were expected to indoctrinate children with the community attitude toward slavery whenever the community on the whole had one, or to avoid the subject entirely. There were, however, notable examples of teachers who expressed their dislike of slavery.

Reuben Crandel, a teacher of botany, was arrested and thrown into prison in 1835 for alleged curriculum of abolition literature. Although it was proven that the "abolitionist" newspapers found in his trunk were wrapping his botanical specimens and the "incendiary" pamphlets were articles opposing slavery, the district attorney sought his execution on a capital offense. The jury cleared him, but eight months in damp confinement caused his death of tuberculosis (Beale, 1941).

In 1857, J. C. Richardson, a Kentucky teacher, was seized by a mob for giving a sermon against the rise of slavery. The mob beat him and threw him into a guarded cabin, expecting to return and further punish him. Two of his students rescued him and held off the mob with their rifles until the teacher and his wife escaped northward. Another Kentucky teacher, John Fee, was more persistent. Although he founded an abolitionist school in the mountains away from slaveholders, he was greeted in another county by a riot, and his school was burned. In all, he was mobbed 22 times and twice left for dead. Finally, he was driven from the state. Three times Fee tried to return, succeeding during the last time under protection of Union soldiers when he reestablished his school that later became Berea College (Beale, 1941).

Socialistic Curriculum

Kenneth Teitelbaum's *A Curriculum for "Good Rebels"* (1993) gives an account of the socialist Sunday school at the beginning of the twentieth century, revealing ways in which radical activity attempted to instill understanding and concern for more equitable social and economic relations. In their effort to encourage children (ages 5 to 14) to become "good rebels," teachers used three kinds of texts:

▼   appropriated mainstream texts

▼   adapted radical materials

▼   focused discussion on socialistic themes

Robert Louis Stevenson's "Where Go the Boats," an example of an appropriated mainstream text that could serve a socialist idea, was used to reinforce a perspective of the interrelatedness of individuals in society: what happens "up the river" will have an effect on children who play "away" a hundred miles or more.

Some texts were adaptions of radical materials that were not originally written for Sunday schools. An adult economics textbook became the basis for a curriculum criticizing capitalism and the ownership of "the machines and the buildings by a few individuals," and offered socialism as an alternative that would put "an end to the relation of master and servant" and ensure equal opportunity for able men and women as well as an equal voice in the management of the industries carried on for the use of everybody (Teitelbaum, 1993). Through such a curriculum, children were expected to gain an introductory understanding of capitalism and the everyday conditions of working-class life in a capitalistic society—poverty, unemployment, and unhealthy and unsafe working conditions. Such content pointed to the need for rebels and stimulated an awareness of how conditions could be improved under socialism.

Other texts featured discussion questions that focused on the relationship between socialistic themes and the social conditions of most workers, like the following:

▼   Name some instances of political injustice.

▼   What is justice?

▼   What do you know about oil wells? Any near here?

▼   Is it easy or hard to get coal or oil?

▼   Who does the work?

▼   Who makes the money?

▼   Who owns the coal mines and oil wells?

▼   Who ought to own and control them? Why?

▼   Would they cost less or more under socialism? Why?

The primary aim of these materials was to show that all things necessary for our support come from the land. The earth, of course, belongs to all people; therefore, no one should be deprived of any of the necessities of everyday living.

Biographic sketches of socialistic leaders and excerpts from the writings of Dickens, Tolstoy, Sinclair, and others were used. Storybooks with accompanying radical lyrics like the following were common:

The earth was made for Brother men
To live in peace, they say;
But men have turned it into hell
In competition's way (Teitelbaum, 1993).

The socialistic curriculum was a model of useful knowledge. The outcomes sought were students' pride in their working class backgrounds; a sense of solidarity with other oppressed groups; a vision of social interdependence, the relationship between current social problems, and the nature of the dominant economic and political interests; and a recognized need for fundamental social change.

PROBLEM-CENTERED CURRICULUM OF THE 1930s

As is discussed in Chapter 5, Harold Rugg and teacher associates in the 1930s created curriculum aimed at helping students understand a changed world.

This curriculum centered on the problems of modern society and introduced students to the ideas of leading thinkers of the time (scientists, sociologists, economists, and writers) that could be used in understanding the problems.

Current Critical Curriculum

In the late twentieth century, some teachers are following the liberation pedagogy of Paulo Freire. Freire (1970) offers a revolutionary model for the Third World by which students learn to problematize their situations, differentiating those social conditions that are determined politically from those determined by natural necessity, and then to take actions that are possible and just. This curriculum has been adapted by Ira Shore and found useful in the industrial society of the West. The goal of these teachers is to empower students to build a just and equal society at peace with itself and other nations and the environment. The teacher invites students to examine problems and structure their investigations of these problems, comaking the curriculum. Typically, students are expected to look at situations with such questions as the following in mind:

▼   What is happening?

▼   How did it get this way?

▼   Whose interests are served by it? Whose interests are not?

▼   What are the consequences of the practice? Or text?

▼   What are its underlying assumptions?

Consider William Bigelow's "Discovering Columbus: Reading the Past" (1989). Bigelow wanted his students to be critical of their textbooks and their society and to ask, Why is it like this? How can I make it better? His approach was first to have students unload the word *discovery*—rip off, steal, invade, conquer—to see that it is a word of the conquerors and to recognize that when the word is repeated in textbooks it becomes the propaganda of the winners. In his introduction to the study, Bigelow feigned ownership of a student's purse on the grounds that he had "discovered" it. He then prepared students to examine critically the history textbooks they had used by considering alternatives to Columbus' enterprise—that the primary motive for his trip was to secure profit and wealth for Spain and himself (Columbus had demanded a 10 percent cut of everything for himself and his heirs).

Bigelow then introduced letters and records written by Columbus and others of the period revealing the generosity of the Indians and Columbus's idea for subjecting and making slaves of the Indians. Moving accounts of how Columbus and his brother sent slaves to Spain and the terror those people experienced were also presented. Even more revolting accounts were presented, telling how Columbus extracted gold from the Indians and the systematic ways the Indians were hunted and killed when they fled when unable to meet quotas for tributes in gold.

After students considered the topic of what "discovery" meant to the victors, they examined textbooks with accounts of Columbus' discovery, including those used in grade schools, and wrote critiques of the texts' treatment of Columbus and the Indians. Guidelines for the critique featured factual accuracy, consideration of omissions, motives given, points of view, function of pictures in the text, reasons given for the portrayal, and groups in our society who might have an interest in presenting an inaccurate view of history.

In keeping with Bigelow's desire that students read texts skeptically, students were asked to question how the text was written, bringing writers' assumptions and values to the surface. The students were able to find instances of omission, avoidance of reality, untruths, and disregard for negative consequences, and were able to give reasons for the rosy accounts in the texts. The relevance of Columbus to present events—U.S. involvement in other countries, motives for exploration, wars for profit—were discussed. Bigelow had evidence that the curriculum was working when students spontaneously asked, "What is your 'interest' in offering this curriculum?"

In his successful book for liberating teaching, Ira Shor (1987) presents the work of teachers in diverse settings who have social criticism and change as their goals. One of these teachers, Marilyn Frankenstein (1987), has developed a critical mathematics curriculum. In her course "Statistics for the Social Science," Frankenstein provides many opportunities for students to examine how subjective choice is involved in describing and collecting data and in making inferences about the world. For instance, students prepare critiques of the official status of the military portions of the federal budget, while at the same time learning about percents and circle graphs. Students find that the government makes military spending appear smaller by including funds held "in trust" (such as Social Security) under Social Service and by counting war-related expenditures under nonmilitary categories. Production of new nuclear materials is charged to the Department of Energy; veterans' benefits are categorized as Direct Benefit Payments. In contrast with the government's claim that 25 percent of the budget is for national defense, student calculations show that nearly 60 percent of the budget is going to pay for past, present, and future wars.

Similarly, students practice arithmetical operations and discuss ways to present the statistics that show that the United States is a welfare state for the rich. They must divide in order to describe tax loophole data, such as "each of the richest 160,000 taxpayers got nine times as much money as the maximum AFDC grant for a family of four." The students learn about the meaning of large numbers when they use their data to consider the services that the total taxes not paid by the rich (7.2 billion) could have provided if the money were included in the federal budget.

Other math skills and concepts are learned from applications that challenge the idea that the status quo is natural, good, and just. Operations with decimals center on problems using data from the U.S. Department of Energy, in which students found the costs of the federal subsidy to the nuclear power industry and recognized that without the federal subsidy nuclear power would be twice as costly—and unable to compete with oil-fired electricity, currently the most expensive power.

Applications of percentages occur when students are given information about such matters as the net profits made by 50 of the 32,000 U.S. food manufacturing corporations and their advertising expenditures, and then are asked to find the percentage of firms that make 75 percent of the profit. The solution serves several social purposes: changing $50 \div 32,000$ to 0.2 percent highlights that only a tiny percent of the firms make most of the profits and leads to political discussions of the agribusiness and corporate monopoly in general as well as a critique of the advertising industry bringing to bear such facts as 70 percent of TV food advertising promotes low-nutritious, high-caloric foods; while only 0.7 percent promotes fresh fruits and vegetables.

Critical Analysis

A joint critical analysis of a curriculum aspect or element by colleagues can form the basis for dialogue and contribute to awareness of desired characteristics of a curriculum. Reasons for teachers' judgments should be revealed.

The following excerpts illustrate typical findings from critical analyses:

Element A
Purpose of Schooling: Curriculum Element A assumes that schools are for the transmission of information, not for the encouragement of student creativity.
Knowledge: Element A presents knowledge as fixed and certain, something discovered by experts. The evidence and logic that supports the facts and ideas presented are missing. Contrary views are also absent.

Element B
Learning: Element B gives students opportunities to explore ideas, conjecture, hypothesize with others, and revise their original ideas. Students are expected to actively construct knowledge, not memorize facts and algorithms.

Element C
Omissions: Element C fails to put ideas in context. There is little help in how to deal with unfamiliar questions and non-routine problems.
Interests Served/Not Served: The concept density of this aspect is very high, and there are few connections to daily living, making the content difficult for those who have never encountered the concepts in concrete situations.
Problems/Solutions: Element C purports to prepare students to enter a domain of knowledge. However, the emphasis on abstractions and failure to consider the perspectives of beginners are likely to discourage students from wanting to study in this field.

Element D
Other: Those who initiated Element D show by this selection of content and treatment of diversity that they encourage ethical relativism and that they legitimize behavior that departs from national cultural values.

▼ ———————————————————————————————— ▼

ACTIVITY 4–1 CRITICAL ANALYSIS OF
CURRICULAR MATERIAL

The relation between the curriculum and society is of great importance. One way to express this interest is to examine how classroom materials might generate particular meanings, restraints, cultural values, and social relationships. Is there any way materials perpetuate social injustice, social class, and economic unfairness?

The purpose of this activity is to identify the implicit assumptions found in a curriculum aspect familiar to you.

1. Select an aspect of curriculum from a school or program known to you; you may wish to examine a lesson plan, an instructional unit, a teacher's manual, an examination, a text, a curriculum framework, a course of study, a grading practice, or any other aspect of curriculum.
2. Analyze the aspect of curriculum you have chosen in terms of what it implies about the purpose of schooling, the nature of knowledge, and how learning best takes place.
3. Determine what is omitted from the aspect, and whose interests are and are not served by this aspect.
4. What problem does the material purport to address, and how adequate is the proposed solution? What are possible unanticipated consequences?

▲ ———————————————————————————————— ▲

RADICAL TEACHERS' NEED FOR EXTERNAL SUPPORT

Teachers who take on social reform need the support of their professional associates and others in the community. Inasmuch as activist teachers go beyond imparting systematic formal knowledge and the limits set by most schools, the cooperation of consultants, parents, and community agencies (print and television media) is desirable. Social projects are likely to make multidisciplinary and integrative curriculum necessary, replacing a curriculum based on discrete subjects. However, in using academic subject matter as tools for exploring meaningful social issues in a critical way, radical teachers reduce the conflict between rigor and relevance.

Some questions exist about whether public schools will permit curriculum innovations designed to counter the disadvantages of class, race, and gender, and to bring about particular changes in their communities. El Puente United Nations Academy for Peace and Justice, a public school in Brooklyn, is a theme-oriented school whose teachers have developed a curriculum that uses the community as a classroom with students examining such environmental issues as the proposed construction of an incinerator in the Navy yard and involving themselves in matters of school overcrowding and racial tension.

Pam Chamberlain, who has developed curriculum aimed at social change in area of homophobia, has found that when the community (especially parent groups) has contributed advice on course content, more information and more controversial topics are included than when the curriculum is designed without parents' advice. She also found, however, that parents with racist and sexist fears are unlikely to challenge homophobia (Chamberlain, 1990). According to Chamberlain, curriculum designed to counter homophobia must go beyond awareness and counseling services. Instead of focusing on gays and lesbians as the "problem," Chamberlain addresses the institution of homophobia by helping students see how the norms of the school pressure students into sex roles and stereotypes, and confirm their fears of differences.

The incorporation of reading materials about community-related nontraditional subjects helps provide a structure for the classroom and can offer a rationale for discussion with other members of the school community. Bringing such materials into the school is a political act—presenting arguments for the curriculum and the specific needs that will be met, organizing a support network, and organizing a campaign among students and the larger community.

CRITICAL PEDAGOGY AND THE CURRICULUM OF POPULAR CULTURE

Critical pedagogy tries to make the familiar strange and the strange familiar. On one hand, it attempts to have students look at popular culture in a new light and to ask (a) what this culture has to do with the issues of class, gender, and ethnic inequality and (b) how and what the culture has done to them and what they no longer want to be. The range of popular culture to examine and interpretations to use is great—cereal boxes, rap music, TV soap operas, cartoons, baseball, and many others. As an ad in a publication put it:

Cult Studs

Q. e.g., Where can you find Hustler post-colonialism, bioethics, film theory, feminist criticism and Kirk on top of Spock?

A. Cultural Studies, coming to a campus near you.

On the other hand, the study of popular culture can provide students with the intellectual tools for entering the high culture traditionally taught in school, with the promise of finding values that contribute to what they are and perhaps provide images of what they and their culture might be.

The concept of high culture has been associated with the ideal of fusing active and contemplative principles—a means by which one can abstract from rather than simply respond to the active world. In the distant past, high culture indicated what was thought to be truly liberalizing and what would open up the riches of civilization—paintings, music, literature, and the like. High culture emphasized what had been thought and written about for centuries regarding human problems. More recently, understanding of political and scientific explanations of a wide variety of phenomena became aims of high culture, with an emphasis on teaching various principles of organization, both quantitative and mathematical.

Criticism of high culture in education centers on the idea that it promotes the class interest of an elite group and preserves the status quo. Alternative ways of achieving traditional goals of abstract thinking are increasingly found in studies in multicultural contexts. High-level thinking in non-European cultures and among the politically disaffected and economically disadvantaged, among others, has broadened the conception of high culture.

The logics of the cultures that children bring to school can offer alternative educational opportunities. The constructivist approaches in Chapter 1 indicate how the conceptual maps of students can contribute to more thoughtful, imaginative, and practical ways of understanding the world. The formal thought systems of the traditional curriculum, however, should be part of their inquiry and construction of knowledge.

Film for Criticism

In his illustration of how film can be used to challenge major themes about American culture, James Banks (1993) draws upon the film *How the West was Won*. In this film, minorities are almost invisible. Mexicans appear as bandits, African-Americans are shunted to the background, and Native Americans are hostile attackers. The film reinforces the notion that the West was won by liberty-loving, hardworking people who purchased freedom for all.

Banks begins his instructional unit on the westward movement by having students share their personal and cultural knowledge of the event; then he screens *How the West was Won*. The faithfulness of this film to traditional historical frontier theory is made apparent. Then transformative perspectives on the West, which challenge mainstream accounts of what happened, are introduced. Segments from films that offer alternative images—*Honor Lost, Dances with Wolves*—are viewed, and students study newer histories, ones that present transformative perspectives on Native Americans in history and culture. The main goal of this curriculum is to help students see different kinds of knowledge, to understand how knowledge is constructed or how it reflects a given social context, and to make their own knowledge.

Jack Weston (1990) also uses the Hollywood Western to awaken critical consciousness, showing how the Western reaffirms individualistic, racist, sexist, and imperialistic values. Students see how the Western stereotypes women in relation to social values and connects sexism to racism and a domineering attitude toward the wilderness. The degradation or villainization of victims as if to justify their exploitation is noted. Students learn that, although Westerns romanticize the conflict and at the same time reaffirm traditional values, behind the myth of the Western frontier lies the exploitation of land and workers for profit, together with resistance to the exploitation.

Alternatives in Dealing with Popular Culture

The idea that students are "dupes" of popular culture—that this culture reinforces sexism, racism, and consumerism—often leads to a curriculum that attempts to inoculate young people against its influence. Many teachers offer instructional units on consumerism, for example, using concepts such as supply and demand, economic stability, advertising, and product promotions whereby students critically evaluate TV and newspaper advertisements. Typical articles in such units ask students to do various things:

▼   Design a survey to show how students are influenced by advertising.

▼   Analyze the uses, appeals, and effects of advertising.

▼   Survey and evaluate the contents of a newspaper.

▼   Test several brands of a given product.

▼   Create advertisements for promoting particular products.

The inoculating approach has been faulted for misunderstanding the relationship of students to popular culture. Many students are sophisticated and critical of this culture. What they tend to lack is an understanding of the importance of popular culture in constructing social relationships and in defining individual and group relations. More than validating the students' existing knowledge, some curricula aim at relating common sense and formal academic knowledge to the study of popular culture.

Ira Shor's curriculum unit "The Hamburger" is an example of a critical curriculum that relates the academic to the familiar (1987). Studies on the theme of the hamburger begin with the students' immediate sources and move to the hamburger's global relations, drawing on history, geography, economics, and aesthetics. The study illuminates modern capitalism and reveals the consequences of decisions by the industry on the environment, health, and labor. The outlook and style of the fast food industries have repercussions that extend far beyond food consumption and ultimately make statements about values, attitudes, and beliefs about life. In conducting such studies, students learn how fast-food practices contribute to their entertainment, certainty, and sense of place; perhaps they even learn to see themselves in a new context. At the least, the study gives students a chance to develop a body of knowledge about modern industry, and the culture that created it.

Sources for Interpretations of Popular Culture

Critical pedagogy need not seek homogeneous interpretations from students. Indeed it should welcome diversity and encourage students to negotiate their own meanings, to argue with the interpretations of others and make sense of popular culture in terms of their own values. To this end, a wide variety of sources is introduced in the study of popular culture:

▼ ——————————————————————————————— ▼

ACTIVITY 4–2   CRITICIZING POPULAR CULTURE FROM A FEMINIST PERSPECTIVE

1. Select a television program, rap artist, talk show, athletic activity (such as body building), or other popular cultural artifact known to you.
2. Review and analyze segments of the chosen aspect of popular culture using the following questions as guidelines:
   a. How are women involved in this social activity or this cultural medium? What roles do women play and are these roles related to social class and race?
   b. What needs to be changed in this medium? What change should occur?
   c. What role can you play in bringing about the desired change?

▲ ——————————————————————————————— ▲

▼ perspectives from academic scholars (ethnic, historical, economics, anthropological and sociological) that represent political views of both those from the left and the right

▼ investigative reports as found in magazines and newspapers (with sources such as *Abstracts of Popular Culture* and *Journal of American Culture* suggesting topics for study and revealing original insights about aspects of popular culture)

▼ students' own studies and interpretations of popular culture

Use of these varied sources helps students see that they can deal with culture and challenge traditional notions of what counts as knowledge and culture. This doesn't mean that student interpretations of culture are necessarily valid, but that they should take part in the social and cultural debates. Just as the views of mature scholars reflect their values, prejudices, and stereotypes, the spontaneous and idiosyncratic interpretations of students must be challenged.

Hence critical pedagogy is associated with practices such as "Others"—an activity that probes students to ask how the situation or discourse could be different: "How would a different gender, social class, historical period, group, sexual preference, or religion alter your interpretation?"

In their language arts curriculum, Raymond Livey and Marita Walm (1993) invite students to collect reviews of programs from television, radio, and other media on a variety of subjects and sources from magazines and newspapers. The students determine commonalities in the reviews and then hypothesize about qualities of a particular form. Next the students test their hypotheses by studying new reviews and write their own review of a book, movie, sporting event, concern, recording, or other specific piece of popular culture. Subsequently, the students study multiple novels prototyping social issues and then move into the real world to test the authors' ideas against other sources of information—for example, by talking with people who are directly involved with the situations like those depicted in a novel.

SUMMARY

This chapter began with accounts of how teachers and the curriculum in the past fomented social change in two ways: taking direct action in reforming a social condition in the interest of justice and equity, and developing a sense of critical agency—the ability to analyze one's self and society and to reflect on how the relations of power, institutions, and popular culture work to keep people powerless and how these relations can be transformed in the interest of greater political, economic, and cultural justice.

Subsequently, the chapter described current curricula by which students problematize their situations, critique texts, and use traditional subject matter for the purpose of revealing deficiencies, institutional and cultural. Attention was given to the factors that support the work of teachers bent on transforming society through controversial curricula.

The chapter ended with a treatment of critical pedagogy and popular culture. Alternatives to the inoculating approach to popular culture were introduced, including those that seek to show how popular culture constructs social relations and defines individual and group relations. The study of popular culture was viewed as an opportunity to raise questions of power and identity. This broadening of curriculum beyond the academic fields was shown to enhance the range of perspectives available to students and to contribute to their understanding of what counts as knowledge and culture.

QUESTIONS FOR DISCUSSION

1. What, if any, responsibility does a teacher have for shaping students' attitudes toward racism and feminism?
2. If you believe that curriculum should help lead society toward change, what is your vision of what that change should be?
3. It is commonly thought that the curriculum best fosters social change when teachers and students work with other constituencies who share their social concerns. Give an example of a desired social change and the popular constituencies that would support it.
4. The curriculum of some teachers aims at helping students recognize the discrepancy between ideals and the status quo, but leaves it up to students themselves to decide what action, if any, is appropriate to take in closing the gap. Should the curriculum stop at intellectual understanding of social problems or should it include an action phase? State reasons for your opinion.

5. Scholars in all fields are offering alternative views of knowledge—math as socially constructed concepts rather than as universal principles, history from the viewpoints of minorities and commoners, literature that represents a variety of cultures and peoples, science with new views of biological determinism. Whose interests are and are not served by the introduction of this new content (interpretation) in elementary and secondary school curriculum?

6. What are some of the ways popular culture is enlarging or thwarting human possibility? How might your curriculum best relate to popular culture?

7. What is the significance of the following quotation for those who want to promote critical curriculum? "It is easy to pull weeds, but difficult to grow flowers."

REFERENCES

Banks, J. (June–July 1993). The canon debate: Knowledge, construction and multicultural education. *Educational Researcher, 22*(2), 4–15.

Beale, H. K. (1941). *A history of freedom of teaching in American schools*. New York: Charles Scribner & Sons.

Bigelow, W. (October 1989). Discovering Columbus: Rereading the past. *Language Arts, 6*(6), 635–643.

Chamberlain, P. (1990). Homophobia in the schools or what we don't know will hurt us. In S. O'Malley, R. C. Rosen, and L. Vogt (Eds.), *Politics of education—essays for radical teachers*, pp. 302–312. Albany, NY: State University of New York Press.

Frankenstein, M. (1987). Critical mathematics education. In I. Shore (Ed.), *Freire for the classroom*, pp. 180–204. Portsmouth, NH: Heinemann.

Freire, P. (1970). *Pedagogy of the oppressed.* New York: The Seabury Press.

Livey, R., & Walm, M. (1993). Shifting perspectives. *English Quarterly, 21*(1).

Shor, I. (1987). *Critical teaching in everyday life.* Chicago: University of Chicago Press.

Teitelbaum, K. *Schooling for good rebels: Socialist education for children in the United States, 1900–1920.* Philadelphia: Temple University Press, 1993.

Weston, J. (1990). Teaching the Hollywood Western. In S. O'Malley, R. C. Rosen, & L. Vogt (Eds.), *Politics of education—essays for radical teachers*, pp. 177–180. Albany, NY: State University of New York Press.

PART

Stories of School Subjects

As curriculum developers, teachers are interested in the intrinsic and philosophical values of their subject matter. A review of curriculum in different fields at different times should enhance this interest, and, by showing the changes that have occurred in all subjects, encourage one to look for new perspectives and possibilities for a field of choice. Descriptions of how the arts, including literature, history, and the social studies, have been taught from the early nineteenth century to the present are found in Chapter 5; descriptions of curriculums in mathematics and the sciences are in Chapter 6. In all instances, the connections between the dominant social thought and power and the prevailing school subjects attest to the human construction of knowledge in the light of given circumstances.

The stories in chapters 5 and 6 are intended to stimulate readers to think about what teachers teach and how they teach. More than that, these stories serve as reminders that there are other ways of teaching subject matter than the ones that have been relied upon.

THE HUMANITIES AND SCHOOL SUBJECTS

Humanities in the school curriculum concentrate mainly upon art, literature, history, and the social sciences. This chapter describes incidents of ways teachers have engaged with learners and the humanities within both the immediate and larger social, political, and cultural milieu. The chapter begins with descriptions of shifting views of the arts curriculum and then presents accounts of the struggle to gain acceptance of English as an academic study. It shows the relation of literature to composition and other language areas. It also reviews enduring conflicts about the nature of English as a school subject (English as literary analysis versus English as personal experiences, and English as a tool for dealing with everyday problems, for example).

This chapter presents curricula for the teaching of history from the perspective of both those who regard history as the description of events and those who believe history to be a body of knowledge that can guide one's actions. Examples of early teachers whose curriculum engaged students in forming historical interpretations from original documents are presented. The weakening of history as a school subject and the introduction of social studies curricula are shown in their political and social contexts. The chapter concludes with a description of the different types of social studies that have been offered as ways to deal with everyday life as well as curriculums that show a connection between social science and social studies.

SHIFTS IN ART CURRICULUM

Kerry Freedman (1987) has shown how school art developed in relation to the purposes of various public interests. Freedman identified four strands of art education that paralleled social influences:

▼ use of art in developing skills for a labor market

▼ art as cultural education and a leisure activity

▼   art as important in the development of moral character and aesthetic taste

▼   use of art for healthful and creative self-expression

Art in Industry

In the late 1870s, art was taught for industrial purposes. Walter Smith, an art teacher, was brought from England to oversee a design education program that became a model. Traditional design patterns were taught in a procedurally described manner, with industrial design courses following practices of industry, using timed and step-by-step procedures for drawing. Particular manual skills were taught for given occupations. In most schools, drawing emphasized the precise copying of illustrations. Children were first taught the parts of shapes, then drew individual shapes, and finally objects. Initially, students made outlines and followed the teacher as he or she copied outlines from a textbook. Later, the drawings of famous sculptures were studied so that children could copy form and shading. Finally, older children might be allowed to do an entire composition of a pastoral scene. The use of color was controlled in order to prevent fanciful experimentation. The practice of preparing all public school children for work through art diminished as manual training schools were established.

Art as Culture and Leisure Activity

In the late nineteenth century, a new middle class sought to show themselves as cultured by studying and collecting art objects. At this time, art museums were established for the public (though they were administered by the wealthy elite). Art appreciation courses were introduced into the public schools to support this acculturation of the middle class.

Art as a leisure activity began with decorative needlework classes in private girls' schools. Then concern in the early 1900s about "unworthy" use of leisure time by citizens resulted in art courses to develop an appreciation for beauty during spare time in place of less wholesome pleasures.

Art for Morality

Moral education through the arts was also an aim in the 1890s until the 1930s. Picture study was introduced to illustrate good character and love of truth and beauty by focusing on the morality of artists' works and "God's handiwork in nature and achievements of men" (Freedman, 1987, p. 71). The pictures used were overly sentimental, such as a "picture of a 'perfect' child with his mother or wild animals tamed by human influence" (Kerry, 1985). Although the moral message was considered more important than the quality of the pictures in classrooms of those teachers with a moral bent, other teachers sought to develop good taste and appreciation of high standards in art by studying masterpieces.

Art in Everyday Life

During the 1930s, the time of the Great Depression, the elite notion of art was replaced in favor of social realism. Much of the art funded by the Federal Art Project, for example, portrayed the life and work of the laborer. An excellent example of art as related to everyday life is found in Freedman's study of the Owatonna Minnesota Project of the 1930s, in which school and community tried to upgrade the aesthetic sensibilities of citizens to enhance the local environment (Freedman, 1987). Art education centered on the beautification of the family's surroundings. Elementary children made decorative objects for the home, while older children focused on commercial art and industrial design, with lessons on consumer and industrial interests (such as posters that would "create a desire for a product") and a unit that taught students the poor conditions of commercial design in America. The adult classes and community lectures focused on efficient, well balanced design in architecture, gardening, and other aspects of community life.

Art for Self-Expression

The concept of art education as creative self-expression shaped the art curriculum after 1900. Child study researchers used children's drawings as the basis for illustrating stages of growth and furthering the idea that children's art unfolds naturally. Child researchers opposed technical, segmented drill and instead allowed children to begin drawing and painting animals and other things that would appeal to their interests and desire. The teacher's role was to provide materials and show students a variety of mediums. Encouraging original expression in producing objects was associated with the belief that art was therapeutic and could contribute to the child's sense of self worth.

Franz Cizek, an Australian art teacher, influenced the American art curriculum by his traveling exhibition of his students' work. He believed that children's art should be free of adult imposition. Victor Lowenfeld, also an Australian educator, became a very influential art educator in the United States (Lowenfeld, 1992). Lowenfeld was also against imposing adult standards on children and in favor of promoting students' efforts in self-expression, releasing them from pressures of contemporary society and developing healthy individuals.

Art for Intellectual Development

Contemporary shifts in the art curriculum have been described by Arthur Efland (1987). Efland tells how in the postwar era art education expanded in affluent suburban areas while the urban poor were denied access. The art programs for the affluent aimed at helping students interpret the meaning of new forms and styles, such as abstract expression, pop art, funk art, minimalism, conceptual art, and performance art.

The art curriculum of the 1960s reflected the trend in science education to pattern school subjects on the ways of specialists in the disciplines were said to structure and derive new knowledge. With federal government funding and support from private foundations, experts from the arts prepared instructional materials for teachers to use in teaching aesthetics. Other experts prepared guidelines for TV programs and for helping students learn "to make" art less and "to see and understand" art more. Differences in the curricula developed by the various specialists reflected conflicting views of art. Some showed concern for the relevance of aesthetics in personal and social life; others featured the acquisition of art and skills as instructional ends so students could not only construct art works of individual character but also analyze and evaluate works and place them in their appropriate cultural and historical context. The art curriculum of the 1960s faded as schools digressed from enriching content and began to focus on accountability, preparing instructional objectives and assessment devices. Measurable skills became the focus, not imaginative products and ephemeral appreciations.

In the 1980s, Discipline-Based Art Education (DBAE) supported by the J. Paul Getty Trust brought renewed interest in strengthening elementary and secondary school study of art through the integration of studio art, production, art history, art criticism, and aesthetics (Clark, Day, & Green, 1987). The DBAE is said to differ from the curriculum of the 1960s in that it has been designed by art educators, not by studio artists and scholars in the field of art. Yet the authors of DBAE have been faulted by Efland for making some of the same as well as some new mistakes:

1. Promoting certain ways of conducting art inquiry and art criticism as if they are the only methods approved by the art community, ignoring the conflicts about purpose and methods that exist in the community.
2. Failing to think through the social consequences of aiming at only providing students with a well-rounded education in art rather than aiming at the highest level of inquiry and understanding as represented by specialists.
3. Using works of art to integrate the disciplines of art rather than using the disciplines to understand the work, a pedagogical formalism emphasizing the structure of the disciplines, not the work of art which the disciplines are striving to understand. (Efland, 1990)

ENGLISH AND THE LANGUAGE ARTS

English as an Imitation of the Classics

There was no "English" in the early nineteenth-century schools; instead there was a mishmash of courses in rhetoric, grammar, elocution, penmanship, spelling, declamation and composition. Then in the late 1800s, college entrance examination requirements shaped the English curriculum in the direction of literature, the logic of grammatical and rhetorical principles. These exams demanded student familiarity with a prescribed list of books representing some period or types of literature, as well as ability to write themes in given "forms of discourse" and to define and classify sentences grammatically. In order to compete with the dominant classics—Greek and Latin—and their assumed value to mental discipline, teachers of English built their courses on the model of the dead languages, which called for memorization of literary selections and reproduction of the geometry of the story.

Albert Roberts' account (1912) of the teaching of English in the high school at the beginning of the twentieth century reveals that most courses were arranged so that literature was an illustration of the work done in composition. Narration, description, exposition, and argumentation formed the basis of the curriculum. In the first year, the initial emphasis was narrative, drawing from such authors as Poe, Tennyson, Browning, and Stevenson. Composition followed reading of the literature whereby students wrote narratives according to its principles. In the second year, the curriculum was based on descriptive types and the writings of Washington Irving, Nathaniel Hawthorne, and George Eliot were often among those chosen. The essay "Bacon and Ruskin" was the instrument for study of the expository works in the third year. Macaulay's essay on Addison and Burke's speech on conciliation generally furnished the principles of argumentation studies during the fourth year.

Other principles used in organizing English courses were these:

▼   with materials chosen as representing some literary period, the study of American authors before the study of more remote authors

▼   with novel studies in the first year, lyrics in the second, the essay in the third, and the epic and drama in the fourth

▼   with emphasized ethical and emotional purposes in the first and second years and the intellectual and critical values of literature in the last two years

The study of literature in this period meant determining the meaning of the author, comprehending the significance of the whole before examining the parts. Subsequent attention was given to structure, chronology, style, and the life of the author as it related to the work.

Literature was the basis for the teaching of composition. From the works themselves, students were introduced to the principles of composition. "Units," "mass," and "coherence" were examined and applied in the students' own compositions. Composition varied from the daily theme to the weekly exercises. Before writing their themes, students made outlines. These outlines were critiqued and revised. When students finished them, the teacher would select two or three papers for class criticism and later read and correct portions of the compositions turned in by the other students. Noteworthy in view of today's "new" assessment procedures was the practice more that 100 years ago of using portfolios containing compositions and other written work that were submitted as evidence of preparation to colleges.

Oral work was also common. Public speaking included declamation, debate, oration, simple plays, and the reading of themes—compositions. Usually, the material was taken from the books read in class in order to deepen and illustrate the literature.

Elementary Curriculum in Language

The elementary language curriculum at the beginning of the twentieth century was criticized in professional journals for putting too much emphasis on the memorization of spelling words and grammar without student understanding. The literature was beyond the reach of many children: *The Christmas Carol*, *The Courtship of Miles Standish*, *The Lady of the Lake*, *The Legend of Sleepy Hollow*, *Rip Van Winkle*, *Snowbound*, tales from Shakespeare, *The Great Stone Face*, *The Man Without a Country*, and *Heidi*. Mechanical mastery of reading—phonics—was incidental to oral reading and the study of literary selections. In the lower grades, much of the literature study was by means of stories told by the teacher. Compositions embraced oral and written reproduction in the forms of riddles, anecdotes, stories, and simple dramatizations. There was some original oral and written work. Capitalization and fundamentals were taught in the lower grades, but formal grammar was left for the sixth and seventh grades.

The following is an illustration of aspects of language taught in elementary schools in the early 1900s:

▼ *Grade 1:* capital letters at the beginning of the sentence; periods at the end

▼ *Grade 2:* capitals for the days of the week and month; use of question marks

▼ *Grade 3:* exclamation points; contractions; capitals in names of places; indention of paragraphs; homonyms

▼ *Grade 4:* apostrophes; commas in a series; writing from an outline

▼ *Grade 5:* divided and undivided quotations; use of commas; and the three-paragraph form

▼ *Grade 6:* subject and predicate; adjective and adverbial phrases; parts of speech

▼ *Grade 7:* complements; modifiers; compound and complex sentences

An Experience Curriculum

Between 1929 and 1935, 175 members of the National Council of Teachers of English engaged in a large-scale curriculum-making endeavor—the production of a guide for the teaching of English, kindergarten through twelfth grade, called *An Experience Curriculum in English* (National Council of Teachers of English, 1935). The term experience set the direction for the curriculum. By experience, the teachers meant many things:

▼ meeting real language situations of life: communicating with others in and out of school

▼ making decisions, taking action, and showing responsibility for the consequences of actions

▼ reliving vicariously lives and events presented through literature

▼ expressing personal thoughts and feelings through written and oral language

Students were encouraged to interact with many sources: films, drama, poetry, newspapers, books, and social activities. However, the experience curriculum excluded materials the teacher thought would be harmful, such as those depicting horrors, sex, sentimentality, and the contravention of natural laws. Grammar (usage) and the technical skills of reading and writing were taught in use, not for use. Teachers assumed that when students do interesting things with language, they are in the best frame of mind for a vigorous and self-motivated attack on their own errors.

The experience curriculum featured units of instruction, each occupying 5 to 15 days throughout the K–12 program. Each unit consisted of a major purpose, or social objective, indicating the activity that would take place, for example, to write an account of a sports event or other school function for the newspaper. In addition, the unit had an enabling objective, which stipulated the academic and other prerequisites for successful attainment of the social objective, for example, to write headlines or leads to secure economy and exactness, using verbal nouns; to give the reader the impression of observing action by using varied sentence structure, concrete details and specific nouns. Units were ordered by "experience strands" of literature, reading, creative expression, speech, and writing.

An Experience Curriculum moved school "English" away from literary analysis and history and toward the study of varied types of language activity—conversation, letter writing, telling stories, dramatizing, reporting, and speaking to large groups. Creative expression differed from the other strands in that it was "done primarily for its own sake," not for external or utilitarian motives.

English as Response to Personal and Social Problems

Beginning in the 1940s, personal and social problems were at the center of the English curriculum for many teachers. For example, Sara Roody's curriculum for the adolescent (1947) introduced "true to life" literature and drew from psychology as a way to reach the new goal of developing student personalities.

Roody gave psychoanalytic explanations for avoiding reality, confronting life problems, and achieving maturity. Typically, literature was selected for its contribution to understanding problems of the family, the American culture, prejudice, and oneself. Important works, such as *The Diary of Anne Frank* and *Catcher in the Rye* entered the curriculum at this time.

Some concern was expressed about the suitability of introducing popular materials. Barbara Martinec (1971) called attention to ways popular novels solved the problems they posed:

▼   Immaturity equated with isolation from the group.

▼   All problems can be solved successfully.

▼   Adults often are not much help.

▼   Solutions are discovered by chance.

▼   Maturity means conformity.

The Academic Tripod as English

Language, composition, and literature comprised the colleges' definition of English in the 1960s. As part of the discipline's approach, curriculum scholars gave a greater role to linguistics in the teaching of language. Teachers attended workshops at which scholars told them to emphasize syntax rather than the parts of speech and to teach usage and the history of language. They also heard that no dialect was more logical or functional than any other.

The teaching of literature reflected the influence of the "new critics," in that teachers taught students to ask questions about the text—its form (How are all parts related?); its rhetoric (Who is the audience?); about meaning (What is the intention and how it is made apparent?); and about values, calling for both personal response and judgments of excellence (Commission on English, 1965).

Close reading was related to the development of composition and language. The academic point of view was that English should be studied for its own sake, not for a presumed utilitarian purpose or personal value. That approach led to reading of standard literary selections. Many major twentieth-century works were omitted because of the pressures of censorship.

English for Growth versus English for Efficiency

From the 1970s through the 1980s, two competing views of English confronted teachers. Some teachers favored the idea of language as an instrument for personal and social growth whereby students used language and literature in their attempt to define and express themselves. Other teachers valued efficiency and the direct teaching of skills thought to be important to reading and writing.

Teachers in the first category followed a curriculum that provided opportunity for reading, speaking, writing, listening through dialogue, and response to literature and the world at large. Storytelling, drama, and discussion, as well as writing, were seen as ways for students to make sense of their lives. Elementary school teachers of the growth orientation created "open classrooms," which offered opportunities for student collaboration and choice. Typically, in the open classrooms, several activities occurred at once. Some students read self-selected materials; others worked at a writing corner expressing their feelings about a picture; and still others listened to recordings of poetry.

In the secondary school, teachers with personal growth as an aim favored mini-courses designed in response to student interests and the passion of the teacher. Generic electives were offered; for example: "The Modern American Novel"; literary history elective: "English Literature"; thematic elective: "Oedipus Rock Opera"; classics elective: "The Great Books"; author elective: "Mark Twain"; an individualized elective: "Paperback Power." Nonprint media, especially films, became the stimuli for classroom discussion and writing. Writing as composition was broadened to include filmmaking and journal writing, and was done for a range of purposes. All called for a sense of audience point of view and awareness of what students wanted to communicate.

In opposition to teachers who favored the growth of curriculum, teachers who were efficiency-oriented saw English as a subject to be studied, manipulated, and mastered. The English curriculum consisted of skills in reading and writing organized into a hierarchy of objectives. Each objective was presented by example or by rule, followed by guided practice, usually in the form of worksheets, and a criterion referenced test to evidence mastery of the objectives. The efficiency curriculum required students to attain competency on particular reading and writing tasks. The specified competencies tended to be minimal and related to daily living—for example, locating the time for a favorite TV program, writing a three-paragraph essay with few spelling and grammatical mistakes.

Current Directions in the English Language Arts

Elementary teachers are putting away their worksheets and no longer focusing on isolated skills. They also are relating various language activities to a common theme. By way of illustration, a first-grade teacher might fill the classroom with books about bears. The teacher and children sing songs and read poems and stories giving facts and fantasies about bears. Children bring their teddy bears to school and later write their own bear stories, poems, and articles. This new activity curriculum gives support to individual and group purposes. Drafts of student writings are shared, and students are encouraged both to make individual responses to literature and to develop common meanings from their experiences with literature and language.

Some teachers want students to acquire the social understandings of literacy, not merely to express their own feelings and opinions. They want students to see how literacy operates in different settings by studying what is read and what is not read in different places by different people and the kinds of meanings that are constructed by texts. Students might, for instance, determine the meanings implied by standardized tests in the school context.

John Willinsky is such a teacher. In one of his programs, he awakened students in the fourth and sixth grades to the importance of literacy in context through a curriculum that sampled 3000 years of publishing. During a nine-day period, students "published" their poetry, using both historical and contemporary techniques. The students began with Homer and the oral tradition to learn the value of reciting a work that is both fresh and familiar. Next, the students experienced the early days of drama with the classroom as the amphitheater. The medieval scriptorium was next as students created illustrated manuscripts and framed their poetry with intricate borders. Then the students matched Gutenberg's movable type and printing presses with their own printer's marks to designate their poster-sized broadsides of poetry. Before each of these activities, a short history lesson described how publishers met the events of the day. Finally, after a visit to a local print shop, Willinsky's students leaped ahead to desktop publishing, issuing their own "small magazine models on such literary innovations as *The Dial* (Willinsky, 1990). Although in the 1990s literature is once again central in the English curriculum, there is conflict about what literature to select. Teachers who are cultural conservatives favor a core of works which they say mirror Western values and transcend time, such as those by Shakespeare and biblical authors. They also want American literature included, as represented by Twain, Thoreau, and Faulkner. Teachers sensitive to the contributions of minorities give greater emphasis to literature that reflects the diversity of America's cultural heritage—Ellison, Rivera, Momaday. Teachers with a concern for social justice select works that honor the value of the female perspective and the working class—Plath and O'Farrell (Moss, 1985).

Further, there are challenges to the idea that literature must be print. Films, videotapes, and recordings are entering the classroom as literature and not merely as supplementary to the written text. Robert Moss' curriculum (1985) is an example of how films such as *King Kong*, *The Godfather*, and *One Flew Over the Cuckoo's Nest* represent a genre worthy of study, as well as providing a springboard to writing. Teachers and students alike are seeking the connection between literary works and other arts—dance, music, painting, and the way all act on our being.

Among the current organization trends in English curriculum are thematic, genre, and student choice. Thematic organization, whereby several texts and activities are focused on a given theme (such as prejudice, family ties, or personal dignity) is popular. The danger with this organization is that the theme may preinterpret the texts and lead to bland generalizations. Although genre is an old way to organize the curriculum, it does allow for the introduction of a wide range of forms, authors, periods, and styles. Teachers on the leading edge let students themselves decide what they are to read and what the theme, if any, will be.

A new fashion in English is to not look for a thematic unit, but at the displacement of meaning: read to find what has been repressed in the process of writing, what is omitted because of social political and historical constraints. Students are taught to look for unexpressed and unacceptable ideas, and to search for contradictions and aberrant meanings, particularly in footnotes and parentheses. Similarly, students are encouraged to write without the pressure of perfect clarity, knowing that writing is a never finished process. In brief, the aim of the new English is for students to respond to texts in light of their own experience and get to see the world anew in their actual pursuit of meaning.

HISTORY AND SOCIAL STUDIES

Conflicting views of history and its use have been present for centuries. In ancient Greece, Herodotus relegated history to the describing of events, while Thucydides argued that it should guide one's actions. Greeks and Romans used stories of heroes to develop characters and patriotism. In the medieval period, study of the saints and popes perpetuated religious doctrine; but during the Reformation, history was used to justify reformed religious beliefs. Comenius wanted world history taught in the interest of international understanding, and Rousseau valued the teaching of facts about common life and depreciated history's focus on kings and the elite. After the Napoleonic Wars of 1800, history was taught in the self interests of nations.

In the United States, answers to the question of why study history have followed two viewpoints:

▼ *traditionalists* interested in transmitting a cultural heritage and developing a national loyalty through the study of history

▼ *functionalists* who would draw upon history and social sciences for their contributions to the understanding of contemporary social and individual problems

Evolution of the Traditional Curriculum in History: The Memoriter System

In the 1800s, separate courses in geography, government, and history were taught in a chronological and structured way to shape values and behavior. Geography for primary students consisted of local geography taught through object lessons and descriptions of the earth as a whole. Intermediate geography emphasized the study of form and locations using maps and atlases. High school courses featured both descriptions and physical geography. In all instances, students were expected to answer a variety of questions and to memorize facts about given localities. The curriculum in government focused on the Constitution, the rights and duties of a people in a republic, the obligations of public laws, and the principles of civil and religious beliefs.

The history curriculum varied with the age of the students. In the early grades, school children were told about the history of the United States and about heroes of the world. In the elementary school, students were given accounts of the principal events of American history. In the academies or high schools, there was considerable variation. College-bound students studied Greek or Roman history, and other students studied American history or English history.

The Memoriter System relied on the use of a textbook from which students were expected to reproduce the exact words of the text. The practice of allowing students to sum up passages in their own words evolved in an effort to help "weaklings" who could not recall the text. Textbooks often featured guidance questions and outlines that highlighted the essentials to be memorized. These essentials were written and rewritten, said backward and forward, the basis for grouping what one remembers of books, sources, and classroom talk (Johnson, 1915).

The following are typical examination questions of the period ("Examination Questions," 1872, p. 38):

1. What river basin does the great central plain of North American include?
2. Name the three great currents of the ocean and tell how they modify the climate of the earth.
3. What was the general order of creation?
4. What parts of the earth are inhabited principally by the Caucasian race?
5. What was the design of the 15th Amendment to the Constitution, and when was it adopted?
6. What was the Louisiana Purchase? When was it made, and what territory did it embrace?
7. What did England and the colonies gain by the French and Indian War?

Circumscribed Inquiry

In the late nineteenth century, Mary Sheldon Barnes (1883), a noted teacher, teacher educator, and author of materials for the teaching of history, was scathingly critical of the Memoriter System and offered—as an alternative to the impacting of information—curriculum aimed at awakening a spirit of inquiry. Instead of viewing students as passive vessels to be filled with historical knowledge, Barnes wanted students to be active learners who, with the guidance of the teacher and the curriculum materials, would draw their own conclusions from rigorous inquiry. Barnes' curriculum relied heavily on selected primary source documents and illustrations of historical artifacts. Students were to develop proper historical and civic perspectives by extracting general truths from the study of "the special fact" embedded in the historical document or artifact.

Barnes (1893) advocated the use of skillfully designed questions to help students work with historical materials. Her teaching manual encouraged teachers to arrange situations where students collected, discussed, and critiqued interpretations drawn from their studies of documents or artifacts. Individual interpretations were expected to be reported in an atmosphere of freedom and honesty, and the conclusions of the class were recorded in simple tabular arrangements convenient for review and examination. A variety of kinds of questions were included:

▼ ——————————————————————————————— ▼

ACTIVITY 5–1   IDENTIFYING CENTRAL CONTENT IN A SUBJECT RELATED TO THE HUMANITIES (ART, MUSIC, LITERATURE, HISTORY)

Select one of the humanities that has been important in your life. Identify one or more of the key concepts, important perspectives, or functions associated with this subject that you would want all students to acquire.

▲ ——————————————————————————————— ▲

▼   *analytical* questions to guide the extracting of information from primary sources and the summaries provided

▼   *synthetic* questions that led students to draw the information together into a coherent image of the past society

▼   *evaluative* questions that asked students to reflect on the ideals, character, and moral qualities of the historical personages and society

Barnes believed that through the use of her curriculum students would learn how to judge and interpret what they see in their own country and help make America the strongest, noblest, and finest nation in the world.

In his recent study of Mary Sheldon Barnes and her work, Stuart Anniel (1990) makes clear that Barnes circumscribed student inquiry by her acceptance of certain fundamental truths about American democracy. There was, for example, a faith in the supremacy of democratic principles in political and social life. She represented the constitutional form of government as allowing for stable political and moral progress and ensuring maximum personal freedom of action. None of her questions, documents, or artifacts took into account the predicament faced by African Americans, the working class, or other groups that often did not share in national progress or experience personal freedom of action. One source, for instance, was an article written by an African American academic who attributed the cause of racial prejudice against African Americans to their poverty and ignorance rather than their color and offered hard work and education as the way to win the respect of whites and a share in the prosperity of the South. This was published at a time when disfranchisement of African Americans, lynchings, and other terrorist acts aimed at African American communities were common in the South (Anniel, 1990). Barnes' treatment of the subject legitimized the violence and suppression of rights by denying their existence. The question that followed such excerpts asked students, "Who is to blame if the Southern black is 'poor and has a bad time now'?" The answer most likely to occur to students was that the fault lies with a black population unable to take advantage of a rapidly growing economy, an answer consistent with the excerpts and the viewpoints found in the newspapers and books of the time.

In brief, Barnes' curriculum did not help students learn to detect and evaluate the kinds of ideological premises that underlined the histories they read. By reinforcing uncritical acceptance, the assumption was that national progress and democracy remedied racial discrimination and other injustices. Barnes unintentionally made injustice invisible and absolved students from having to give personal attention or to take action toward resolving national problems not directly touching their lives.

SOCIAL STUDIES VERSUS HISTORY

In the early twentieth century, history lost favor to the teaching of social studies. Questions of direct concern to individual communities, such as those related to public health, immigration, alcoholism, and housing, became more important than questions about how people lived in the past. The rest of this section provides an account of directions taken in the social studies curriculum during much of the twentieth century. Only in the current decade has historical literacy regained prominence and replaced social studies in the school curriculum.

Traditional History in the Curriculum of the 1990s

In the 1990s, the Bradley Commission on History in Schools focused on studies indicating that many students were unfamiliar with historical and geographical facts and knowledge believed necessary for understanding complex social and political questions (Gagnon, 1989). The commission's recommendation called for more courses in history at all levels. Also, the staff at the National Center for History in the Schools defined the historical understandings they thought students should acquire before graduating from high school (National Center for History in the Schools, 1992). Teacher associates at the Center created teaching materials—units of instruction—in accordance with the Center's criteria for use in the schools.

The new traditionalists' curriculum emphasizes historical facts, significant historical documents, knowledge of historical chronology, democratic heritage, and the nation's political institutions. This curriculum contrasts with the social studies curriculum, which centered on social issues and problems. The new courses in history, geography, and government aim at developing history's "habits of the mind" such as these:

▼   connecting the past to the present

▼   perceiving past events as they were experienced by people at the time

▼   comprehending the diversity of culture while acquiring a sense of a shared humanity

▼   grasping the complexity of historical causality

▼ recognizing the importance of individuals who have made a difference in history

Although this new curriculum has many similarities to the old traditional curriculum, there are some differences. Memorization of names, dates, and places is out; case studies and narratives are in. In preparing their units, teachers look for engaging stories from each era of history. The units present specific "dramatic moments" which illuminate landmark events. Students examine a crucial turning point in history and learn that choices had to be made and that there were consequences. The dramatic moments are based on primary sources—documents, artifacts, journals, diaries, newspapers, and literature from the period under study. The unit must recreate for students a sense of "being there," while giving students opportunity to practice the role of historians, analyzing the sources, making interpretations, and constructing their narratives that relate relevant factors. Units are selected for distribution by the Center on the basis of their historical interest, liveliness, use of primary sources, and contribution to the students' historical and cultural literacy.

Authors of the new curriculum would say that this curriculum differs from the curriculum of Mary Barnes in that they have made a conscious effort to introduce the role played by people at many levels of society, in many regions, from different backgrounds—women, minorities, and the common people. They have also faced tensions in conflicting national values: aspirations for freedom versus security, liberty versus equality, and unity versus diversity. They have attempted to counter older histories that suggested the inevitability of progress and destiny by giving more emphasis to the importance of human agency. Nevertheless, the themes and units of the new curriculum, such as the development of society, institutions, culture, and democracy, imply progress and a common purpose.

Teachers in Oakland, California; Portland, Oregon; Milwaukee, Wisconsin's Immersion Schools; and elsewhere where members of ethnic groups are concerned about unfavorable treatment of certain groups in the history taught in schools have rejected the new traditional curriculum (Hillard, 1990). Instead these teachers and parents have developed curriculums that present the group's heritage told in their own way. These curriculum aim at increasing self-concept and countering historical interpretations that favor dominant interests and that fail to present a history that gives students from the respective ethnic group a sense of hope for their future.

Changes in Social Studies

Social Function Curriculum In the early 1930s, thousands of teachers throughout the United States constructed units of instruction aimed at preparing students to perform major social functions. The particular functions were identified by a state or local curriculum authority. In Virginia, for example, hundreds of teachers working in production committees developed units of instruction dealing with nine functions:

1. protection and conservation of life, property, and national resources
2. production and consumption of foods and services
3. recreation
4. expression of aesthetic impulses
5. transportation and communication
6. exchange of goods and services
7. expression of religious impulses
8. education
9. extension of freedom and distribution of rewards of production

   With few exceptions, activities in each grade addressed these functions. For example, first graders who learned to cross a street properly were achieving something related to the protection and conservation of life. Centers of interest for sequencing the activities in each category were these:

▼   *Grade 1:*   home and school life

▼   *Grade 2:*   community life

▼   *Grade 3:*   adaptation of life to environmental forces of nature

▼   *Grade 4:*   adaptation of life to advancing physical frontiers

▼   *Grade 5:*   effects of discovery on human living, effects of the machine on human living

▼   *Grade 6:*   provision for cooperative living

For example, in the fifth grade, the function of expressing aesthetic impulses in conjunction with the center of interest—the effect of discovery on human living—resulted in one teacher posing the question, How was recreation influenced by frontier living? This, in turn, suggested a detailed activity "designing a sampler."

Life Adjustment

Learner concerns about everyday life and persistent life situations became the foci for social studies curriculum in the 1940s. Florence Stratemeyer (1957) defined *persistent life situations* as those that recur in different ways as one grows from infancy to maturity, situations involving health, personal relations, natural phenomena, moral choices, and political structures. Activities and content were selected as they contributed to an individual's ability to deal with situations confronted by students of different ages (Stratemeyer, 1957).
   In the elementary school, life adjustment curriculum often took the form of an area or culture study or a social project through which students contrasted their own responses to persistent situations with those of other people in other

places. At the secondary school level, life adjustment meant teaching whatever was useful to students, such as applying and qualifying for a job; critically reading newspapers, advertisements, and the fine print in contracts; and learning to use community resources in solving personal problems.

Generalizations as the Basis for Social Studies

Harold Rugg and his teacher associates in the 1930s created social studies materials aimed at helping students understand a changing civilization and its programs. Rugg set a precedent in his attempt to identify the problems of modern society and the key generalizations for dealing with these problems through analysis of the works of leading "frontier thinkers" in science, literature, economics, and social sciences. In Rugg's curriculum, problems and issues such as socialism, unions, corporate wealth, corruption, world interdependence, ecology, and immigration were the foci for study. Generalizations were grouped by the category of problems to which they related. In the category of "war," for instance, were generalizations regarding the influence of climate and conquest, political coordination, alternatives for gaining access to resources, psychological factors leading to war, and the consequences of accepting a common purpose for humankind (Billings, 1927). The use of generalizations showed the commonalties among problems and interconnections of economic, social, and political movements.

Rugg's texts contained extensive bibliographies, dramatic episodes to show how people are living and have lived, autobiographies, travel and personal diaries (both actual and fictional), suggested research projects, and discussion topics. Typically, students were given data such as maps and the history of trade routes for an area and then presented with a problem like determining the best location for a city in the area. Later, the actual location would be revealed and discussed.

As with circumscribed inquiry, the problem and generalizations approach can be faulted for bias on the part of the curriculum developers. Although Rugg opposed nationalism in the social studies, he was biased toward democratic principles in his selection of content and his presentation of the problem of contemporary life.

Social Science as Social Studies

University scholars in the 1960s fragmented the social studies program by developing materials that isolated the social sciences—economics, anthropology, political science, geography, sociology. Teachers were uncertain about which discipline to teach and concerned about the limitations of relying on the contributions of any one discipline to understand social problems. The content of each discipline was organized to advance knowledge in that subject, not to address problems that covered subject areas. Soon people became disillusioned with a curriculum that featured competing structures of disciplines and that seemed more appropriate for future academic specialists than for all citizens.

▼ ────────────────────────────────── ▼

ACTIVITY 5–2   DEFINING A FIELD OF KNOWLEDGE

It is unlikely that teachers of the arts and social sciences have a common concept of these fields, yet a teacher's "cognitive map" of a field indicates there is a key factor in how that teacher constructs curriculum in that field. Use the following questions in defining your own definition of a field of interest to you.

1. What do you think it means for someone to know X? If someone is an expert in this field, what would you expect them to know and do?
2. What are some of the major areas that make up X as a field or discipline?
3. How are the areas related to each other?

Your responses might be compared with the definitions given by colleagues.

▲ ────────────────────────────────── ▲

Problem Solving in Social Science

By the 1970s, another social studies curriculum emerged, one called by its critics "The Smorgasbord" curriculum and by its proponents "The Relevant" curriculum. Topics such as race, poverty, civil rights, environmental contaminants became the foci. Ethnic awareness and student activism were encouraged. The *mini-course*, a brief course on a limited topic of importance to crucial issues, appeared in many secondary schools. The issues of curriculum were justified as contributing to the decision-making ability of students, preparing them for participation in a democratic society. Accordingly, students identified aspects of problems, gathered and analyzed relevant data, reached conclusions, and sometimes took action to ameliorate the situation. Critics faulted the curriculum for its lack of continuity, its localism, and its departure from academic and cultural traditions.

Current Social Studies Programs

Historical literacy has regained its prominence in the school curriculum. The trend in elementary schools is toward integrated units built around a historical period. An interdisciplinary unit, such as "Life in Colonial New England," encourages children to draw, paint, read, write, and role-play aspects of life in the past. Geography and historical narratives are central. Lessons throughout the unit are connected by major concepts or themes like change, traditions, or values. Attempts are made to have children not only experience the lives of those in the past but also see how some of these experiences are part of their lives today.

The trend in secondary schools also is toward inculcation of a set of traditional beliefs and values, drawing upon history, government, institutions, and culture to illustrate fundamental ideas. Not all teachers are following the trend to historical literacy. Some secondary school teachers follow the social science approach and provide scientific explanations for aspects of social life. The systematic study of economics, sociology, or political science characterizes their courses. Other teachers keep to a problem-solving curriculum, placing world, nation, and local problems of the day—ecology, AIDS, homelessness, gender, trade, community—to the forefront. Their curriculum draws from a wide range of subjects in a focus upon one or more of the problems that entail students taking action consistent with their findings and conclusions. Teachers with a predisposition to social reconstruction sometimes subvert the historical literacy curriculum by shaping their history curriculum so that students center on key issues like treatment of minorities and women as they compare the past and present. The issue becomes the filter for the study of history.

SUMMARY

Much of the history of the arts curriculum still hangs on, creating tensions and opportunities for something different. This chapter has reviewed art curricula aimed at technical proficiency, creative expression through engagement, sustained attention and problem findings, and the knowledge structure of the arts when they are seriously pursued. Authentic practice in studio classrooms, museums, critiques, performances, and artist residencies suggest the nature of future arts curriculum. Invention rather than verification and experience rather than isolated skills may be the way art contributes to ways of learning.

The roots of the English language arts have also endured. English as a study of language as a formal system and as part of a social and cultural heritage reflects a classical past. Curriculum based on the tripod of language, literature, and composition is a response to the search for a body of learning which the field lacks. Literature is still taught as the basis for moral and historical studies and for studies of structure and style. The current popularity of thematic approaches to literature together with an emphasis on creating multiple interpretations through reader response, whole language, and studies of popular culture are viable alternatives for teachers as they develop curriculum for English.

Different curriculum for teaching history have been described: the Memoriter System, circumscribed inquiry, and the newer history curriculum (which aims at developing history's "habits of the mind"). Social studies curriculum are shown to be responses to public and social agendas of officials, interest groups, and members of local communities. At the same time, these curricula have attempted to represent the knowledge of academic scholars. Variation among social studies curricula corresponds to the different motivations of teachers—those who see its purpose as promoting certain values; those who want students to know history, geography, and economics; and those who want students to acquire knowledge and values for improving the society.

QUESTIONS FOR DISCUSSION

Arts

1. Which of the following goals are appropriate for the school's arts curriculum?
   a. *Personal development*: Arts, such as painting, music, dance, drama, and clay modeling should center on student expression of feelings, releasing tensions and overcoming frustrations.
   b. *Aesthetic judgment*: The arts curriculum should aim at the development of aesthetic sensibilities, harmonizing art with ideals of character and conduct.
   c. *Realism*: Students should learn to produce an excellence in art that is measured by faithfulness in representation of actual things.
2. Should school art courses include more material from art history and criticism than the hands-on-activities that now characterize many arts classes? Why? Why not?
3. How should the arts curriculum be related to the ordinary concerns of people and to their everyday activities?

English and Language Arts

1. Should English programs inculcate ideals and values? If so, which ones and on what bases are they to be selected?
2. How can the language curriculum address the personal nature of language and the individual as the unit of meaning while serving the social enterprise of language and the need for shared meanings?
3. Consider your own experiences in the study of English and the language arts. What trends in the field have you encountered? What was valuable and what was missing in each?

History and Social Studies

1. Much curriculum work in the field of history rests on the belief that understanding the past and the present world will motivate individuals to transform society into some improved form. Is this a valid assumption? Give reasons for your answer.
2. Which of the following social studies traditions are most appropriate for today's curriculum?
   a. *Citizenship transmission*: A set of beliefs and fundamental ideas should be perpetuated through study of history, government, and institutions of the society.
   b. *Social sciences*: The methods of knowing and knowledge gained by the social sciences—economics, sociology, political science, and anthropology—should comprise the content of social studies as a school subject.

c. *Social problems*:   The social problems identified by students should become the basis for reflective inquiry, including data collection, analysis, interpretation, drawing conclusions, and taking action.
3. Which aims would you promote through a curriculum in history?
   a. to develop historical empathy
   b. to comprehend the interplay of change and continuity
   c. to understand the significance of the past for our own lives
   d. to recognize there are multiple interpretations of historical events

How can these aims best be achieved?

REFERENCES

Anniel, S. A. (1990). The educational theory of Mary Sheldon Barnes: Inquiry learning as indoctrination in history education. *Educational Theory, 40*: 45–52.

Barnes, M. S. (1883). General history in the high school. *The Academy, 4*: 286–288.

Barnes, M. S. (1893). *Teachers manual.* Boston: D. C. Heath.

Billings, N. A. (1927). *Determination of generalizations basic to the social studies curriculum.* Baltimore, MD: Warwick.

Examination questions. (August 1872). *The California teacher, 10*(2): 37–39.

Clark, G., Day, M., & Green, W. D. (1987). Discipline-based art education: Becoming students of art. *Journal of Aesthetic Education, 21*(2): 129–196.

Commission on English. (1965). Freedom and discipline in English. New York: College Entrance Examination Board.

Efland, A. (1987). Curriculum antecedents of discipline-based art education. *Journal of Aesthetic Education, 21*(2): 57–94.

Efland, A. (1990). Curricular fictions and the discipline orientation in art education. *Journal of Aesthetic Education, 24*(3): 67–81.

Freedman, K. (1987). Art education as social products in the cultural society and politics in the formation of curriculum. In Thomas Popkewitz (Ed.), *The formation of school subjects* (pp. 63–85). Philadelphia: The Palmer Press.

Gagnon, P. (Ed.) & the Bradley Commission on History in Schools. (1989). *The case for history in the schools.* New York: Macmillan.

Hillard, A. G., III (Ed.). (1990). *Infusion of African and African-American content in the school curriculum.* Proceedings of the First National Conference. Morristown, NJ: Aaron Press.

Jackson, P. W., Ed. (1992). *Handbook of research on curriculum.* New York: Macmillan.

Johnson, H. (1915). *Teaching of history in elementary and secondary schools.* New York: Macmillan.

Kerry, E. J. (1985, November). *The purpose of art education in the United States from 1870 to 1980.* Paper presented at the History of Art Education Symposium, State College, PA.

Lowenfeld, V. (1947). *Creative and mental growth.* New York: Macmillan.

Martinec, B. (1971). Popular—but not just a part of the crowd: Implications of formula fictions for teenagers. *English Journal, 60*(3): 39–44.

Moss, R. F. (1985). English composition and the feature file. *Journal of General Education, 37*(2): 122–143.

National Council of Teachers of English. (1935). *An experience curriculum in English.* W. William Hatfield, chairman. New York: Appleton-Century Co.

National Center for History in the Schools. (1992). *Essential understandings and historical perspectives all students should acquire*. Los Angeles, CA: University of California.

Roberts, A. E. (1912). The teaching of English in the high schools of the United States. *The School World, 14*(159): 81–83.

Roody, O. (1947). Developing personality through literature. *English Journal, 36*(6): 299–304.

Stratemeyer, F. B., Forkner, H. L., & McKim, M. G. (1957). *Developing a curriculum for modern living* (3rd ed.). New York: Columbia University, Teachers College Press.

Willinsky, R. (1990). *The new literacy redefining reading and writing in the schools*. New York: Routledge.

MATHEMATICS AND SCIENCE IN THE SCHOOL CURRICULUM

This chapter deals with the problem of making choices about what to teach in mathematics and science. It begins with mathematics and, by examining math curriculums at different historical periods, notes what school mathematics has been and is about. Early programs aimed at using math to understand the society and the teaching of arithmetic so people could carry out personal business and meet the requirements of many vocations are among the curriculums that reflect early choices in aims and content. The relationship between the mathematics of specialists in the universities and the mathematics taught in schools is described. Features of current curriculums in school mathematics are presented, including not only those that reflect the traditional goals related to citizenship, employment, and the development of reason but also newer goals and content based on the needs of a technological society and the belief that students should construct mathematical ideas as they pursue interesting problems.

The chapter goes on to review the shaping of elementary and secondary science curriculum and the conflict between science as knowledge versus science for living, between the teaching of scientific knowledge and curriculum that encourages actual practical capability. The importance of object lessons, nature study, and scientific generalization in early elementary curriculum is shown. Curriculum aimed at the teaching of science processes is contrasted with curriculums that either give priority to science content or place science in a broader context of environmental studies and life experiences. Secondary school science curriculum in physics, chemistry, and biology are reviewed to show how teachers have varied in their views regarding what should be emphasized:

▼ pure science content and its disciplinary logic

▼ learning science as technology and as personal development

▼ applied dimensions of science, such as found in newer, environmentally-oriented, integrated science curriculums

Major social influences on the science curriculum in different historical periods are presented to show how some of the earlier influences are still observed in present situations and to recognize how other interests are competing for priority in the emerging science curriculum.

Just as with the arts and social studies, the curriculum of mathematics and science has changed greatly throughout the past one hundred years. All of the areas follow a common pattern, swinging from a practical orientation (centered on the world of work and response to social developments) to an academic and intellectual orientation (whereby college and university scholars influence the content of the elementary and secondary curriculum) to a humanistic orientation (concerned with individual expression and participation in the construction of knowledge). The pattern has repeated itself at ever more frequent intervals. As the practical curriculum loses its connection to the state of knowledge as conceived by academic scholars, the stage is set for the introduction of the intellectual orientation. However, the abstract curriculum that results from this influence, in turn, is associated with loss of student motivation or with declining enrollments, and a corrective shift to a curriculum with a humanistic orientation follows.

MATHEMATICS FOR REASONING AND FOR USE

The United States was the first country to establish arithmetic as a special subject. David Kamens and Aaron Benavot (1991) attribute this early commitment to numeracy as part of the new nation's ideal of progress and political freedom. The ability to count was related to making the community aware of social problems. Statistics was the basis for national action on a wide range of issues.

Inasmuch as numbers were thought to be objective and value-free, they were more persuasive than opinion in political debates—the beginning of America's scoreboard mentality. In the 1840s, for example, numerical reasoning was used to assess the value and effects of slavery. Throughout the eighteenth and nineteenth centuries, calculating was seen as a way to both produce and measure progress. The counting of population and exports was part of American political life. Statistics were used to draw attention to the need for morality and to assess the efficacy of social practices such as inoculation against small pox. Throughout United States history, tension has existed between those who wanted mathematics taught for its disciplinary value in developing students' ability to reason carefully and logically and those who wanted it taught as a useful tool in daily life and in particular occupations.

Non-Formal Mathematics

Prior to the nineteenth century, there was little emphasis on the teaching of mathematics in colleges or in the Latin Grammar School. The academies and private teachers gave instruction in arithmetic and other practical mathematics. The developing need for mathematics in commerce, surveying, and navigation was met through the academies, subapprenticeships, and self-study. Textbooks of the time featured examples appropriate for given occupations, which students were to follow, similar to today's vocational manuals.

College Entrance Requirements and the Math Curriculum

Arithmetic was not a requirement for Harvard until 1802. At that time students were expected to have knowledge of the four operations with integers, tables of measures, fractions, and the "rule of three" (ratio and proportion as "A is to B as is C to the unknown"). It was thought unfeasible to teach arithmetic to primary students until Pestalozzi illustrated how to present it concretely and in an interesting fashion. Influenced by Pestalozzi, Warren Colburn in 1826 introduced lessons that featured a sequence of questions and exercises of increasing difficulty and that differed from former materials in putting more emphasis on explanation than on rules to be memorized. Colburn also prepared materials for introducing students to algebra through a series of problems requiring reasoning from students and only simple intuitive use of equations.

In 1820, algebra became a required subject for entrance to Harvard, and applicants were to have an understanding of simple equations, comprehending also the doctrine of roots and powers and arithmetical and geometrical proportions. Little change occurred until 1872, at which time the following requirements were established: arithmetic, algebra, and plane geometry. These requirements and the textbooks college professors wrote shaped the mathematics curriculum for the secondary and elementary schools of the period. Arithmetic was taught incidentally in the primary grades; basic arithmetic in grades 2–6 and intuitive algebra and written work in grades 7–8; algebra in grade 9; and plane geometry in grade 10.

In general, the same courses that had been offered in colleges were included in the curriculum of high schools and academies, and the same textbooks were used. The math curriculum for the elementary and secondary schools reflected the logic of adults more than the learning perspective of students. It followed the traditional classification of subjects that divided the content of mathematics into arithmetic, algebra, and geometry instead of equations, ratio, measures, similarity, functional dependence, scale, variation, and the like, making it difficult for students to see that these concepts are the same notions and operations in each subject. This practice hid the observation that the same concepts made use of in new ways could be related to show new connections.

Practical Uses of Mathematics

In the early twentieth century, the mathematics curriculum in the elementary and secondary schools became more centered on practical and vocational goals than on disciplinary values. Social factors influencing this change included a larger population of non-collegebound students, concern about the large numbers of students who failed disciplinary courses, and the growing influence of psychologists who discredited the mathematicians' claim that mathematics would improve one's thinking faculty, especially the ability to reason in all situations.

The arithmetic curriculum of elementary grades at this time focused on the four operations, fractions, common tables of measures, the decimal point, decimal fractions and percentages. Instruction in the seventh and eighth grades centered on percentage and its applications and business arithmetic.

A variety of approaches—such as drill work and exercises in actual measuring and computing—was used to teach arithmetic in the primary grades. Children sometimes did the purchasing of foodstuffs for the day's luncheon, using current prices that they had obtained. For part of the day, children solved problems that appealed to them or played games involving numbers. The use of splints in learning place values and the addition of three-digit numbers was popular (Smith, 1917). Children in the upper elementary grades confronted different kinds of applied problems: application of a rule, narrative problems, grouped problems, problems without numbers, oral problems, and problems in real situations. In rural areas, they might learn laying out and measuring fields, finding the value of crops, putting up fences and buildings, and farm economics. In the city, an equally broad range of real life problems was drawn from industry, home economics, and civic expenditures.

At the beginning of the twentieth century, the traditional course in algebra was modified by reducing manipulations, postponing difficult topics, and increasing the application of algebra and the solving of equations. Similarly, courses in geometry were made less difficult by eliminating materials on limits and incommensurables, and adding informal proofs and graded theorems for students to prove in place of the required theorems to be memorized.

From the 1920s through the 1950s, conflict existed in the secondary school between those who wanted to teach traditional mathematics to all and those who wanted to vary the content according to future roles, making the subject chiefly an elective (Stanic, 1987). That those of the social efficacy persuasion won the day is evidenced by the decline in numbers of secondary school students who took algebra and geometry during the period. Many teachers did not believe that all students should study mathematics throughout the secondary school years and opposed the teaching of discipline views of mathematics—the logical organizing of subject matter as defined by university scholars—to future laborers. Accordingly, a variety of courses were developed to meet the different "needs" of those preparing for the following things:

▼ general education

▼ certain trades

▼ engineering

▼ specialized studies in math

The prevailing view was that after finishing a junior high course giving students some idea of the general nature and use of arithmetic, intuitive geometry, practical algebra and the meaning of demonstration in geometry, only those students who had ability and interest in mathematics or who expected to enter a college or technical school were required to pursue the subject.

Paradoxically, as the place of mathematics in the school curriculum declined, the contributions from professional study and research in mathematics with the colleges and universities were unparalleled. Also, the widening gap between the mathematics taught in schools and the knowledge of specialists set the stage for reform and attempts by mathematicians to control the school mathematics curriculum.

Scholar Preparation of the Elementary and Secondary Mathematics Curriculum

Mathematics in 1960 gained the upper hand in shaping elementary and secondary mathematics in the direction of disciplinary and cultural aims at the expense of utilitarian aims. University curriculum projects in mathematics funded by the National Science Foundation gave as their rationale the importance of mathematics in science and technology and the need to modernize the curriculum to reflect newer developments in the mathematical sciences—statistics and pure and applied mathematics (University of Illinois, 1959).

Changes in the elementary curriculum included the introduction of new topics—probability, geometry of physical space, positive and negative numbers, graphs, sets, Venn diagrams, and numeration systems other than the decimal. Instead of a focus on the processes (algorithms) of arithmetic and the authenticity of the grocery store, the curriculum of mathematics centered on the properties of numbers by introducing the mathematical sentence: "What number for N will make this sentence true: $56 + 28 = N + 56$?" The curriculum of the junior high school lost application to social situations, instead directing study toward the structure of mathematics and the interconnections of the various branches. New activities were created to help students discover concepts for themselves, similar to Colburn's inductive method involving Cuisenaire rods, multi-base blocks, geoboards, and abaci for teaching the various numeration systems. Some teachers encouraged group activities in constructing models, computer programming, and exhibitions showing probability, and growth patterns.

In the high school, first-year algebra became more abstract and featured generalizations of equalities and solution sets. There was an emphasis on the concept of function and graphical representations of function theory, showing how changes in one variable resulted in or were caused by changes in another. Geometry was revised to allow students to use their knowledge of algebra in proving theories by coordinating methods. More attention was given to proofs that are unacceptable because they rest on unproven incidence relationships as a way to show how difficult it is to prove "obvious" statements and reject false statements.

The curriculum of math scholars was faulted for introducing too many mathematical details and lack of applications to real-life problems. Many parents did not see the reasons for introducing the structure of mathematics in place of arithmetic. Reports of a decline in basic math skills as measured by conventional tests also contributed to a return to teaching minimal mathematical skills in the elementary schools and college preparatory algebra and geometry in the secondary schools. Some teachers, however, maintained aspects of the reform—the notion of sets and the use of sets of objects to explain the various operations; the use of "big ideas" in mathematics such as patterns, graphing, and activities that encouraged students to solve problems rather than to follow a set of rules or steps to get a correct answer.

Current Trends in the Mathematics Curriculum: Problem Solving and Practicality

Under the auspices of the National Council of Teachers of Mathematics, a cross-section of mathematicians, teachers, and teacher educators developed a framework to guide reform in school mathematics throughout the 1990s (Commission on Standards for School Mathematics, 1991). The framework encourages the teaching of a broad range of math topics—number concepts, computation, estimation, data analysis, model building, discrete math, function, algebra, statistics, probability, geometry, and measurement. However, these topics are not taught in isolation but in ways to show their connections. It is suggested, for example, that number theory be used in grades 5–8 as the basis for bonding many individual facets into a whole, such as the commonalities among various arithmetics.

The current direction in mathematics curriculum differs from the traditional curriculum in three essential ways:

1. The presentation is problem-oriented. Instruction revolves around concrete word problems whereas the traditional curriculum proceeded from concept to concept.
2. Classes are conducted to encourage active participation of each student. A constructive view of learning dominates, one that holds that individuals must construct their own understanding of math principles and concepts. Hence, children are encouraged to rely more on one another and less on the teacher in judging whether and why their answers are right. The teacher tries to find out what individuals are thinking and then helps them refine their ideas and encourages them to invent ways to solve problems.
3. By contrast with the traditional division of math into algebra, geometry, algebra II, trigonometry, and calculus, the curriculum is organized around five or six major problems per year. Each time a problem comes up, new tools and concepts (regardless of whether they are from algebra or geometry) are introduced until the problem is solved.

Teachers are expected to develop learning opportunities in accordance with the following goals:

▼ *Valuing of mathematics*:   The goal is a combination of the old cultural appreciation of mathematics for its beauty and power and the importance of mathematics to the present scientific and technological world.

▼ *Confidence in one's own math ability*:   There should be opportunities for students to be successful in using math in their own situations.

▼ *Problem solving*:   Students should explore individually and in groups both classroom and real-world problems.

▼ *Communication:*   Students should read, write, and discuss ideas using the signs, symbols, and terms of mathematics.

▼ *Reasoning*:   Students should make conjectures, gather evidence, and build arguments about the validity of a conjecture.

Current issues of both the *Arithmetic Teacher* and *The Mathematics Teacher* describe the curriculum developed by individual teachers in accordance with the guidelines. Dan Brutlag and Carole Maples (1992) developed a four-week unit "Beyond the Surface" to help middle-grade students relate many mathematical concepts and tools to one another, to other subject areas, and to personal growth. This unit deals with sealing surface area–volume relationships and was built around four general principles that promote the making of connections by students:

1.   A significant context of interest to the students that connects and anchors mathematical ideas should be used. To this end, the teacher selected ideas from the student world that involved relationships among scale, similarity, surface area and volume. Popular literature and movies suggested that students were familiar with scaled-up or -down versions of animals, plants, and people. Hence, the unit began by asking whether such fantastic things as killer bees are as large as airplanes? Are there really blimp-sized bananas? Can human beings shrunk to the size of grasshoppers? Are these things possible, or will they exist forever only in the movies? The answer to the question lies in the mathematical relationship between surface area and volume. In order to comprehend biological information about the relative effects of size (and hence biological possibilities), students needed to have a sophisticated understanding of the mathematical concepts of similarity, scale, surface area and volume.

2.   Students should construct their own concepts through concrete, active tasks. Accordingly, students explored several tasks at the beginning of the unit to answer the questions, What is surface area? and What is volume? They built objects out of Cuisenaire rods held together by putty. Because the rods were centimeter rods, the volume and surface area could be found by counting. Gradually, students devised their own algorithms and formula to make the counting easier. In one of the tasks, students worked in groups

to build different objects all having a volume of 22 cubic centimeters and to find the minimum and maximum possible surface area for objects built with all six rods. After looking at the class data, students wrote their conclusions and gave their reasons.

In answer to the question of how surface area and volume change as objects are scaled up in size, students were assigned to two group tasks. In the first task, students built a "rod dog" out of centimeter rods and then built a similar dog with dimensions twice those of the original. The surface areas and volumes for the two dogs were counted and compared. In the second task, each group was assigned particular scale facts. Each group used these facts to build an enlargement of the original dog out of centimeter-grid paper, found the surface area and volume for their dog, and recorded their data on a table to be used with an overhead projector.

3. A mathematical relationship should be represented using several mathematical tools. In the "Beyond the Surface" unit, students represented the same information using models, diagrams, tables, graphs, and formulas. It is assumed that students who are able to apply and translate among different representations of the same problem situation or of the same concept will have both a powerful set of tools for solving problems and an appreciation of the consistency and beauty of mathematics.

4. Students should reflect on the connections of their mathematical experiences by writing in journals, making presentations, discussing in seminars, and working on projects. Throughout the unit, students wrote about their experiences and understandings. At the end of the unit, each student completed an individual project rather than a traditional chapter test for assessment. To complete the project, students had to reflect on the ideas learned and show what they learned in a creative, open-ended way. Options for projects included the option to build models of three similar houses, finding the scale factor, surface area, and volume of each and to comment about the relationships; and the option to invent a new friend about half the student's height, to devise a method to find the surface area and volume of the student and half-sized friend, and to comment about the relationships.

Controversy about the Present Math Curriculum

Not all teachers are committed to curriculum that offers the same topics to all students. The early-twentieth-century approach of differentiating the math curriculum on the basis of career aspirations is alive. The mathematics curriculum proposed by Paul Burke (1990), for instance, offers one required course for all high school students followed by elective courses that would offer mathematical topics appropriate for the preprofessional training of scientists and engineers. The required course would be of a practical nature and center on such topics as percentages, logic, and statistics. The study of percentage would include compound interest received on savings or paid on credit cards and mortgages; the unemployment rate, inflation, growth of cells, and special cases

▼ ── ▼

**ACTIVITY 6–1   DESCRIBING THE
"MATHEMATICAL VISION" OF TEACHERS**

1. Interview one or more teachers about the mathematical visions they hold.
2. Consider asking these questions:
   a. What are their goals for their mathematics program? What kinds of mathematics learning do they hope their students will experience?
   b. What do they see as worthwhile mathematical tasks or important mathematical ideas?
   c. Do their programs emphasize problem solving, communication, reasoning, conjecturing, and making connections among mathematical ideas? Are there commonalities in their thinking? Why?

▲ ── ▲

that confuse many people (such as tenths of a percent and figures over 100 percent). Logic would be broadly conceived with examples from all fields in hopes that it would transfer; arguments by counterexamples, definition of terms, and induction would be included. Statistics would include the reading of complex graphs and tables with data from newspapers, almanacs, and other reference materials; the strengths and biases of surveys, polls, lists of best sellers would be noted; the concepts of average, weighted averages, median, and the percentile would be applied. The strengths and weaknesses of regression equations would be shown through study of such questions as the relation between education and income. The use of standard deviations and confidence intervals would be applied to real-life situations.

SCIENCE AS KNOWLEDGE VERSUS SCIENCE OF LIVING

Science education has long been an area of contention. Throughout much of the nineteenth century, many people viewed science as of little use to the average citizen, something easily forgotten; some thought science inferior to Latin and Greek in developing the reasoning faculties of students; and others saw science as hostile to organized religions, undermining religious beliefs and authority. David Layton (1973) tells how in 1840 a "science of common things" was introduced in primary schools in England as a way to relate science to people's lives. He relates the short-lived duration of this program and how it was followed by science in an abstract form—a textbook-based discipline entailing laboratory work aimed at the discovery of knowledge rather than a science addressing the personal interests of students and the social needs of society.

A review of the elementary and secondary science curriculum in the United States in the nineteenth and twentieth centuries shows a continuous debate about the primary goal of science education—knowledge or a better life.

ELEMENTARY SCIENCE CURRICULUM

Object Lessons

Science made its appearance in the elementary school about 1850 as object teaching. Objects taken from the wide range of phenomena of nature—dew, frost, hail, wind. Animal and inanimate objects—all that could fall within sense observation—were the materials for study, not models or pictures. Children were encouraged to differentiate among the objects seen and touched—the shade of color or the variation in surfaces. The role of the teacher was to draw the child to correct observations and exact inferences through suggestions and questions, not by telling or making direct statements. The purposes of object lessons were these:

▼   to gain knowledge of common things

▼   to cultivate the capacity to observe

▼   to develop reasoning ability

Unfortunately, many teachers had difficulty adjusting lessons to individual variations of students' interests and abilities within the large classes. Sometimes the lesson tended to be highly formal and to neglect the interpretation and understanding of events and phenomena. Objects were placed before children who were asked to name it, describe its parts, and state the relationships among the parts. From the observation of single objects, students were led to compare them with others, taking the first step toward classification.

Nature Study

By 1870, object teaching had evolved into nature study. By contrast with science in the secondary schools of the time, which was directed toward the acquisition of knowledge of scientific principles, nature study in the elementary school dealt with natural things and processes as they related to daily life.

The exact shape that nature study took depended on the season of the year and the locality of the school. Common, however, were these:

▼   studies of the weather (daily systematic readings and chartings of the thermometer and barometer, wind direction, and other meteorological observations)

▼   celestial studies (finding the altitude of midday of the sun throughout the year)

▼   physical geography (river courses, hills, valleys, sand, stratification of rocks)

▼ study of plants and animals (structure and germination of seeds, influence of light on green plants—usually taught through the care of a class garden that served as a laboratory for the fundamental condition of growth; insects, worms, frogs, and domestic animals offered abundant sources of study about how animals move, feed, breathe, grow, and care for offspring)

An important aspect of the nature study curriculum was that the same materials and phenomena could be studied by students of different ages. The students' continued and growing interest in the phenomena was considered more educational than introducing new and unrelated subject matter by grade level.

Nature study's goals were to develop interest in objects and processes of nature, to give training in accurate observation and in classifying facts, and to provide useful knowledge of nature as it affects human life. Nature study was used to correlate learning in many areas. Modes of expression—drawing, dancing, acting, constructing, writing, and composing music—were featured as students responded to the emotional stimulation of a field trip or other experience with nature.

Physiology and hygiene were correlated with nature study in such activities as comparing form and uses of human body parts with those of animals. The industrial and physical aspects of geography were introduced through nature study, and, of course, the applications of number were both necessary and numerous. For example, one group of students took as their inquiry the problem of determining the rate at which plants multiply as indicated by the seed production at a vacant city block covered with wild verbenas. Students measured the area as one-quarter acre and calculated the average number of plants per square yard. They then found out how many seeds were contained in each plant and the number that failed to mature, indicating an average of 1700 seeds available for growth. Based on the proper distribution of good seeds and the assumption that each would produce a plant, students determined that the quarter-acre could be populated each year for succeeding years and that in the fifth year it would provide enough seeds to furnish plants as thickly as those found on that quarter-acre on an area equal to sixteen times that of the entire earth (Jackman, 1904).

By the 1920s, enthusiasm for nature study began to wane. There were criticisms that the nature-study curriculum lacked organization, that students tended to study a disconnected series of object lessons, that a chaos in goals—aesthetic, ethical, intellectual, and civic—were pursued. Nature study was faulted for expecting the teacher to be an expert naturalist and for failing to introduce vital elements of scientific method and content: The teacher gives lists of flowers, birds, or constellations to study each month, but no suggestion for the meanings that may be developed.

Generalizations from Science

The study of science tended to replace nature study in the 1920s. This change in orientation is seen in the curriculum developed by Gerald Craig and his coworkers at the Horace Mann Elementary School (1927). The process for developing this curriculum is itself of interest to curriculum makers. Craig first prepared a list of specific objectives for elementary school science that conformed to scientific generalizations fundamental to modern life; contributed to health, economy and safety; and were considered essential for understanding phenomena of interest to children. These objectives were submitted to parents and other educated laypeople for ranking as to importance. These judgments were supplemented by the judgments of scientists and social forethinkers as found in authoritative source books of science. In addition, Craig and his fellow teachers tried to find out from children what questions in nature and science interested them most. The generalizations from science that best answered the questions were included. Assignment of the objectives to grade level was based on the assumed order of complexity. There were specific topics and major generalizations for each grade level:

▼   *Grade 1:*   change of seasons; effects of cold weather; where plants and animals live; plants and seeds; sun, moon, and stars

▼   *Grade 2:*   plants and seasonal changes, animals and seasonal changes, water, ice, steam, air, and weather, heat and light from the sun, magnetism, plants as food, ways electricity help

▼   *Grade 3:*   how animals protect themselves and care for their young, how seeds are scattered, the sun and moon, cause of day and night, food of animals

▼   *Grade 4:*   the earth we live on, economic value of animals, social life of animals, air, soil, gardening, molds, bacteria, electric wiring, fossils, importance of water

▼   *Grade 5:*   hibernation, migration, causes of fogs and clouds, metamorphosis, moon and its movement, conservation of nature, balance of nature, protective coloration, how plants grow

▼   *Grade 6:*   the story of the earth, the solar system, reproduction, methods of adaptation

The topics are interrelated from grade 1 to grade 6 by certain themes. Migration, hibernation, metamorphosis, parental care, and community life, for example, are all adaptation. Examples of the kinds of generalizations that comprised the course objectives and essential meanings to be taught are these:

▼   Nature's laws are invariable.

▼   Man's conception of truth changes.

▼   The earth is one of a number of bodies that revolve around the sun.

▼   The earth rotates on its axis once every 24 hours, causing day and night.

▼   All life depends on vegetation, and vegetation languishes outside the temperature range of 55 degrees to 10 degrees centigrade.

▼   All life has evolved from very simple forms.

In the 1950s, some scientists faulted the social utility approach to elementary science education, saying it was not science but only "snippets of information about favored topics as weather, nature study, magnets, and series of 'Gee Whiz' topics" (Seeborg, 1960). Other weaknesss in the generalization-oriented curriculum were these:

▼   Topics were presented as results to be accepted on faith with little experimentation.

▼   There was a failure to show how scientific conclusions are derived by induction and deduction.

▼   The connections between all natural phenomena was not revealed to students.

Science as Processes versus Science as Concepts

Federal support for elementary school science began in 1961. The curriculum projects undertaken with this money were conducted by academic scientists and used a variety of approaches. The leaders of the American Association for the Advancement of Science project "Science—A Process Approach" (Gagné, 1966) held that science consisted of the processes scientists used, not the concepts with which they worked. Hence this curriculum was designed to teach the scientific processes of classifying, measuring, observing, and inferring. Materials were made available for these purposes. Children were encouraged to question and hypothesize about the phenomena presented and to conduct experiments using numbers and making inferences in testing their hypotheses. Children were taught how to summarize and communicate their findings.

Other scientists, notably the developers of the Science Curriculum Study (SCIS) at the University of California at Berkeley, centered their effort on producing materials and ways of teaching fundamental science concepts (Karplus & Thier, 1967). Two major categories of concepts were chosen—description ("What happens?") and an explanatory or interpretive concept ("Why does it happen?"). Concepts were arranged in a hierarchy by degree of abstraction. Major ideas from both biological and physical science were drawn upon. The major concepts by grade level were these:

▼   *Grade 1:*   organisms and material objects

▼   *Grade 2:*   life cycles and interaction of systems

▼ *Grade 3:* population and subsystems

▼ *Grade 4:* environment and relating of positions and motion

▼ *Grade 5:* community and energy sources

▼ *Grade 6:* ecosystems and models of electric and magnetic interaction

Boxes of equipment and materials together with instructional units were part of the program. Three different kinds of lessons were featured:

1. Children are left on their own to explore and discover while playing with collections of objects.
2. Children are helped to invent a concept that is new to them and to find meaning from the exploratory experiences. (The invention lesson also provided guided practice in using new labels and categories.)
3. Children discover the usefulness of the new concepts by applying them in their own situations.

Only about 30 percent of elementary schools used any of the curriculum developed by the scientists, and by 1980 there was evidence that teachers were not providing hands-on experiences so that students could get greater insights into the basic concepts of science. Instead a return to the textbook approach and an emphasis on the memorization of scientific facts had occurred (Harms & Yager, 1981). Increased control by state authorities through testing that demanded selection of "right" answers to fragmented questions contributed to the decrease in student practice of scientific processes and inquiry using concepts from several subject areas. Nevertheless, some elementary school teachers developed science curriculum to meet local needs, moving away from science as a discipline to the social significance of science, and some teachers followed ecological approaches centered on human interests and called on interdisciplinary sources.

Alan Harden and Meghan O'Connor at the Loyd Center for Environmental Studies in Somerset, Massachusetts, have implemented a curriculum that casts students in the role of environmental consultants hired by a builder of a restaurant. Before the consultants' field investigation, they receive instruction for their jobs. They learn to use topographic maps, field equipment, and pacing measures. Biological concepts, such as succession and natural cycles, are explained. Information about the various forms of local wildlife and the importance of wetlands for the town are presented. Students then take field trips to inspect the building site and land. They identify the kinds of vegetation, sediment, and wildlife at the site; and then examine current land use and the effect further development would have on the ecosystem. Later in class, students prepare a report of their findings, which they present at a simulated town meeting.

Current Directions: Social Problems and Themes

Among the goals for science in the 1990s are the prior generation's goals of developing student skills for scientific investigation and facilitating students' acquisition of concepts that approximate those of scientists. Other goals, however, are getting equal attention: to prepare students for technological problem solving, to equip students to make decisions about science related social issues, and to help them be independent, life-long learners of science.

Science for All America, the report issued by the American Association for the Advancement of Science (1989), envisions an ideal elementary curriculum that demonstrates the connections that exist among the different disciplines and helps students understand their changing world. Accordingly, California has asked that elementary school teachers develop their classroom science experiences around major themes such as energy, evolution, patterns of change, scale and structure, stability and interaction. The theme *evolution*, for example, is treated in grades 1–3 through the study of the diversity among living things and in grades 3–6 through the study of how living things adapt to their environment in order to survive and how the various studies of living things help them keep alive and grow. Activities in physical, earth, and life sciences are related to the themes, and students try to draw connections from concepts being studied to daily experiences and previously learned ideas. In many schools, science is used as a vehicle to enhance reading, math, and the arts, much like the science curriculum of the 1920s.

Under a grant from the Packard Foundation, nearly 300 elementary teachers developed a theme for the year that would relate the different subjects and would design first-hand real-world science activities (Greene, 1991). Under this curriculum, students read and write about science. Working in groups, they investigate and solve problems requiring measurement and computation, and express their understanding through art, music, and movement. One first-grade class (using the theme "Over in the Meadow") experimented, drew conclusions, and recorded their observations on such topics as the senses, weather, rocks, and soils, birds of prey, metamorphosis.

SCIENCE IN SECONDARY SCHOOLS

The traditional curriculum divisions of physics, chemistry, and biology have evolved from other subjects and have experienced periodic swings in content and direction, from that which is useful in daily life to that which prepares one to enter the scientific community. Also, when the lag between what scientists know and what schools teach becomes acute, the curriculum is bent toward the disciplines. The abstractions of the discipline, in turn, invite student and public dissatisfaction and a return to a more personal and society-relevant science curriculum.

Physics in Secondary Schools

Physics as a Natural Philosophy.   Great changes in technology in the period 1750–1870, including the introduction of machines such as the steam engine, contributed to the popularity of natural philosophy, the study of mechanics, hydraulics, pneumatics, optics, electricity, and magnetism. Natural philosophy emphasized practicality; much of the content was taught in academies and through self-study. Textbooks in the field, for example, seldom demanded mathematical formulas and instead supplied illustrations to represent and clarify the principles presented (Woodburn & Ellsworth, 1965).

Physics as Preparation for College.   The classical concept of education in colleges only yielded to science in 1872 when Harvard accepted physics as one of its entrance requirements. Four years later, Harvard profoundly influenced the high school physics curriculum by stating which experiments would be acceptable (experiments that demonstrated what was already known) and stressing the intellectual values and the study methods by which scientific facts and laws had been discovered, rather than utility, as an end.

Between 1887 and 1900, colleges dominated the physics curriculum through entrance requirements that formalized the topics and promoted an instructional approach that was a combination of didactic lectures, textbook memorization, and laboratory work that aimed at a so-called rediscovery of the laws of physics.

Physics as a Practical Science.   The early 1920s saw a reaction to the college-dominated curriculum and a return to more practical courses. Physics textbooks from 1900 to 1950 attempted both to describe the physical world and to show the applications of physics to everyday life. A 1924 textbook, for instance, introduced material on the automobile, radio, engines, radiation and radioactivity, and waterpower (Fuller, Brownlee, & Baker, 1924). A negative reaction to the social utility approach to physics began in the early 1950s. Academicians faulted the existing curriculum for its trivial content and absence of fundamental concepts.

Physics as Research.   Some scientists formed the Physical Science Study Committee (PSSC) and developed a high school course in physics that presented physics as a system of inquiry. Emphasis was placed on having students confront physical problems in the laboratory, exploring them from various directions and developing the tools necessary for solving them. The PSSC laboratory activities allowed for new discoveries and departed from the old lab activities that were solely for verifying previously won conclusions. The curriculum also introduced a limited number of "themes"—the measurement of time and space, matter, and the causes of motion—to which selected content could be related, rather than attempting a general coverage of physics. For example, after conducting an experimental treatment of electricity and magnetism, students tried to relate their findings to previous work in measurement, motion, the particle nature of matter, force, wave, conservation principles, and physical model-making for the story of the atom. Through films showing experiments, demonstrations, and discussions, students were led to see how classical theory alone could not explain the frequency threshold of the effect and the need for a new model that would simplify the view of matter and radiation.

The PSSC course was taught in half of the high schools of the United States during the 1960s and became the prototype for other curricular projects in biology and chemistry. Although the science content for PSSC and the other programs was accurate and the support materials designed for use in the classroom were excellent, the program did not endure. The number of students taking physics and chemistry dropped from 51 to 40 percent, and in the 1980s less than one third of America's high schools offered a course in physics taught by a qualified teacher. Without experience in designing and conducting experiments, many teachers had trouble teaching students to be scientists. Further, whereas the chief concern in the 1950s was to produce advanced science researchers, 30 years later the chief concern was to educate all citizens for participation in a highly scientific and technological world. The preparation of a workforce that depends on advanced technology became the priority.

Physics for Decision Making.   The physics curriculum of recent years has emphasized the technical and social aspects of physics, the goal of giving an up-to-date picture of the role physics plays in both pure and applied science, technology and society. It is taught as a human activity with cultural, historical, ethical, and social understandings. The new physics curriculum aims at preparing students to use science and technology in dealing with value-related social decisions.

One such curriculum consists of ten thematic units—comparing, weather changes, music, traffic, electrical machines, energy and quality, matter, light sources, ionizing radiation, and electronics (Lijnse, et al 1990). The thematic approach allows for flexibility and relates physics to everyday life. Each unit begins with an orientation of this relationship—how an understanding of physics might be helpful in using technological devices, making a consumer decision, or undertaking a socioscientific study. This orientation is followed by basic knowledge and skills concerning the topic. For example, a unit on weather change introduces questions for determining the weather; forecasting; methods for measuring temperature, air pressure, and the like; as well as how to interpret weather charts—all involving knowledge and skill. After study of the compulsory part of the unit, students work in problem-solving groups dealing with special questions about clouds, precipitation, fronts, pressure areas, and other weather-related phenomena. The knowledge acquired in these groups is used to address the integrating questions about forecasting.

In the thematic curriculum, concepts are taught in the contextual situation in which they have to function, moving the study of physics away from its study as a discipline and toward the study as a functional and relevant resource. Supplementary units, however, are available for students who want more insights into the systematic structure of physics including the topics of force, motion, energy, and force fields.

Chemistry in Secondary Schools

The early academies and public high schools taught a practical chemistry that could be applied in the home and in agriculture. These courses were largely lecture and demonstration. After the Civil War, laboratory work in chemistry was offered in most schools. The period 1872–1900 saw domination of the chemistry curriculum by colleges, as with the physics curriculum. Chemistry texts were organized by the logic of the subject. An issue at the time was whether laboratory work that consisted of observation and the introduction of generalizations should only affirm the textbook. Formalism, as opposed to inductive method, increased under the influence of college teachers of chemistry, and as formalism increased, the percentage of students enrolled in chemistry declined from 11 percent in 1890 to 7 percent in 1905.

After World War I, industrial chemistry became more important for the nation. High school chemistry courses became more applied and taught such information as how to remove stains and how to test for adulteration in foods. At least 14 different types of chemistry courses of an applied nature—such as technical chemistry, textile chemistry, and dairy chemistry—were offered.

In the 1960s, the federal government, through the National Science Foundation, funded programs such as the Chemical Education Material Study. This curriculum followed an inquiry approach and introduced both laboratory work and theoretical concepts (such as rates and mechanisms of reactions, chemical bonding, structural ideas, and the systematization of chemistry in terms of the periodic table). The goal was to have students attain a highly mathematical and logical form of science. The program succeeded in revising the teaching of chemistry so that courses reflected modern knowledge of the subject. However, the disciplinary approach to chemistry did not increase student interest, as indicated by falling enrollments.

Currently, the teaching of chemistry has a constant stream of new curricula. In some of the new courses, chemistry is taught as part of a general science course. In other courses, it is combined with biology, geology, physics, and other subjects. In general, much attention is given to the application of chemistry to everyday life and to industrial uses through the study of plastics, detergents, medicines, insecticides, and other products.

Biology in Secondary Schools

Biology teachers today differ among themselves about biology as a school subject. Some follow an evolutionary approach, with an emphasis on adaptation and change; others take a functional approach, highlighting physiology. Many favor an environmental approach with a focus on ecology and conservation, and a few have a genetic and molecular approach. The latest approach is an applied biology approach that uses biology to solve human problems. In part, these differences in orientation reflect the 100-year history of the field.

Biology as Natural History.   In the early 1800s, the academies and prep schools offered courses in natural history in which students studied plants, animals, and nature, and acquired medical information, especially as related to herbs and botany. In their courses, students described and classified living things and were taught to view the "wonderful harmony of nature and its relation to moral behavior" (Rosen, 1959, p. 480). Specialized courses in zoology and botany also had a natural history approach, with an emphasis on the classification of animals and plants. Human physiology became part of the curriculum in 1839. Because many of the authors of physiology texts were physicians, the courses stressed anatomy and body functions.

Biology as a Mental Discipline.   After the Civil War, botany shifted its aim to mental discipline and introduced the laboratory method as an appropriate instrument for attaining this goal. The morphology of plants became a focus. Similarly, under the influence of Louis Agazzi, who taught high school classes and brought other teachers to his laboratory, the focus of zoology changed from natural history to comparative anatomy and the classification of animal life from man to protozoa, with mental discipline as the major aim. After 1865, the temperance movement succeeded in having physiology textbooks devote pages to the evils of alcohol and tobacco, which diluted the mental discipline emphasis and adversely affected the popularity of physiology.

Integrated Biology.   In the 1870s, the concept of a general biology course that would integrate botany, zoology, and human physiology was promoted. Thomas Huxley and Henry Martin (1876), for instance, held that study of living bodies, plants, and animals is really one discipline. Due to problems in organizing an integrated course, for many years teachers followed a "fern and worm" method (in which those two organisms were studied as prototypes of their respective kingdoms). Until the 1900s, biology courses were highly academic, demanding attention to structural details and following laboratory instructions to confirm prespecified observations.

Practical Biology.   The academic and disciplinary orientation for biology lost ground through the first half of the twentieth century. Instead the subject was regarded as useful for both collegebound and non-collegebound students. Knowledge of biology was seen as helping citizens deal with problems of health, hygiene, food preparation, sanitation, and conservation of natural resources. Where laboratory work had formerly been justified as promoting the faculties of observation and willpower, psychological evidence cast doubt on the possibility of training students' powers of observation and denied the existence of general faculty of observation. Teachers responded by justifying such work as developing thinking skills and the scientific method.

Courses of the times were often organized around projects and problems involving field trips and the local environment. Textbooks introduced a number of generalizations derived from scholarly studies—microorganisms are the immediate cause of disease; all life came from pre-existing life and reproduces its own kind; food, oxygen, and certain optimal conditions are essential for the life of living things.

Biology Updated.   By 1960, the disparity between what was taught in high schools as biology and what scientists thought essential was great enough to warrant a change in the curriculum. The Biological Science Curriculum Study (BSCS), a committee of high school teachers, administrators, and research biologists, expressed its concern about the failure of biology courses to deal with such issues as organic evolution, the nature of individual and racial differences, sex and reproduction in the human species, and the problem of population growth and control. The committee also faulted courses for not developing understanding of biological concepts and organizational ideas such as the genetic continuity of life, and for not accurately portraying scientific activity. The committee created three versions of the same course (Glass, 1962):

1. a molecular approach, including genetic evolution
2. a community approach with attention to ecological problems
3. a cellular approach with emphasis on physiological functions

In all stances, supplementary material—such as films to stimulate original investigations and articles to assist students in their inquiries—was available.

By the end of the 1970s, nearly half of the school districts in the United States were using the BSCS materials. The social atmosphere of the 1970s supported the teaching of biological education as relevant for a broad range of students, not just for those planning careers in science. Many teachers adopted an ecological perspective combined with the aim of developing decision-making skills for citizenship. They taught biology in relation to important aspects of contemporary life—in the context of population growth and need for family planning, stress and mental health, proper food preparation and use, and others.

Current Biology Curriculum.   Currently, biology teachers are asked to develop curriculum in accordance with the recommendations of Project 2061 of the American Association for the Advancement of Science (1989). Its widely encompassing recommendations aim at helping students become familiar with the natural world in its diversity and its unity, understand key concepts of biology, and apply biological knowledge to connections among the sciences. It recommends such practices as showing how the transformation of energy occurs in physical, biological, and chemical systems and how evolutionary changes appear in stars, organisms, and rocks.

SUMMARY

This chapter described curricula in mathematics and science during different historical periods, to provide readers with an understanding of current curricula in these fields. Past patterns in the teaching of mathematics as a fixed set of concepts and skills to be mastered, for example, may conflict or impede the goals of a new era. Analytical rather than mechanical skills are now the priority. However, some older views of mathematics such as statistical analysis of social issues are very much in order.

▼ —————————————————————————————————————— ▼

ACTIVITY 6–2 RELATING A SCIENTIFIC
DISCIPLINE TO A SCHOOL SUBJECT

A school subject differs from a discipline in that a school subject should be consistent with the purposes of the school and the reasons for teaching the subject, including social and personal relevance. Mastery of an organized field of knowledge may be necessary for an expert, but the general education of a citizen may not require the same degree of specialized knowledge.

Consider a class you might teach. What are some of the reasons students in the class should study X (an aspect of science)? What areas would you want students to experience? What makes X difficult for students? What can be done to make the study of X more satisfying for students and to enhance their success with the subjects? Compare your answers to the curriculum in X at different historical periods.

▲ —————————————————————————————————————— ▲

Current math curriculum provides students with experience through which they "do" mathematics rather than learn about it. Doing mathematics involves solving real problems, building math models, abstracting, inventing, and explaining.

A range of science curriculums has been implemented in elementary schools—object lessons, nature study, science generalizations, and process approaches. Currently, the elementary school science curriculum combines many of the old curricula, focusing on observations, natural and created environments, and scientific investigations. In the past, the science curricula of the secondary schools took two different approaches: those curriculums that prepared students in a discipline for further study and those that aimed at developing citizens who could participate in the political and social choices involving science and its applications.

Today's science curriculum is likely to incorporate many older ideas. Chemistry, for example, is borrowing another generation's curriculum in emphasizing student familiarity with chemical reactions and field and laboratory experiences in applied areas like food, building materials, and consumer products. Also, physics curricula are likely to feature concepts useful in everyday life yet present an authentic view of the history, nature, and methods of physics. The trend in the biology curriculum is to show connections to physics and chemistry and to help students become familiar with the natural world through the application of key science concepts. It remains to be seen whether teachers can develop a science curriculum that can serve both the interests of those in a scientifically-based workforce, keeping pace with rapid scientific knowledge and technology, and the interests of those who want a scientifically literate citizenry that can benefit from the personal and social applications of science.

QUESTIONS FOR DISCUSSION
Math

1. Which of the following ideas should guide curriculum development of mathematics?
   a. *Empiricism*:   Math has been derived from studies of physical objects; hence, the math curriculum should include manipulation of objects and the application of math concepts to problems of the real world.
   b. *Reasoning*:   Math is not bound to statements that respond to the way things really are, but only to conclusions that follow by logical necessity from the premises defining given mathematical systems. Hence, the teaching of mathematics should aim at understanding the intellectual rigor and logic of abstract mathematics.
2. How can newer topics such as probability, statistics, and estimation best be related to other topics of arithmetic, algebra, and geometry?
3. It appears that most teachers emphasize algorithms and procedural skills rather than conceptual understanding of the mathematical ideas underlying these skills. How do you account for this finding, and what should be done about it?

Science

1. What knowledge from the domains of science and technology are central to citizens' decisions about such matters as toxic waste, life-support systems, conservation of natural resources, and AIDS?
2. Give reasons for or against the science curriculum concentrating on:
   a.   more scientific theories and concepts, less on facts
   b.   the cutting edges of science and technology
   c.   methods of scientific inquiry
3. The science curriculum has been faulted for presenting ordered pieces of someone else's knowledge rather than helping students develop their own knowledge by exploring a repertoire of phenomena in the physical and natural world. Should the science curriculum consist of ways of engaging students in a wide range of engaging phenomena, giving less attention to scientific views and focusing more on the processes students use to make sense of the phenomena? Why? Why not?

REFERENCES

Brutlag, D., & Maples, C. (1992). Making connections: Beyond the surface. *The Mathematics Teacher, 85*(3): 231–234.

Burke, P. (1990). Should we stop force-feeding math in high school? *Virginia Journal of Education, 84*: 14–15.

Colburn, W. (1826). *Colburn's first lesson: Intellectual arithmetic upon the inductive method of instruction.* Boston: Hilliard Gray, Little and Walker.

Commission on Standards for School Mathematics of the National Council of Teachers of Mathematics. (1991). *Curriculum and Evaluation Standards for School Mathematics*. Reston, VA: National Council of Teachers of Mathematics.

Craig, G. (1927). *Certain techniques used in developing a course of study in sciences for the Horace Mann Elementary School*. New York: Columbia University Teachers College, Bureau of Publications.

Fuller, R. W., Brownlee, R. B., & Baker, D. C. (1924). *First principles of physics*. Boston: Allyn & Bacon.

Gagné, R. M. (1966). Elementary science: A new scheme of instruction. *Science, 151*(3706): 49–53.

Glass, B. (1962). Renascent biology: A report on the AIBS biological sciences curriculum study. *The School Review, 701*: 1–43.

Greene, L. C. (1991). Science-centered curriculum in elementary school. *Educational Leadership, 49*(2): 42–46.

Harms, N. C., & Yager, R. (1981). *What research says to the science teacher* (Vol. 3). Washington, DC: National Science Teachers Association.

Huxley, T. A., & Marten, H. D. (1876). *A course of practical instruction in elementary biology*. New York: Macmillan.

Jackman, W. S. (Ed.). (1904). *Nature study: National Society for the Study of Education: The third yearbook*. Chicago: University of Chicago Press.

Kamens, D. H., & Benavot, A. (1991). Knowledge for the masses: The origins and spread of mathematics and science education in national curriculum. *American Journal of Education, 99*(2): 137–180.

Karplus, R. & Thier, H. *A new look at elementary school science*. Chicago: Rand McNally, 1967.

Layton, D. (1973). *Science for the people*. London: Allen & Unwin.

Lijnse, P., Kortland, K., Eijkelot, H. M. C., Van Genderen, D., & Hooymayers, H. P. (1990). A thematic physics curriculum: A balance between contradictory forces. *Science Education, 70*(1): 95–103.

Project 2061. (1989). *Science for all Americans*. Washington, DC: American Association for the Advancement of Science.

Rosen, S. (1959). Origins of high school general biology. *School Science and Mathematics, 59*(60): 473–489.

Seaborg, G. (1960). New currents in chemical education. *Chemical and Engineering News, 38*(49): 97–105.

Smith, D. E. 1917. Arithmetic. In Louis Rapeer (Ed.), *Teaching elementary school subjects* (pp. 207–252). New York: Charles Scribner & Sons.

Stanic, G. M. A. (1987). Mathematics education in the United States at the beginning of the twentieth century. In Thomas S. Popkewitz (Ed.), *The formation of the school subjects* (pp. 145–176). New York: Falmer.

University of Illinois Committee on School Mathematics and the Advisory Committee of the School Mathematics Study Group. (1959). Chicago: University of Illinois.

Woodburn, J. H., & Ellsworth, S. (1965). *Teaching the pursuit of science*. New York: Macmillan.

PART

Textbooks as Opportunities for Curriculum Development

Textbooks are a vehicle for determining what and how to teach and learn. In adopting textbooks, boards of education affirm versions of society's valid knowledge. However, teachers and students interpret these books in multiple ways, reconstituting the text and deciding what to emphasize, deemphasize, select, and exclude.

In the next two chapters, there are three foci. First, we address the basis for a systematic and critical examination of textbooks. The basis is necessary so that teachers can identify the positive and negative features of textbooks, expose implicit assumptions, and find potentials for learning and teaching. Second, attention is given to the role of the teacher in the selection of textbooks and their use in the classroom. This role includes both participating with school boards and parents in textbook selection and developing with colleagues individual school policy regarding textbooks and their use. Third, there is an account of the ways that teachers respond to the characteristics of textbooks in different subject matters and how they mediate these books through their own explanations, claims and opinions, and how they help students apprehend the content of textbooks and apply their own background knowledge and social situations in constructing new meanings from texts.

ASSESSING AND SELECTING CURRICULUM MATERIAL

This chapter reviews the knowledge needed for autonomous consumers of curricular materials, especially textbooks. Claims are made as to why this knowledge is needed by beginning teachers. Three different kinds of assessment tasks are presented:

1. applying technical and pedagogical standards
2. recognizing assumptions about subject matter, learning, and the teacher's role
3. making critical judgments about the text's contribution to justice, equity, and human need

Attention is given to issues in the use of political criteria, censorship, and its flip-side—the addition of content in response to pressure from special interests.

The processes of textbook adoption are described and critiqued. The roles of teachers and students in these processes are clarified. The chapter concludes with a discussion of school-level decisions about textbooks and the setting of a policy for their selection and use.

Teachers have been classified according to their levels of capacity in curriculum development. One scheme proposes the following levels (Silberstein, cited by Ariav, 1991, pp. 187):

▼ Level 1—*Autonomous consumers*: teachers who can use ready-made curriculum materials such as textbooks (These teachers know how to assess and select materials and how to adapt materials to particular teaching situations.)

▼ Level 2—*Consumer developers*: teachers who can develop materials of limited scope to supplement and enrich ready-made materials

▼ Level 3—*Autonomous developers*: teachers who can plan, design, and develop an entire course of study, often in areas with no or few existing materials

There is no assurance, of course, that a level-3 teacher will perform at that level when working in an unfamiliar subject area and social context.

KNOWLEDGE FOR AUTONOMOUS CONSUMERS

This chapter is concerned with the knowledge necessary for performing as autonomous consumers. Often such knowledge is overlooked. Deborah Ball and Sharon Feiman-Nemser (1988), for instance, found that teacher education programs tend to aim at level 2 or level 3, neglecting level 1, although the competencies of level 1 may be prerequisite for achieving the higher levels. Many teacher educators promote the idea that good teachers do not use textbooks and guides but develop their own curriculum—units of instruction and courses— instead. In the student teaching experience in school settings, however, novice teachers use textbooks in teaching reading, math, science, social studies and other subjects. Either their cooperating teacher expects them to use the textbooks, or they resort to the books as a way to deal with the demands of classroom teaching when they do not have the time or expertise to plan in different subject areas for unfamiliar students. Not all student teachers are able to use textbooks effectively. Some follow teacher's guides, mechanically moving through activities without understanding what they are doing. Others are not sure how to adapt the textbooks appropriately.

Ball and Feiman-Nemser recommend that teacher-educators consider the contextual constraints and the limits of beginners' knowledge and instead of telling them not to "teach by the book," to help them learn how to teach from textbooks—to use textbooks and guides as instructional scaffolds, as tools for understanding more about a topic and how it is learned. Most textbooks show ways to organize content and offer suggestions for helping novices proceed and evaluate their effectiveness. This does not mean that teacher-educators must give up preparing teachers for levels 2 and 3. What student teachers learn from textbooks may help them move toward building their own units of study, units that are defensible in terms of subject matter and responsiveness to students.

An appropriate activity for student teachers is to identify the discourse of a textbook—to recognize the central questions that the text purports to answer. Experienced teachers can help them with this task and show them the significance of a topic and how to avoid getting bogged down in details. Student teachers should learn how the central questions or discourse have been treated previously in the curriculum and how the responses to these questions as given in the texts will be extended in subsequent study. This activity, of course, is an introduction to "thinking like a curriculum person."

All teachers gain from the practice of analyzing textbooks and accompanying guides prior to use. This analysis contributes to understanding the subject matter, offers ideas as to how to represent it, and stimulates the teacher to look at content from the learner's perspective. Typically, some of the concepts and procedures introduced in textbooks will be unclear to the teacher and should be clarified with the assistance of colleagues and other texts or references. New ideas for representing content may be found in the drawings, illustrations, metaphors, examples, and activities in the text.

Viewing the text from the learner's perspective is especially difficult for teachers who are unfamiliar with the intended student population. When actually using the text with students, it is important for the new teacher to find out what in the learners' backgrounds might be useful in making connections to the text and to give opportunities for students to talk about their experiences with the texts. By doing this, the teacher becomes aware of student thoughts and the need for going beyond the text, and the students create new meanings for themselves and the text.

TEXTBOOK ASSESSMENT

In assessing textbooks for the purpose of determining their potential meaning and suitability, teachers perform three tasks:

1. They evaluate the technical and pedagogical aspects of the textbooks.
2. They determine the value and assumptions about the subject matter, learners, teacher's role and educational purposes embedded in the text.
3. They engage in critical judgments about the text's contribution to justice, equity, and human need.

Applying Technical and Pedagogical Standards

Changes have occurred recently in the basis for judging the difficulty of textbooks and their value for effective learning. Few teachers today rely on the older practice of applying readability formulas, which take into account the length of sentences and the number of syllables in words but ignore connectors that make text easier to read. Increasingly, teachers attend to both *features in the text* known to effect comprehension—content difficulty, organization of ideas, author's style—and *characteristics of the learner* that determine the appropriateness of the text—learner's background, purpose, and interest. Teachers are more concerned about the match between the textbook and the learner's background of experience and whether provision can be made for developing the necessary background. Nevertheless, the words of Lee Cronbach regarding technical and pedagogical criteria are as applicable as ever:

> Does the text create readiness for the concepts and accomplishments to be taught in subsequent grades? Does the text assist the pupil to understand why certain responses are superior to others for given aims, rather than present them as prescriptions? Does the text make provisions for realistic experience, through narration, proposal of supplementary experiences, laboratory experiences and laboratory prescriptions, so that students will be able to connect generalizations to reality? Does the text formulate explicit and transferable generalizations? Are the text explanations readable and comprehensible? Does the text provide for practice in application either by suggesting activities or by posing sensible problems in symbolic

form? Do these problems call for the use of generalizations under realistic conditions and require the student to determine which principles to use as well as how to use them? Does the text provide an opportunity to use concepts from many fields of study in examining the same problems? Does the text help the learner recognize the intended outcomes from his work? Does it provide him with means of evaluating this progress along these lines? (Cronbach, 1955, pp. 90–91)

Framework for Pedagogical Analysis

The theoretical framework that underlies pedagogical analysis of textbooks holds that learners generate meaning by integrating old and new information. To be effective, textbooks must explicitly help learners integrate information. An analysis tool based on this framework has been developed and used effectively by teachers (Educational Development Center, 1990). This instrument requires that teachers consider how well textbooks provide for three phases of the learning cycle:

1. getting students ready to learn
2. engaging students in the learning activity
3. having students demonstrate competence and extend their knowledge

Consider the following illustration of the criteria used in the different phases together with samples of the kinds of strengths and weaknesses in science and social studies textbooks identified by teachers using the instrument.

Phase I: Getting Students Ready to Learn

Criterion	*Establishing Focus.* The textbook should make clear what is being learned, why it is important, and how it relates to other learning.
Findings	+ "The textbook made explicit the relationship between previously learned concepts and upcoming content." − "Textbooks rarely provided pre-reading activities other than an overview."
Criterion	*Activating Background.* Textbooks should help students activate their relevant prior knowledge.
Findings	+ "Some teacher's editions suggested activities for teachers to use in activating prior knowledge." − "There was no guidance for assessing and dealing with students' pre or misconceptions about upcoming information."
Criterion	*Previewing Concepts.* The textbooks should separate major themes and concepts from extraneous information.

Findings   + "There were graphic organizers highlighting key concepts and their relationships."
– "There was little guidance for determining the most important information."

Phase II: Engaging Students in the Learning Activities

Criterion   *Active Learning and Connecting Old and New Information.* The textbook should help students make the connection between old and new information through active reading techniques.

Findings   + "The teacher's edition provided an extensive repertoire of activities that emphasized active learning."
– "The textbook promoted passive learning, teacher-directed lecturing, and silent reading."

Criterion   *Study Strategies.* The textbook should promote strategies for learning.

Findings   + "The text showed students how to construct their own graphic organizers."
– "The textbook relied on verbal questioning by the teacher to monitor student progress. There was no guidance in self monitoring."

Criterion   *Experimental Activity.* The textbook should promote experimental hands-on and real-world activities.

Findings   + "The texts provide a variety of hands-on learning activities offered to stimulate interest."
– "There was frequent use of hands-on activities, but mostly for reinforcement or follow-up, not to introduce new concepts or to tap prior knowledge."

Criterion   *Cooperative Learning Strategies.* Textbooks should encourage cooperative learning strategies at all phases of learning.

Findings   + "Two of the texts fostered group study, team reading, peer teaching, and culminating projects."
– "The texts did not provide for small group learning."

Phase III: Having Students Demonstrate Competence and Extend Knowledge

Criterion   *Multiple Ways to Demonstrate Mastery.* Textbook should encourage having numerous opportunities for demonstrating success.

Findings	+ "Some of the books showed teachers how to maximize the number of student responses including the use of memory, translation, interpretation, application, and evaluation questions." − "Acceptable student responses were linked to single 'correct answers'."
Criterion	***Acknowledging Diversity in Students' Strengths and Interests.*** Textbooks should provide a variety of activities for students to demonstrate their learning.
Findings	+ "There were suggestions for using role play, debates, experiments, and demonstrations as alternative ways to evaluate student learning." − "There was little direction for using post-instructional activities."
Criterion	***Extending/Applying Learning.*** Textbooks should offer approaches to apply learning in the classroom, in other educational settings, and in relevant nonschool situations.
Findings	+ "The teacher's edition provided a range of activities that would relate to the local community and encourage home involvement." − "Enrichment activities were geared to the most successful students only."

EMBEDDED VALUES AND ASSUMPTIONS ABOUT SUBJECTS, LEARNERS, TEACHERS, AND EDUCATIONAL PURPOSES

Major Questions Texts Address

Evaluating a textbook requires one to recognize the major discourse, question, or issue that the text purports to address. A mathematics textbook, for example, is likely to have for its statement or implied question, "What does it mean to learn mathematics?" The answers given in the text, what must be inferred from its content, may be conceptual understanding, proficiency in doing textbook problems using specified algorithms, practical application of math in everyday life, or something else.

Similar discourse on major questions is found in textbooks in all subject areas, and the ranges in contributions to discourse are real. What it means to learn art may be answered by texts that highlight appreciation or production or expression. Some art texts may imply that art education means finding only beauty in the environment and not learning to perceive the ugly.

One may infer from particular textbooks in science that science education means developing intellectual power, or gaining familiarity with scientific

▼ ─── ▼

ACTIVITY 7–1   ANALYZING A TEXTBOOK
FROM THE PERSPECTIVE OF A THEORY OF
LEARNING

1. Select a familiar textbook (together with accompanying teacher's guide, activities, skills, test questions, or other supplementary material) or one that you might be expected to use.
2. Using the criteria developed by the Education Development Center that focuses on the learning cycle (described in the preceding section), analyze the strengths and weaknesses of the textbook in terms of the framework provided.
3. In the interest of saving time, you may decide to sample particular pages in the material.

▲ ─── ▲

information, or learning to bring a scientific perspective to social and personal problems. In answering the question "What does it mean to learn science?" some science textbooks imply that it means getting students to see science as a noncontroversial field, while other textbooks imply a different answer by featuring the conflicts that exist within the scientific community and drawing attention to the controversies that rage over the social consequences from scientific and technological policies.

Textbook answers to the central question of what it means to study history and social studies can be found by examining the book's approach to current social problems (featured or ignored), history (simple or multiple interpretations), and stance on citizenship (passive or active).

English and language arts textbooks differ in their contribution to the issue of what it means to be literate. Some textbooks imply that it means learning basic skills and language conventions; others that it is familiarity with the literature that unites the culture and the ability to communicate in writing; and still others that it means making alternative interpretations and that texts, reading, and writing are for one's own purposes.

Values and Unstated Assumptions

Writers of textbooks promote their own values. Examination of textbooks in economics shows that most are biased in promoting economic freedom, private property, decentralization of government, competition, and the use of extrinsic incentives as values. The people preparing new social studies textbooks tend to value national identity and religion and prize the nation's unity over its diversity, except as that diversity contributes to common outlooks.

In contrasting old and new textbooks in math and science, one will note a change from an idealistic philosophy to a philosophy of pragmatism. Older texts assumed that a given structure or reality to the world existed and could be discovered through objective and logical methods of science and mathematics. A

corollary was that the textbooks should transmit those aspects of this knowledge authorized by government. Writers of the newer science and math texts are more likely to assume that knowledge is created (not discovered) and that this knowledge reflects the values and experiences of given communities of scholars. Accordingly, some new math and science textbooks attempt to help teachers establish a classroom community that reflects the values, methods, questions, and ways of communicating (special terms as symbols) of the larger scientific and mathematical communities. Students are expected to construct knowledge as they confront problem situations, speculating and making predictions, trying their own solutions, and explaining and justifying them. Problem solving in the newer books does not involve the stereotypical textbook problems ready-made for students, but problems that arise from students as they attempt to achieve their goals in the classroom. Knowledge is created as students convince their peers that their solutions are valid as demonstrated by evidence and logic.

Assumptions about the teachers' and students' roles that underlie materials based on the constructivist perspective are in the direction of intellectual autonomy. Both teachers and students are obliged to resolve their problems for themselves, and they are not required to use any particular solution method. An undifferentiated conception of ability operates. Students are regarded as showing high ability whenever they persist in solving personally challenging problems. The teacher's role is one of framing problematic situations and facilitating solution processes; students are expected to explain their solution methods to one another and to respect one another's efforts.

An Analysis of Art and Music Textbooks

Wanda May, Tamara Lantz, and Sara Rohr (1990) have illustrated how the usefulness of textbook analysis can reveal the partisan interests served by textbooks, calling attention to serious omissions. In one of their analyses, that of an elementary textbook series in art, they found that the textbooks focused primarily on design elements rather than on developing the understanding that art has personal meaning to the creator. Because of the series' emphasis on art products and how they are made and used, the investigators concluded that the series presents art as a "commodity." It was clear that these texts perpetuated the myth that art means independently making a product, without regard to how the social influence or context bears on the question of beauty.

In another of May, Lantz, and Rohr's analyses (1990)—that of a music textbook series—the investigators isolated patterns and themes from frequency counts, conceptual mapping, and charting content that was emphasized, underrepresented, or omitted. Among their findings were those showing that the textbooks presented *how* people engage in musical activities rather than *why*. Most of the musical material was historical rather than contemporary. There was an absence of controversial issues presented in and by music. The music textbook series avoided multiple interpretations, controversy, and the possibility of critical student discussions. The texts implied that students were incapable of understanding their own social situations or understanding different cultural contexts.

ACTIVITY 7–2   FINDING SUBTEXTS
IN TEXTBOOKS

Whether selecting textbooks or teaching students to question the text, teachers attend to the *subtext*—hidden meanings and messages that serve the author's intentions and polemics. Samuel Wineberg (1991), studying the effects of subtext, presented an excerpt from an American history textbook to eight historians and eight high school students. All were asked to verbalize their thoughts as they read the excerpt and to rank its trustworthiness as a historical source along with seven other sources, including an eyewitness account, newspaper articles, and historical fiction.

Directions

Read the following excerpt and determine the hidden meaning that the writer wants the reader to carry away. Also, evaluate the historical soundness and trustworthiness of the excerpt.

> In April 1775, General Gage, the military governor of Massachusetts, sent out a body of troops to take possession of military stores at Concord, a short distance from Boston. At Lexington, a handful of "embattled farmers," who had been tipped off by Paul Revere, barred the way. The "rebels" were ordered to disperse. They stood their ground. The English fired a volley of shots that killed eight patriots. It was not long before the swift-riding Paul Revere spread the news of this new atrocity to the neighboring colonies. The patriots of all of New England, although still a handful, were not ready to fight the English. Even in faraway North Carolina, patriots organized to resist them. (Steinberg, 1963)

Responses of Historians and Students

You may wish to compare your reading with those of the historians and students in Winesberg's study. You probably identified the subtext as aggrandizing the heroism and resolve of the people who began the Revolutionary War on the American side and the justice of their cause. That was the subtext or latent meaning that eight historians constructed from the excerpt. They also ranked the excerpt last of the eight sources in trustworthiness. The reasons for the lack of trust centered on the fact that neither the British and nor the American sides ever portrayed the Minutemen as "standing their ground" or "barring the way"; the textbook author's labeling of the encounter at Lexington as an "atrocity" that started events sets off association of other "atrocities"—the Holocaust, My Lai, Kampuchea; the way the description of the Colonists went from "embattled farmers," to "rebels" to *patriots* which was not in quotation marks, possibly because the author regarded them as *real* patriots and

▼ ————————————————————————— ▼

ACTIVITY 7–2   *continued*

not rebels in a negative sense; the author's appeal to the underdog by drawing a David and Goliath contrast—"embattled farmers versus the troops of King George"; and the hedging on who fired the first shot together with an implied causal relationship between the statements "The rebels stood their ground" as the "English fired a volley of shots."

The students, on the other hand, rated the passage as the most trust-worthy of the eight documents. They thought the excerpt was "just reporting the facts"—the rebels were ordered to dispense and they stood their ground—straight information and a neutral account of the events at Lexington Green. Wineberg points out that although the students have strong factual knowledge of the American Revolution, they did not see the subtexts in what they read. Before students can see subtexts, they must believe they exist.

▲ ————————————————————————— ▲

CRITICAL JUDGMENTS ABOUT EQUITY, JUSTICE, AND CONTRIBUTIONS TO HUMAN NEED

Textbooks, as well as other aspects of curriculum and instructional practice, can be subjected to critical analysis. In addition to the suggestions for conduct-ing critical inquiry as given in Chapter 4, many teachers wish to use the follow-ing strategy in their critical analysis of textbooks:

1. Show historical and political connections to the text.
2. Identify what group the textbook rewards and who it deprives.
3. Interpret the metaphors, images, and arguments, that are present in the text.
4. Consider the different potential meanings likely to be confronted by the readers.

Historical Connections

In their attempts to uncover the historical origins of certain aspects of a text—content, format, methodology—teachers consider the social circumstances that gave rise to the features. Should it be found that the same social circumstances do not exist today, then the appropriateness of the features for the present can be questioned with a view of effecting change. For example, one can examine foreign language textbooks to see the extent to which they reflect the influence of such historical needs as (a) the need for social stratification based on classi-cal culture and mental discipline obtained through literature and grammar, (b) military needs for oral competencies in a foreign language met through audio/lingual procedures, or (c) the need for social integration and face-to-face communication in a second language resulting in a natural approach involving contextual cues and genuine dialogues.

Political Connections

Wider political influence from the left on textbooks became apparent with the civil rights movement of the 1960s and the increased political pressure on publishers of textbooks from groups concerned about social and personal values. Publishers have responded to controversial issues such as those concerning sex roles, religion, parent/child relations, health (AIDS and abortion), evolution, ecology, population growth, and the problems emanating from these issues in one of these ways:

▼ Avoided the issue.

▼ Emphasized alternative views in an attempt at balance.

▼ Taken a firm position on the issue.

State legislatures and boards of education, under pressure from minority communities and those concerned about the inclusion of women in nontraditional roles, have set policies requiring schools to use only books that fairly represent minorities and women in their content. Most states require that all textbooks pass a "legal compliance" screen before they can be considered for adoption. It should be noted, however, that many textbooks that pass the legal requirement for better representation of members of minority groups and women are faulted by minorities for their superficiality; "tinkering"; or depiction of women, African Americans, Asian Americans, and Hispanic Americans in photographs and other visuals, without discussion of their real roles in history or present-day society. May, Lantz, and Rohr (1990) noted in their textbook evaluations that ethnic or gender "representativeness" was cosmetic. Despite the introduction of diverse culture and historical contexts, both series were found to be lopsided toward white, male, and Western culture. In the art textbook series, objects were stripped of their culture and historical context in the interest of analyzing the elements of design inherent in the objects. In the music textbook series, females were underrepresented and misrepresented in terms of composers, conductors, and lyrical content (for example, women were noted for singing lullabies or as the object of men's lyrics). Although the illustrations of students were diverse by gender and culture, even incorporating a physically handicapped youngster, these pictures were unrelated to the text (May, Lantz, & Rohr, 1990).

Potential political messages of textbooks are recognized by those who are sensitive to the overt and implied meanings. For example, at this writing educational authorities in Mexico are facing a political crisis over a newly issued social studies textbook series. Much of the criticism of the series is in response to changes in the historical treatment designed to support President Carlos Salinas' relations with the United States and his policies affecting land ownership and use. Gone from the new texts are the traditional stories such as the "Niños Heroes," cadets who died in the defense of the Castle of Chapultepec during the American invasion of Mexico in 1842. Also, the new text no longer says that the United States "took" one third of the Mexican territory but reports only that the United States augmented its territory by two million kilometers. Critics also see a connection between the modernization plans of Salinas and the textbook treatment of history. Porfiro Diaz, the nineteenth-century Mexican dictator, is no longer portrayed as one who protected the land-owning aristocrats and enslaved the Indians. Instead the texts praise President Diaz for his role in attracting foreign investment and promoting economic development.

In view of these and other changes in historical interpretation, many teachers in Mexico have begun a rebellion over the official textbooks. The powerful National Union of Educational Workers, for example, has asked all teachers to not restrict their teaching to the use of the new text but use their own "baggage" and alternative sources. The union is also preparing its own supplementary materials.

Censorship and Pressures to Include Certain Content

In the United States, advisory groups have examined textbooks for their treatment of evolution, environmental issues, religion, and ethical issues in science. Liberals have detected conservative bias and conservatives found liberal bias. Different groups have worked to censor textbooks believed to conflict with their views on religion, lifestyles, and morality. People for the American Way, a Washington-based organization opposed to censorship, reported in 1992 that attempts to censor school texts surged by 50 percent across the nation and that the censors were successful 40 percent of the time. Most frequently charged were literature texts such as *Of Mice and Men*, *Catcher in the Rye*, *The Color Purple*, *The Adventures of Huckleberry Finn*, *The Grapes of Wrath*, and it is noteworthy how few titles of the thousands published in the academic fields are censored. However, one can interpret this finding as evidence that censors have been effective in getting publishers to suppress controversial issues. Indeed some teachers prefer not to use texts that are likely to be controversial.

Several points should be made regarding the use of political criteria, censorship and its flip-side, the addition of content in response to pressure from special interests:

▼ Finding bias in a textbook is not necessarily a cause for rejection of the book. The overall merits of the textbook should be taken into account, and teachers might regard a serious omission or a questionable interpretation as an opportunity for disabusing students of the impression that a text is an absolute authority. Students can learn to question the text; see what is missing, what needs clarifying; and think about the adequacy of the content to the problem it purports to address. Teachers can help students to see human motives in texts and to learn how to separate the truth from the half truth. Of course, the teacher will supplement the information and views of the biased text.

▼   Teachers have both the moral and legal authority to resist censorship. The fundamental First Amendment principle of nonsuppression of ideas protects the teacher. The U.S. Constitution does not permit the official suppression of ideas. However, materials used in the public school must be educationally suitable; the decision to accept or reject material must not be on the basis of ideas expressed but on whether the material fosters or hinders the intellectual, emotional, and social development of students.

▼   Although particular groups have been successful in getting publishers to include information of importance to their causes—environmentalists (rain forests), industrialists (capitalism), scientists (molecular structure), AIDS activists (AIDS), cultural literacists (Greek mythology), and many others, inclusion of more material does not ensure that the added content will be treated in depth. In her study of American textbooks, Harriet Tyson-Bernstein (1988) concluded that the addition of topics for political reasons results in superficial treatment and the absence of the integrating concepts necessary for building student understanding. The best response of teachers to the plethora of controversial topics in textbooks is (a) to select fewer topics from the textbook to study and to relate the selected topics to a common theme, problem area, or discourse and (b) go to other sources for additional information on the selected topics.

Metaphors in Critical Analysis

Metaphors and the use of analogies in the critical analysis of textbooks sometimes reveal what is not readily apparent in the textbooks and suggest new ways for helping students gain access to their content. For example, the metaphor of the machine presents an analogy between the characteristics of some textbooks and a world view in which reality is comprised of self-contained units that can be brought into relation with each other. The components are integrated and arranged in sequential order. Textbooks that present a continuum of skills and concepts and that assume a taxonomic or hierarchical ordering of content are similar to machines. Critical analysis of the learning tasks and the sequence have little validity—that the whole is greater than the sum of its parts and that there is no optimum order for acquiring the skills or concepts. The failure to account for human agencies in learning is a central criticism of programs modeled after machines.

The "story" as a metaphor for all texts is currently popular. A story or narrative is said to be the "natural" way to acquire meaning (Bruner, 1986). The elements of situations, characters, intentions, problems, resolutions, themes, lessons learned by the characters, and lessons generated by the readers are effective in integrating knowledge. The story metaphor carries the connotation that the presentation is but one version of something and leaves open the possibility of other accounts from different perspectives.

"Modern poetry" offers an analogy that is useful in suggesting what teachers must do in helping students relate to textbooks. Such poetry is highly condensed, a complex puzzle with many clues and missing pieces. Readers must infer meaning from the elements that are omitted. To the extent that textbooks resemble modern poetry, teachers should prepare students for understanding the texts. Chapter 8 deals in detail with the ways teachers mediate and adapt the text for better learning and for different goals. However, at this point, consider four problems confronted by students in understanding texts:

1. vocabulary for which students need to become familiar with both the denotative and connotative meanings of words in the text
2. need to overcome the disparity between the author and student frames of reference (Teachers must mediate the mismatch between the students' world views and that of the textbook.)
3. need to understand the syntax of the textbook (including the particular organizational patterns and symbols used in books about different subject matters)
4. incompleteness of text

Just as the reader of modern poetry is expected to assemble the meaning of a poem in a unique way, so readers of textbooks have to be taught to find what in the text is personally significant.

TEXTBOOK SELECTION

Textbook Adoption

The selection of textbooks occurs at several levels. In 23 states, state boards of education list textbooks that local districts can purchase with state funds. In other states, local school boards approve books that can be used. Board adoption is for the purposes of control and focus. The state board of education in California, for instance, approves only textbooks that match the state curriculum framework and policy. Textbook selection functions as a way to support state curriculum and pedagogical reforms. Selection from among the different books on the approved list is usually a decision for individual schools.

Increasingly, representatives of teachers and parents participate on committees that review and recommend textbooks to the state and local boards. However, committees making recommendations often are expected to apply criteria specified by the board. Also, there is a trend to grant teachers in given schools waivers so they can obtain textbooks not on the approved list, if they show that a special student population or program requires something different.

At the elementary school level, teachers usually select, at regular intervals, a textbook series in a single content area from among the approved texts. Secondary school teachers typically make departmental decisions regarding the textbooks that will be used in the particular departments. Members of committees reviewing textbooks for possible adoption at state and local levels have been criticized for the superficiality of their reviews.

The criteria sheets are faulted for listing too many factors and failing to weigh the more important factors. The instruments used by such committees average 70 items (Comas, cited in Tyson-Bernstein, 1988, p. 69). Most host committees must attest that recommended texts meet legal standards—are free of partisan content and provide equal opportunity, support current scholarship, and can be adapted to a range of learning needs. Recommendations for better reviews call for making more time available for conducting the review, discussing the major issues in the curriculum under consideration and the overarching principles that subsume the details of the content, and selecting teaching strategies appropriate to content goals.

Teachers have more influence in making recommendations for textbook adoption at the local level than in statewide adoptions. The local committee is usually made up of experienced and inexperienced teachers who represent a variety of student populations and teaching conditions. Representative members of the community, parents, and, in some cases, students, serve on adoption committees, sharing their expertise and perspectives. A broadly chosen committee is necessary for defending choices in textbooks in the event those chosen are attacked by special interests.

The adoption process at the local level begins with a review of the subject-matter and grade-level expectations for which the books are to be considered. Analysis of the existing curriculum ties textbooks to existing curriculum goals rather than permitting the textbooks to define the curriculum. The developing of criteria for selection of books to be placed on an adoption list is a major task. The criteria presented in the first section of this chapter are recommended candidates. Other factors may be important to a particular committee—content breadth across subject matter, accuracy of content, depth of treatment, capacity to stimulate students. Fewer than 20 items should be developed, and they should be weighted according to their importance.

When comparing textbooks, committee members may reduce the factors to those on which books may differ. Bad and good examples can be taken from various textbooks to define the criteria and to use as models in making evaluations. Tryout of the evaluation instrument and procedures will reveal the need for clarification and revision, an opportunity for the committee members to explain and justify their views. The committee's task of evaluating textbooks can be made easier by dividing the work. Some people are better than others at assessing overall coherence, some at assessing community sensibilities, some at judging academic integrity, and others at predicting the textbook's appeal to students.

Procedures for analyzing and comparing examination copies of textbooks vary. Among the most popular strategies are these:

▼   conducting side-by-side comparisons where the same element in all books is compared

▼   developing a strand or concept throughout the series

▼   checking to see whether the questions, activities, test items, methodology, and content are consistent in the materials

It is desirable for the committee to arrange for short-term tryouts in which a teacher tries a sample from the instructional units and reports on both the specific criteria and general features are given. These tryouts should be conducted with a range of teachers and students.

Publishers and their representatives can be helpful to adoption committees, clarifying questions that arise before, during, and after the review.

School-Level Textbook Decisions

At the school level, formulating textbook policy for a particular school is an opportunity for the staff to engage in curriculum inquiry. For what does the school want to be known—academic achievement, creativity, inquiry, critical thinking, or the cultivation of student interests? When agreement has been reached about the ideals or ethos that the staff envisions for the school, textbooks can be evaluated for their possible contribution to this ethos and to other goals.

A decision should be made about how the textbooks are to be used—as a classroom set or as common resources to be drawn upon whenever a particular class is pursuing an inquiry. The sharing of textbooks allows for the selection of multiple textbooks, increasing the resources available to students. The policy of multiple texts rests on the assumption that no single textbook is adequate for all parts of a subject curriculum or serves all students. The policy of locating textbooks at a particular center—a math and science center, a language and social science center, a music room—also increases the range of instructional materials available for a particular study. Textbooks in centers can be used by many different classes throughout the school day, in contrast to the placing of books in classroom sets that are typically used only during an instructional period. Of course, other considerations (such as the importance of each student having his/her own textbook for homework) should be taken into account.

The school's textbook policy should be made only after reflecting on other ways than textbooks for achieving the school's goals. The value of using trade books, periodicals, teacher-made materials, and films are cases in point. The use of other experiences—laboratory, community service, independent investigations—to teach those elements of the curriculum best taught by nontextbook activity should become part of the policy.

School faculties use similar criteria and evaluation procedures to those of textbook adoption committees, as they select textbooks both from titles on approved lists and from wider sources. In the interest of time constraints, only the most promising of the textbooks under consideration need to be fully studied. Individual teachers may look at different textbooks in the same series or teach sample lessons from one of the textbooks. Tryouts allow teachers to find out which aspects of a textbook help them achieve their goals.

▼ ── ▼

ACTIVITY 7–3   MODIFYING AN INSTRUMENT FOR SELECTING A TEXTBOOK SERIES

The instrument on pp. 150–152 was recently used by a textbook committee in evaluating mathematics texts.

1. What are the views of mathematics implied in this instrument?
2. What principles of learning are held by the authors of this instrument?
3. What would you delete or add to the instrument?

▲ ── ▲

The practice of involving students is also recommended. Student rating, having students rate three textbooks dealing with a common topics, is suggested. Both teachers and students gain by seeing different interpretations of a common topic and by considering different reasons for valuing a particular book. Criteria for use in student ratings are usefulness of the text, the author's intention, and supporting evidence for the ideas presented.

SUMMARY

Analysis of textbooks is more than attending to copyright dates, the attractiveness of texts, the representations, illustrations, and other surface features. New tools of analysis include the following things:

▼ pedagogical criteria that put student learning above ease of teaching and that reflect the constructionist's view that textbooks should be designed to encourage student interaction with the text and the creation of meanings rather than to transmit information to passive learners

▼ critical criteria that directs attention to ideologies implicit in textbooks, including assumptions regarding knowledge (fixed or fluid), cultural values (dominant or diverse), authority (text, teacher or classroom community)

▼ the stance taken to the central question which the text purports to deal (The connection of the textbook to the economic and political interests in the larger context are part of the analysis.)

Textbook adoption policies by state and local boards of education are viewed as attempts at curriculum control. Through the adoption process, policy makers send their messages about what should be taught. There is more teacher participation in textbook selection committees than in the past, and boards of education are more disposed to grant schools and teachers waivers to select books not on approved lists in order to meet the needs of special programs and students. The

RATING MATHEMATICS TEXTBOOKS

How To Use the Rating Form

1. As a group, rank the sections I–V of the rating form in order of priority. Give a weight to each of the five sections by percent, making sure the percentage total is 100.

2. Individuals next rate all applicable items within a section on a scale of 1–5, the lowest rating being 1 and the highest 5.

3. Total the rankings for each section.

4. Divide the total for each section by the number of items rated, and multiply the result by the assigned percentage for that section to obtain the section rating.

5. Total the section ratings for the text's final rating.

Note: **Evaluate student text and teachers' manual, if available, as a unit.**

Title _____

Publisher _____

Copyright Date _____

Evaluator's Name _____ Final Score [_____]

Section I—Content

Section Rating

_____
% weight   [_____]

1. Problem solving and problem-solving strategies are placed throughout the book. _____

2. Realistic and everyday situations are reflected in the problems. _____

3. Mental arithmetic and techniques for estimating and checking the reasonableness of results are developed. _____

4. Computation skills are developed with whole numbers, decimals, fractions and percents without overemphasizing complicated computations. _____

5. Geometric shapes, concepts, and properties are presented and geometry is used in solving problems. _____

6. Techniques for measuring and the basic concepts of measurement (unit, instrument, accuracy) are developed through activities involving distance, area, capacity, weight, time, temperature, and angles. _____

7. Skills for constructing, reading, and interpreting tables, charts, and graphs are developed. _____

8. Key concepts of statistics and probability are developed, giving opportunity for data collection, organization, and analysis, as well as the exploration of chance. _____

9. The concepts of variable and the use of algebraic expressions in solving problems are developed. _____

10. Exercises and investigations relate mathematics to science, art, and social studies. _____

11. Other _____

_____

_____

Section II—Content Explication

_____
% weight

Section Rating
[   ]

1. Lessons often begin with open-ended problem situations that interest and challenge students, require students to formulate math problems, and stimulate creative solutions. _____

2. Some lessons are designed for students to work in small groups throughout the problem-solving process. _____

3. Representations of content are varied—verbally, numerically, graphically, geometrically, or symbolically. _____

4. There are opportunities for students to explore and explain concepts and to defend their thinking. _____

5. Students interact with each other—not just the teacher—in discussions, debates, and projects. _____

6. Other _____ _____

_____

_____

Section III—Student Activities and Assignment

_____
% weight

Section Rating
[   ]

1. A variety of operations and solutions techniques are required. _____

2. Activities require students to decide on the method of calculations to use. _____

3. Activities require students collect data from the classroom, school, and community. _____

4. There are exercises of varying difficulty for each concept developed. _____

5. There is a balance in exercises between skill reinforcement and applications. _____

6. Other _____ _____

_____

_____

Section IV—Teacher Materials (Guide or Manual)

Section Rating

_____
% weight

[   ]

1. Procedures for analyzing student misconceptions are suggested.   _____

2. There are illustrations of how to integrate other content areas.   _____

3. There are illustrations of how to question, respond, clarify, and extend student learning.   _____

4. There are suggestions for manipulatives, games, and other easy-to-use materials that are relevant to desired outcomes.   _____

5. There are suggestions for evaluating student understanding through class discussions, written and oral explanations, and student work.   _____

6. There are suggestions to the teachers for conducting assessment through student portfolios, work samples, self assessment, and complete work.   _____

Section V—Physical characteristics

Section Rating

_____
% weight

[   ]

1. The text is attractive and identifiable as a mathematics text.   _____

2. The print size and type are suitable for the student.   _____

3. The artwork is functional and the layout is appropriate.   _____

4. The index, table of contents, and glossary will facilitate flexibility in using the text.   _____

5. The cover and binding are durable.   _____

6. There is an absence of stereotypes based on race, ethnicity, gender, or handicap.   _____

_____   _____   ×   _____
Total points   Number of items rated   Weight

Total rating (transfer to Final Score box on first page)

setting of a textbook policy by teachers at the individual school site is an opportunity for curriculum dialogue and justification for decisions about what should be taught and how. Guidelines for effecting the policy have been presented.

QUESTIONS FOR DISCUSSION

1. In what circumstances would one seek a textbook characterized by breadth of topics, events, and wide perspective rather than a textbook offering deep treatment of a few topics?
2. There is no evidence that "better" textbooks find their way into classrooms where there are state adoptions. How do you account for the failure to find differences?
3. Should teachers have the freedom to choose textbooks without restriction, or should they have to choose from among titles that are on the board approved lists? Why? Why not?
4. Would you rather have 40 copies of the same textbook in a subject area or 40 copies made up of different textbooks in the same area available in the classroom? Why? How would you teach differently under the two conditions?
5. In rank order, list the five most important criteria to use in selecting textbooks.
6. In 1992, an appellate division of New York's Supreme Court ruled that a college does not have to allow community members to inspect film materials used in a controversial sex-education class. The court said that showing the materials outside the classroom with no instruction or context would have a chilling effect on academic freedom. If someone wants the material, they should buy it or take the course. Should such a ruling apply to textbooks in the elementary and secondary schools?
7. What statement regarding censorship of textbooks should be included as part of an individual school's textbook policy?

REFERENCES

Ball, D. L., & Feiman-Nemser, S. (1988). Using textbooks and teachers' guides: Dilemmas for beginning teachers and teacher educators. *Curriculum Inquiry, 83*(4): 401–423.

Bruner, J. (1986). *Active minds, possible worlds*. Cambridge, MA: Harvard Education Press.

Cronbach, L. J. (1955). *Text materials in modern education*. Urbana: University of Illinois Press.

Educational Development Center, Inc. (1990). *Improving textbook usability*. Conference Report. Newton, MA.

May, W., Lantz, T., & Rohr, S. (1990, April). *Whose content, context, and culture? Elementary art and music textbooks*. Paper presented at the meetings of American Educational Research Association, Boston, MA.

Ariav, T. (1991). Growth in teachers' curriculum knowledge by the process of curriculum analysis. *Journal of Curriculum and Supervision, 1*(3): 185–200.

Tyson-Bernstein, H. (19988). *A conspiracy of good intentions: America's textbook fiasco*. Washington, DC: The Council for Basic Education.

Wineberg, S. S. (1991). On the reading of historical texts: Notes on the breach between school and academy. *American Educational Research Journal, 28*(3): 495–519.

MEDIATING AND ADAPTING TEXTBOOKS

This chapter continues the knowledge base for autonomous consumers of curriculum materials by focusing on how teachers can mediate and adapt materials in different subject matters. Multiple uses of textbooks and specific ways of augmenting, restructuring, and circumventing textbooks are presented. Similarly, suggestions are given for how to make a text more accessible to students, to bring different interpretations to the text, to better serve the local community, and to bend the text to the larger goals of the teacher and students.

A textbook is a curriculum document that offers content and method and that follows some principles of sequencing. Different textbooks in the same field promote different educational goals and vary in their degree of specificity and prescriptiveness. However, teachers mediate the curriculum of the text in many ways. A teacher's adherence to the textbook depends on the degree to which the teacher views the text as the content authority and whether the teacher has a conviction about what should be taught.

Few teachers expect students to read textbooks in isolation from the classroom discourse. For most teachers, textbooks are instructional tools that must fit the teacher's view of the "correct" way to use the textbook: follow the text, teach the text, and test the text; or to use it as a reference for students to draw on as they pursue their classroom investigations. The view in which the teacher relies on the textbook as the primary definition of curriculum and single source of information is more likely to occur in poverty areas where home and community have no other academic resources and the teacher is unaccustomed to generating knowledge from the local environment.

Using textbooks as inquiry is illustrated in the current practice of *discourse synthesis*, the process of integrating ideas and information from multiple source texts to create new texts (Spivey, 1980). In elementary classrooms, students may be asked to select, organize, and connect information from three or four textbooks related to a topic of importance to the student or groups of students. Studies of how teachers use textbooks show that most teachers do teach by the book. The teacher's own beliefs and preferences, the context in which teaching occurs, the subject matter and grade level, and the particular students in the class all make a difference in how the curriculum of the textbook is implemented.

MEDIATING MATH TEXTBOOKS

In her study of textbook use in fifth-grade math classes, Susan Stodolsky (1989) looked at the extent to which teachers followed the topics, materials, and suggestions of textbooks and accompanying teachers' manuals. Stodolsky confirmed that teachers varied considerably, ranging from close adherence to extreme autonomy from the adopted math textbook. Although what was taught was almost always in the books, most teachers skipped topics and chapters and did not follow the sequence of the text. Least agreement was in the use of suggested activities from the teacher's edition. Most teachers ignored the suggestions for enrichment activities and student-centered group projects in favor of teacher-centered written and oral activities emphasizing mastery of algorithms. Teachers did not expect students to learn independently from math textbooks but did assign the problems in the text after instruction by the teacher. Investigation of math instruction at the secondary level also indicates that teachers are more likely to omit topics than to add them, and to make minor deviations (such as more drill or graphing) rather than significant changes (such as reorganizing the text by commencing with equations).

Widely used math textbooks of the mid-1980s rarely posed real problems. Textbooks of this period seldom gave students opportunities to symbolize, explain, hypothesize, or expand concepts. Instead the texts expected students to recall, reproduce, and iterate (Nicely, 1985). Newer math books include more suggestions for extended problem solving, and teachers like Vera Kerekes in Oakland, California, are using textbooks as the basis for entire math courses in the problem-solving mode (1990). Instead of discussing functions, for example, students in Kerekes' class make up curves that represent real-life situations. Although the first example comes from the textbook, others come from the daily newspaper and the students' own experiences. Students draw different curves to show relations such as the height of a person as a function of time, or income as a function of education. Each new type of function (linear, quadratic, exponential) is introduced by presenting data that students graph and use in inferring relations between variables. Strategies such as guessing, building a model, developing charts, working backwards, drawing a picture, and looking for patterns are encouraged.

Increasingly, math teachers are providing activities to provoke different interpretations by students. In their discussions, regarding various solutions to problems, students give explanations for their proposals. These discussions are believed to further individual construction of knowledge through conceptual conflict and resolving of contradictions. The discussions are also viewed as opportunities for the teacher to understand the mathematical thinking of the child. In a primary classroom, one child may say that a solution to addition of two-digit numbers is thinking of them as made up of tens and ones, while another student believes it best to count 46 ones. The idea is not to combine solution procedures to get a joint solution but to develop explanations that are meaningful to someone else and to make sense of another's attempt at solving the problem.

It takes much time to introduce newer ideas for teaching math, such as actively involving students in solving problems at concrete and abstract levels, using several representations, applying math to novel situations, inventing strategies, and assessing the reasonableness of solutions. Accordingly, teachers who want to promote these constructivist practices must alter their textbooks. There is no way that they can "cover" all the topics in the textbook if they want to "uncover" the child's thinking. Rosemary Schimalz (1990) illustrates the textbook modifications that teachers are making in response to a changing pedagogy. She recommends that when planning for the year, teachers teach first the topic in the textbook of which most members of the class are unsure, instead of starting with topic one of chapter one. Next, the teacher makes an outline of topics quarter by quarter, totally ignoring the preceding topics. A less crowded timeline permits topics to be introduced at a slower pace and allows several days for physical, verbal, and manipulative activity involving diverse problem solving. Topics that have been skipped can be dealt with in review sequences that take place during the first five to ten minutes of the day.

REPLACEMENT UNITS

There is a growing trend for elementary teachers of mathematics to use units that replace what textbooks provide. Replacement units usually feature five weeks of instruction and address one main idea, such as multiplication or fractions. The units are models of constructivist teaching and learning. Activities in the unit engage students in thinking, reasoning, and creating their own theories, investigating patterns, trying to solve problems and to justify solutions. Most units offer challenging problem-solving situations for students to investigate and to use ideas from several strands of mathematics—multiplication, geometry, probability, statistics, patterns, and functions.

Some of the more popular replacement units are: *Math by All Means* (Burns, 1991), *Math Excursions 2* (Burk, Snider, & Symonds, 1991), *Seeing Fractions* (Corwin, Russell, & Tierney, 1991), *Polyhedraville: An Investigation of Three-Dimensional Geometry* (Beyond Activities Project, 1992), and *Work Jobs* (Lorton, 1972). Most of these units have been developed by classroom teachers. Marilyn Burns, author of many replacement units, presents samples of children's work and thinking drawn from her own experience (1991). Similarly, *Math Excursions* (Burk, 1992), which offers projects and investigations that relate mathematics to the lives of children and integrates other subjects, was prepared by three classroom teachers whose units reflect their search for better ways to manage math instruction. The development of these units involved extensive testing and feedback from children. Some of the teacher authors acknowledge the inspiration given by the late Mary Baratta Lorton, who created outstanding activity-centered materials for the teaching of mathematics (Lorton, 1972).

AUGMENTING SOCIAL STUDIES TEXTBOOKS

In her investigation of textbook use, Stodolsky (1959) found that social studies teachers often conduct additional activities both related and unrelated to the textbook and its content. Although the topics in the book are taught and usually taught in sequence, distinct and unrelated topics are introduced simultaneously during instruction. Unlike in math, more than topics in the textbook are the object of instruction in social studies. Also, the use of multiple sources—films, newspapers and other texts—is much more common in social studies than in math.

Most social studies teachers use the textbook as the starting point for classroom discourse and activity. Teachers try to relate the text to real problems in the students' lives—to issues and current events. The necessity for this practice is supported by findings regarding inadequacies of social studies textbooks (Beck, McKeown, & Gromoll, 1989):

▼ assuming an unrealistic assessment of the intended learners' backgrounds for understanding the concepts and main points of the content

▼ having unclear content goals for portraying social situations

▼ giving little consideration to the messages students are to come away with

▼ offering inadequate explanations (Major concepts and events often go unexplained, and there is a lack of information that would connect facts, events, and ideas.)

Social studies teachers must decide what are the purposes of the courses for which the text is intended. Is it to be a survey course, or is it to focus in depth on several themes or concepts while ignoring many major events and personalities? Does it attempt to introduce political, economic, and intellectual aspects of society or to eliminate some of these areas? Should the teacher supplement the text by introducing state and local matters of importance? Aside from decisions about content, social studies teachers must decide whether the course and materials are to be used for ethical judgments and critical thinking, particularly with respect to the evaluation of evidence and the logical consequences of social actions.

RECONSTRUCTING TEXTS THROUGH READING INSTRUCTION

In his study of literary texts, George Hillocks (1990) faulted literature textbooks organized by genre or chronology for not giving students opportunity to cumulatively develop critical abilities. Disparate writers or works are clumped together by literary form or chronology, so that each work is treated as an end in itself, rather than as preparation for reading other works. Because knowledge gained about one writer is unlikely to be applicable to the next, students are unprepared for independent reading of subsequent selections and forced into the role of passive recipients of knowledge about individual writers and works. The students depend on the teacher for explanations of the content.

Hillocks (1990) describes how teachers depart from the separate works of literature approach, which textbooks tend to use, to provide students a chance to develop concepts for independently interpreting new works. Concepts such as personality, the hero, courage, justice or genres, conventions, and levels of meaning are the basis for studying literary selections. One teacher's sequential unit began with satire in cartoons and comic routines that used diatribe and exaggeration to ridicule the satirists' target. Then students used that knowledge to examine simple satires based on irony and to develop the understanding that irony operates through contrast. Later, students were introduced to satiric fables that depended upon both exaggeration and irony and required students to interpret symbols in order to identify the targets and the reasons for the satire. Finally, more complex satiric works, such as *Animal Farm* were introduced, and the students were able to construct meanings of literature for themselves using their increased knowledge about literature.

If a teacher believes that students should generate meaning from literature and relate it to their lives, the teacher goes beyond introducing the selection itself to teaching students ways of approaching it. For example, in her treatment of literary text, one teacher taught students four things (Sdottir, 1991):

1. *translation:*   to understand the literal meaning of the selection
2. *connotation:*   to understand the symbols in the selection
3. *interpretation:*   to see how the meanings symbolized reveal the author's purpose and world view
4. *appreciation and evaluation:*   to see how the literature has meaning for the students' own lives

In similar fashion, Gordon Wells offers five different modes of engaging with the written text (Wells, 1990):

1. Teachers help young children with the *performance mode* by attending to the alphabetical principle, syntax clues, and other linguistic conventions.
2. In teaching the *functional mode*, teachers introduce materials that will help students achieve some purpose, such as an instructional manual for a new product.
3. The *informational mode* is taught as students consult texts to find facts on a matter.
4. The *recreational mode* is featured as students explore a world aesthetically in enjoying the literary experience.
5. In the *epistemic* or *critical mode*, students read a text in order to understand what it *can* mean, giving their alternative interpretations and asking "Is this text internally consistent? Does it make sense in relation to our own experiences?"

In using basal readers, teachers tend to emphasize the performance mode of engagement with a secondary emphasis on the informational. Although the stories and poems of basal readers may elicit recreational and epistemic modes, teachers frequently ask students to recover the literal meaning of these texts instead. Even with literature-based reading programs, there is more emphasis on literal comprehension and the drawing of inferences predetermined by the text or teacher than on encouraging the use of recreational and epistemic modes.

At all grade levels, teachers who employ reader response approaches in their teaching are likely to offer instruction in all modes of engagement. Primary school teachers who engage beginners in shared story readings where they learn that texts represent a world that can be explored, challenged, and even improved upon (epistemic and recreational reading) find that the students are more motivated to master the performance mode of engagement so they can read for themselves. Students are willing to acquire the knowledge and strategies necessary for participating in literary discourse when made aware that texts represent an author's contribution or stance on a central discourse or issue and that they themselves have something to offer regarding this discourse, drawing on their own experiences and outlooks.

In helping students learn to read for information purposes, especially when reading in the content fields and when preparing for academic examinations and tests of comprehension, *reciprocal teaching* is highly successful. Accordingly, the teacher models strategies for comprehending textbooks, such as summarizing main ideas from text, making predictions about what will follow from passages, generating questions about the text and trying to answer them, and clarifying through rereading any aspect of the text that is not understood. After the teacher models the strategies in reading a passage, students are encouraged to imitate the strategies on a subsequent passage, followed by the teacher modeling again on the next page, and so forth. Initially, the teacher must prompt by definition, example, and praise as students attempt to apply the strategies. However, with a few days of experience, students are able to use strategies on new passages. Internalization of these reading strategies is of value in helping students become independent in gaining information from texts.

Reciprocal teaching occurs when teacher and students talk to each other about the meaning of a segment of text, each taking turns in leading the dialogue. The dialogue is structured to feature four strategies:

1. *generating questions about the content:*   Students ask themselves, "What questions might a teacher ask about the passage?" Then they try to answer the questions. "If you are having a hard time thinking of a question, summarize first."
2. *summarizing the segment:*   "Remember, a summary is a short statement in your own words." "It doesn't include a detail."
3. *clarifying aspects of the text* that are not understood: "What doesn't make sense?"
4. *predicting upcoming content* from cues in the text and prior knowledge: "What do you think will come next?"

▼ ── ▼

ACTIVITY 8–1   IMPROVING ABILITY TO LEARN FROM TEXTBOOKS: RECIPROCAL TEACHING

Demonstrate for yourself the effectiveness of reciprocal teaching by conducting the following experiment:

1. Create a pre- and posttest by generating questions about two selections from a textbook, preparing ten questions for each selection. Five of these questions should be factual questions whose answers are directly stated in the text, and the other five should require an inference to be drawn from information in the text. Both selections should be unfamiliar to the student(s).
2. Ask the student(s) to read one of the selections and then answer the questions for that selection. Review the answers and record the number of literal questions and the number of inferential questions that were answered correctly. These scores will serve as the baseline comprehension pretest scores.
3. Conduct reciprocal teaching of the strategies for at least three 30-minute sessions.
4. Ask the student(s) to read the second unfamiliar selection and answer the accompanying test questions that serve as the posttest.
5. Score the posttests and compare the pre- and posttest scores, noting both the total score and separate scores for literal and inferential comprehension.

▲ ── ▲

Both teacher and students silently read a sequence or paragraph from the textbook and then the teacher begins to model each of the strategies, indicating what must be clarified by rereading or asking someone, posing a question about the segment and trying to answer it (self-monitoring of comprehension), summarizing the passage, and predicting what will follow. Then the teacher and students silently read the next paragraph, followed by the students attempting to apply the four strategies with the teacher prompting as necessary and encouraging the students. Turn taking continues throughout the session. Initially, the teacher constructs paraphrases and questions for the student to mimic, "A question I would have asked would be . . ." However, after about four to eight 30-minute sessions, students are capable of assuming the role of dialogue leader.

Often students are expected to gain particular understandings from textbooks. They are asked to study the text and obtain content knowledge on which they will be tested. This type of reading differs from reading for pleasure, or for fulfilling one's own purposes, or for creating new interpretations of text. Reciprocal teaching is a highly successful technique for helping students increase their ability to acquire knowledge from textbooks in many subject areas and learn a set of strategies that are useful in independent learning from textbooks. Indeed, it is not unusual for students to improve by 60 percent or more their comprehension of texts after being taught the strategies through reciprocal teaching (Palincsar & Brown, 1984).

Although reciprocal teaching leads to dramatic improvement in student comprehension of text, it is important that students know they can get the same excellent results when they apply the strategies in reading other textbooks. The technique can be adapted to group instruction and peer tutoring.

CLARIFYING SCIENCE TEXTBOOKS

The textbook is the dominant instructional resource for the teaching of science at all levels. Books are used more often than hands-on science in the lower grades or than laboratory or field-based science learning in the upper grades. Presentations and demonstrations are still the typical way to clarify the text. Science textbooks at the elementary level present science primarily as a body of knowledge and only secondarily as a process for creating new knowledge. Topics and concepts are highlighted and information, facts, and processes are introduced within topics.

Science textbooks at the secondary school level have been criticized for their encyclopedic coverage of topical material and heavy concentration of technical vocabulary. Further, the content of these books is structured into unconnected areas of biology, chemistry, and physics. Without effort by teachers, students are unlikely to consider the social implications of science and technology or to think about the implications of these fields for their individual lives.

There are teachers who introduce topics beyond those in the textbooks as elective or digressions. Such topics as oceanography and ecology may be introduced because of the teacher's interest or local influences. Teachers with higher knowledge of science ask about material not in the textbook and require students to synthesize material; while teachers with less knowledge tend to use questions that require recall of information found in the text. Without teachers supplementing textbooks, by introducing hands-on activities, projects, serious questions about the earth's environment, and the like, the science curriculum is likely to be disconnected from real life. The textbooks themselves tend to reinforce students' conceptions of science as a fixed body of knowledge rather than an active process of inquiry into the nature of the world.

The assumption that ideas in science must be constructed by learners, not transmitted, has implications for textbook use. Teachers are now more aware of students' extant knowledge and how it conflicts with scientific frameworks. Accordingly, instead of having students read about Newton's laws, photosynthesis, molecular theory, and planetary movements, teachers first find out what students think about the phenomena to which these scientific theories relate. By taking account of students' naive conceptions, the teacher can anticipate some of the difficulties students will encounter with texts. Just by clarifying the usefulness of naive conceptions in everyday life—the sun rises and sets—and contrasting them with the nature of scientific explanations, students are better prepared to learn the latter. Even better is an inquiry approach that challenges and builds a background of experience before reading. The inquiry begins with a focus upon a problem and students pursue answers to unexplained phenomena. At the same time they try to use evidence and logic in justifying their procedures and answers before their peers.

Consider the lesson one science teacher presented prior to reading the text. Knowing that the text would present the concept that air expands when heated and contracts when cooled, the teacher distributed materials containing a clear plastic tube, tube cap, clay, candles, matches, rulers, and some plasticene clay. Students were to examine the materials and place the capped tube over a burning candle standing in a tray of water. The students observed the water rising in the tube and then addressed the problem focus: "Why did the water rise in the tube?"

The naive explanation that water rose to replace the oxygen being used up was found to be incomplete as students found they could create a rise ranging from 35 to 50 percent of the volume of the tube by manipulating variables in the system, including the addition of more candles. Further, students viewed a film loop of three mice in a sealed jar that contained a burning candle. When, contrary to their predictions, the mice did not die when the burning candle went out, students inferred that oxygen remained in the jar. Then students predicted what would happen if the cap on one of the plastic tubes was replaced with a balloon and the tube placed with two or three candles set in clay anchored to form an airtight seal. The students watched as the balloon first filled with air and then contracted to the point of being sucked into the tube.

Another experiment followed, in which a small amount of liquid detergent was placed around the perimeter of the candles prior to lowering the tube. Students then speculated about the resulting bubbles, which formed on the surface of the water outside the tube and how these bubbles related to the water rise inside the tube. At this point, students were asked to explain how all the activities were related, leading to the concept that air expands when heated and contracts when cooled.

Opportunities for students to use the new concept were presented, such as predicting what would happen in such situations as placing a hard-boiled egg on top of a milk bottle containing a burning towel, opening and reopening a refrigerator door, and submerging a hot can of duplicating fluid that has steam rising from its open lid in an aquarium of cold water after replacing its cap. Only after these experiments did students turn to their textbooks to compare their observations and conclusions with the text's corresponding photos and explanations (Dantorio & Beisenherz, 1990).

▼ ─── ▼

ACTIVITY 8–2   ADAPTING THE TEXTBOOK

There are many reasons for adapting a textbook: to make the text more accessible to students, to bring different interpretations of the topics and issues addressed by the author, to better serve the local community, and to bend the text to the larger goals and purposes of the course or class.

The two processes in adapting textbooks are: (1) analyzing the textbook, capturing the strengths of the material, and identifying aspects that should be mediated; (2) deleting, substituting, adding, and reorganizing the text itself and using framing questions and activities by which students construct their own meaning from the text.

In this activity, you are asked to adapt a textbook of interest to you. You will first analyze the textbook and teacher's guide, if available, and then state how you will adapt this textbook in light of the analysis. Your analysis should indicate the need for adaptation and provide support for your decisions regarding the textbook and its use. You may wish to prepare your own analytical scheme or adjust the scheme suggested in this activity as necessary to make it more appropriate for a given subject matter or grade level.

Textbook Analysis

1. *Consequences and stance.*   Compare your own purposes and goals for the course or class with the stated and implied purposes of the author of the textbook. Clues to the author's intentions may be found in the preface, introductions to the chapters, teaching and learning suggestions, problem exercises, and presentations of content. Of course, you must be clear about the purposes or major questions, problems, or concepts that are central to your course or class before identifying conceptual discrepancies. Identify the major organizational themes of concepts that bring coherence to the textbook, and reveal the author's stance and possible contributions to the discourse of the class. What is the author's approach to the subject matter? Are the treatments of topics oversimplified, incomplete, or inaccurate? What is missing?
2. *Pedagogy.*   What are the author's assumptions about teaching and learning? What does the textbook imply about the role of the student? Does it assume active or passive learners? Are students expected to construct knowledge from information in the text or reproduce this information? Are students expected to follow the text or to discuss and evaluate it?

▲ ─── ▲

Is the textbook prepared as "teacher-proof" material in which question and procedures are scripted and the text is the authority for what is to be learned? Or does the textbook imply that the teacher is the intellectual authority who may construe the content for multiple purposes? Or does the textbook lend itself to shared authority, whereby teacher and student reorganize the book in developing their own meanings from the text and in using the content for their own purposes?

3. *Situational relevance.*   Consider the textbook from the viewpoint of your own students and community. What is the appeal of the book for your students? How well does it match their background of experience? Does it draw on the experiences of these students? Will students have success with this textbook? Under what conditions?

   To what extent are the textbook's topics, issues, and concepts relevant to the local situation? Do they serve high priority community needs? Do they conflict with local tradition and forms of knowledge? How might the community be used both in the development of the concepts and in their application?

4. *Practicality.*   How practical is the textbook? Consider such issues as the depth of treatment versus coverage and the time available. Does the textbook support learning in other content areas or fragment the program? What supplementary materials, if any, are required? What other sources would be more effective and efficient than the textbook in attaining class goals?

Adaptation

After completing your analysis, indicate how you will respond to the discrepancies between the text and your own class goals and purposes. What topics and activities in the text will you feature? What will you eliminate? How will you prepare students for dealing with the text? How will you find out what students already know and believe about the subject matter of the text? How will you introduce the key questions, issues, problems, or discourse of the textbook and show the connection to the discourse of the classroom? What elaborations will be necessary in clarifying the text? What alternative interpretations must be introduced to balance the author's views, to preclude over-generalizations, and to provide inquiry? How are students expected to apply the content of the text? Is there any way students can use the textbook in contributing to life in the local community?

SUMMARY

There is great variation in the way teachers use and mediate textbooks. Some teachers deemphasize textbook-centered learning and instead teachers and students reconstitute the text. Although much of classroom work is built about the text or based on it, what the teacher decides to emphasize or embellish makes a difference in what students learn. At the same time, the different background knowledges of students and the way students interact with the text produces new meanings and interpretations.

This chapter has shown how the nature of the subject field influences the kinds of adaptations that take place. Newer trends in adaptations, such as the replacement unit, have been presented. Teachers who foster many modes for engaging texts and a climate for discussions are more likely to succeed in introducing students to a world not immediately obvious and in helping them understand their own thinking and feelings.

QUESTIONS FOR DISCUSSION

1. Contrast the ways textbooks are used by teachers with a *transmission* view of learning whereby students are expected to receive information from the text with the ways textbooks are used by teachers with a *constructive* view that encourages students to construe concepts as they interact with teacher and peers.
2. Should textbooks be viewed as a means for students to learn and study independently, or should they be regarded as a teaching tool that requires mediation by the teacher so the students interpret the text properly? Give your reasons.
3. Consider a textbook with which you are familiar. How would you adapt the book for use with limited English speakers?
4. Where would you place intellectual authority in your classroom: with the text, with you, with students and teacher as a community of discourse?
5. One of the problems in using multiple textbooks as resources in the study of a given topic is that many students are unable to access or comprehend the texts. How would you address this problem?
6. How do you feel about having students rewrite aspects of their textbooks for their peers, summarizing the key ideas and giving their own interpretations?

REFERENCES

Beck, I. L., McKeown, M. G., & Gromoll, E. W. (1992). Learning from social studies texts. *Cognition and Instruction, 2*(2): 99–158.

Beyond Activities Project. (1992). *Polyhedraville: An investigation of three-dimensional geometry.* Chico, CA: California State University.

Burk, D., Snider, A., & Symonds, P. (1992). *Math excursions: Project based mathematics for second graders.* Portsmouth, NH: Heinemann.

Burns, M. (1991). *Math by all means: Multiplication*. Sausalito, CA: Math Solutions Publications.

Corwin, R., Russell, S. J., & Tierney, C. (1991). *Seeing fractions: A unit for the upper elementary grades*. Sacramento, CA: Department of Education.

Dantorio, M., & Beisenherz, P. C. (1990). Don't just demonstrate: Motivate. *The Science Teacher, 57*(2): 27–29.

Hillocks, G., Jr. (1990). Literary texts in classrooms. In P. W. Jackson & S. Harouteman-Gordon (Eds.), *Eighty-ninth yearbook of the National Society for the Study of Education: Part 1. From Socrates to software: The teacher as text and the text as teacher* (p. 180). Chicago, IL: National Society for the Study of Education.

Kerekes, V. (1990). A problem-solving approach to teaching second-year algebra. *Mathematics Teacher, 8*(6): 431–432.

Lorton, M. B. (1972). *Work jobs*. Menlo Park, CA: Addison-Wesley.

Nicely, R., Jr. (1985). Higher order thinking in mathematics textbooks. *Educational Leadership, 42*: 26–30.

Palincsar, A. M., & Brown, A. (1984). Reciprocal teaching of comprehension. *Cognition and Instruction, 1*(2): 117–175.

Schimalz, R. (1990). The mathematics textbook: How can it serve the standards? *Arithmetic Teacher, 38*(1): 14–16.

Sdottir, S. G. (1991). Ways of seeing are ways of knowing: The pedagogical content knowledge of an expert English teacher. *The Journal of Curriculum Studies, 25*(5): 409–421.

Spivey, M. N., & King, J. R. (1980). Readers as writers comparing from sources. *The Reading Research Quarterly, 24*(3): 7–26.

Stodolsky, S. (1989). Is teaching really by the book? In P. W. Jackson & S. Harouteman-Gordon (Eds.), *Eighty-ninth yearbook of the National Society for the Study of Education: Part 1. From Socrates to software: The teacher as text and the text as teacher* (p. 180). Chicago, IL: National Society for the Study of Education.

Wells, G. (1990). Talk about text: Where literacy is learned and taught. *Curriculum Inquiry, 20*(4): 369–405.

PART

Creating Curriculum in the Classroom

The chapters in Part 5 are for those who want to perform in curriculum as either autonomous consumers who can develop materials of limited scope to supplement existing materials or autonomous developers who can plan and design curriculum in wide areas with few existing materials.

Chapter 9, *Curriculum and Planning*, introduces the reader to key concepts in curriculum planning. The relationships between organizing centers or curricula foci and the organizing elements of content are highlighted. The relationship of an instructional unit to course goals and to daily plans are also clarified. Three forms of instructional units are described and illustrated: the thematic unit, the subject-matter unit, and the inquiry unit. Alternative procedures in planning these different kinds of units are shown.

Chapter 10, *Generating and Designing Units of Instruction*, specifies the components of instructional units and contrasts the principles that are used in constructing thematic units as opposed to either subject-matter or inquiry units. Examples of each type of unit are presented, illustrating unit planning at both elementary and secondary school levels.

CHAPTER

CURRICULUM AND PLANNING

This chapter addresses the preparation of preinstructional plans by teachers—the visions and frameworks to guide the curriculum that will be enacted in the classroom. Contrasts are drawn among long-range, daily, and unit plans. Major attention is given to the development of instructional unit plans. Characteristics and illustrations are given for different kinds of unit plans—thematic, subject-matter, and inquiry units. Two important curriculum concepts are featured:

1. The *organizing center*, which is the focus of study for students that guides the selection of activities for a unit
2. The *organizing element*, which identifies the content to be introduced in the study and which forms the basis for continuity among instructional units, courses, and long-term goals

   The importance of the teachers' world view in planning instruction is emphasized. Given the same curriculum theme and common educational goals, it is unlikely that teachers will generate similar activities and common interpretations of subject matter.
   Curricula are initiated as teachers visualize what might occur in a classroom, tentatively answering their own questions about content, materials, student learning activities, time allocation, and other aspects of a framework to guide future action. Curricula are created as plans are revised and implemented. When the interactions among students and teachers result in new content, interpretations, ways of working, and purposes, curricula are created. The feelings and meanings generated from classroom experiences may comprise a curriculum and, indeed, curriculum may continue to form as the meanings of classroom experiences unfold throughout a lifetime.

LONG-RANGE, DAILY, AND UNIT PLANNING

Although teachers engage in long-range planning as well as daily planning, course and daily plans are regarded by teachers as less important than the planning of instructional units. Long-range planning, typically done during the summer months, usually consists of reviewing materials to be used during the coming year, rearranging topics, and adding and deleting content to be taught. A broad outline, together with ideas for how the content is to be taught, is formed on the basis of a mental review of the events of the past year and of newer materials and ideas (Clark & Peterson, 1986). Detailed long-range planning tends to be counterproductive because of unpredictable changes in schedules, students, and interruptions.

Daily plans are usually nested within the unit plan and depend on the progress of a class in that unit. The daily plan of most teachers consists of a mental picture of the content to be taught and the sequence of activities that might occur, supported by notes and lists of important points that the teacher wants to be sure to remember. Daily plans are likely only to be written in detail and in a prescribed form when the teacher has to comply with administrative requirements for turning in plans on a regular basis or when the plan is to be used by a replacement or substitute teacher.

The planning of an instructional unit offers the teacher an opportunity to initiate a curriculum that is responsive to a local situation, individual students, and the teacher's own passion. Unlike curricula presented in textbooks that isolate knowledge into subject-matter compartments, a teacher's unit plan may forge connections among subject matters as well as connecting to life in a particular community.

PLANNING AS MAPPING

One notion of curriculum has been associated with the idea of movement toward a destination—a "race course", a set of experiences, a stream of activities, a journey involving increasingly wider ranges in modes of thinking. Hence, the metaphor of the map is sometimes used by teachers in creating their instructional unit plans. Accordingly, the plan specifies the steps for reaching a predetermined goal. However, maps are seldom complete, and they require frequent revision. Travelers using the map may decide to change their original destination and route for reasons of feasibility and interest. They may seek a new map or make their own.

In their planning or curriculum mapping, teachers vary in attitudes about flexibility of the plan and their relative concerns about the quality of the learning experience or about the attainment of a goal. Units of instruction take on the characteristics of open and closed maps:

▼ *Thematic units* are open maps of broad focus that allow for many subthemes and encourage unexpected outcomes.

▼ *Subject-matter units* are closed maps that focus on prespecified topics with less opportunity for students to determine the central questions, subtopics, and the sequence in which content is presented.

▼ *Inquiry units* are focused upon a central question or problem to be solved. Usually the question or problem has been chosen or defined by students although the teacher may have provoked the inquiry. Inquiry units feature task responsibility and allow for study of sub-topics of interest to individual students when pertinent to the inquiry.

DESCRIPTION OF INSTRUCTIONAL UNITS

Thematic Units

The broad focus and instructional units as related subject matter can be seen in the brief descriptions of "The Circus," "Hermanitas," and "Hudson River Valley."

"The Circus."   Herbert Kohl (1976) tells how he went about creating a thematic unit in preparation for the school year. He chose the theme "circus-time" because it combines danger and discipline, farce and high seriousness, and because few students can be indifferent to the many aspects of life and fantasy encompassed in the circus. Kohl began by going to the circus to remind himself of what it was all about. Then he analyzed what he saw and speculated about what could be studied through the circus. His general map of the circus looked something like the illustration in Figure 9–1.

Next Kohl developed subthemes, matching them with activities for the classroom. For example, the subtheme *tightrope walking* was turned into balancing, which brought forth such content ideas as vertigo and other balancing games, floating and sinking, gymnastics, center of gravity (equilibrium and the ear), balancing a checkbook, and associated weights and balances (scales and measures). Classroom activities included making balancing toys; making a seesaw and balancing things on it; building balanced structures with Lego blocks; walking a straight line on the floor, then on blocks, and then on chairs; talking about fear of height and how feelings affect performance; writing about confidence, imagining walking the wire 100 feet up, and measuring actual heights.

Kohl thought about the best time to introduce the unit—before or after a circus would come to town—and the resources available. He was lucky in that a former student who had attended Ringling Brothers Clown College could come

FIGURE 9–1
General map of the circus

	Animals	
Jugglers		Clowns
Tightrope walkers		Freaks
Pitching tents		Parades
Moving	Posters	
	Art	
	Music	

to class and show his clown faces and tricks which, in turn, led to the children's evolving their own clown characters listening to the opera Pagliaci, making masks, and creating short plays with masked super heroes.

All teachers would have their own ideas about what activities might go on under the circus theme. Instead of circus performers coming to the class, volunteers from local theater groups could visit and make theater real for the children. Other teachers might have the students decorate the class with old circus posters or record other aspects of what they remember about a circus. At one time, Kohl brainstormed the circus theme with his first graders, producing a map that looked like Figure 9–2.

From the map, groups studied the different aspects of the circus and then performed part of a class circus. Some classes may create a circus with students as performers, or perhaps training their own pets to do tricks or dressing up for a parade or playing music to accompany the performers; other classes may prefer to build a model circus with balancing toys and clowns, papier mâché animals, and carts that move, parade, and do tricks. The portable circus can be performed in other classes. In brief, the possible curricular responses to a circus or other themes are varied.

Themes also lend themselves to the planning of interdisciplinary units at the secondary level where teachers from several fields organize their courses around five or six common conceptual themes likely to evoke intellectual and emotional responses from students, such as those of "Women, Race, Social Protest" or "The Protestant Ethic and the Spirit of Capitalism." A question such as "Is war ever justified?" may be answered by students from the perspectives of history, literature, and science.

"Humanitas." In the program "Humanitas," more than 267 Los Angeles secondary school teachers have formed individual school teams for the purpose of developing interdisciplinary units around central concepts and producing their own curricular materials. Typically, members of a team represent English, social studies, and art. Materials related to a theme come from a variety of sources—primary sources, novels, newspaper articles, plays, videos, art exhibits. Humanitas teachers may use a final examination as a planning technique in order to identify significant issues to discuss, clarify their objectives, and guide their selection of materials and activities. The teams develop cooperatively early in the planning process an end-of-unit essay. This essay requires students to synthesize what they will be learning in all their "Humanitas" classes. The following is a typical essay question from a unit on Culture and Traditional Societies taught in a ninth-grade class.

FIGURE 9–2
Circus theme map

	clowns	
people on stilts		trapeze artists
midgets	circus	beautiful costumes and parades
trick animals		elephants

▼ ── ▼

ACTIVITY 9–1   BRAINSTORMING
FOR A THEMATIC UNIT

1. Select a theme (abstraction, event, person, institution, or other phenomena).

    If in a group situation, all should spontaneously express their ideas on the theme. Encourage weird or ridiculous ideas as well as the usual kind. Don't reject another's idea, but try to build on it. If one cannot build on an idea, give a completely unrelated idea. Record all ideas expressed.

    If alone, freely associate ideas related to the theme and try to connect the theme to a discipline (art, music, science, history, religion, literature, etc.) or to functions (recreational, vocational, health, political, etc.).

2. After you have formed a list of subthemes, consider the kinds of activities—projects, experiments, readings—that might be undertaken in a unit addressing the subthemes. Consider also the kinds of knowledge students might create from activities and resources suggested.

▲ ── ▲

The cosmology of a traditional culture permeates every aspect of that culture. This is illustrated in the following three culture groups: the Eskimo, the Southwest Indian, and the Meso-American. Specifically discuss the spirit world that each group believed in, and explain how it influenced their culture and values. Include examples from your reading in art history, literature, and social institutions to illustrate and substantiate your analysis. Finally, to what extent, if any, does the spirit world affect us today?

"Hudson River Valley."   Working solo, teachers can make their curriculum more interdisciplinary by realigning the subjects they are already teaching. For example, one teacher in Pelham Middle School in New York focused on a theme of great local importance, the Hudson River Valley. She encouraged students to examine maps of the valley (geography), to read about the valley's past (history), to read legends of the Hudson River (literature), and to write their own legends (writing). Students also studied the geometry of the River's bridges (math), examined the river's water purification (science), and became familiar with Hudson River artists. The culminating activity was a trip on the river and the preparation of essays on the relationships between the river and the people in which students drew on everything they had learned in class.

Subject-Matter Units

Some teachers prefer to integrate the content of their course within a subject matter or academic discipline.

"The Vietnam War."   Darrell Meadows has developed a four-week unit, "The Vietnam War," for high school social studies that relates geography, political

science, ethics, history, and other social sciences (Meadow, 1990). Meadow's unit begins with an introduction stating the reasons for the study. He points out the need for students to understand the history and culture of Vietnam, as well as the roots of U.S. involvement, so they can draw lessons from that war. He then presents the major goals, concepts, and student activities for the unit. An example of a goal is "that students will learn to think objectively and critically about conflict and its resolution in international relations" and of a concept "the geography of Vietnam has had a fundamental impact on its history and development." Examples of activities are these: role playing, group discussions, and written reports to foster critical thinking; readings, library research, guest speakers, and video presentations to inform students about the history and culture of Vietnam; map construction and readings to learn about geography and its role in Vietnamese history.

"The Vietnam War" unit also features a preliminary reaction guide for establishing baseline beliefs of the students, like these:

▼ "Only when a nation is invaded does it have the right to go to war."

▼ "Even though some Americans may oppose war with another country, once war is declared, each person should give the government full support."

This unit also includes a study guide, semantic maps for major concepts, copies of historical documents, such as the Gulf of Tonkin Resolution, a bibliography and a listing of art sources, drama, poetry, films/videos, documents and community resources.

"Fractions for the Primary Grades."   Most subject-matter units begin with the teacher constructing a conceptual map outlining the major ideas within the subject. A unit "Fractions for the Primary Grades" begins with the map shown in Figure 9–3.

Accordingly, the unit's activities follow the ordering of the map (Payne & Towsley, 1990):

1. Students begin by sharing equal-sized pieces, such as a cheese square between two people, a pie among four plates, and a set of books among five shelves. The activity is oral and emphasizes "fair share" and "equal parts." Wholes such as apples, candy bars, and circles are partitioned and named as fractions, halves, thirds, fourths, and tenths.
2. Next, fraction slips are introduced, and students count the pieces of the fraction slips forward and backward, showing the pieces of the slips as they count—zero, thirds, one third, two thirds, three thirds, and so on.
3. The names of fractions—"one fourth," "two halves," and the like—are given aloud, and students match the name with corresponding part of their fraction slips. Students then show the parts giving the appropriate name.

FIGURE 9–3
Subject-matter unit map for fractions

Equal pieces
Counting
Matching names with fractions
Real problems
Comparisons
Equivalence and estimation
Symbols for fractions

4. Students share common objects—sandwiches, fruit—naming the fractional parts as they confront the problems of sharing the objects.

5. Using their fraction slips, students determine which is more—one tenth or one fourth? (They explain why a tenth sounds bigger but is smaller.) Then they compare the same number of pieces of different sizes (two thirds and two tenths), more than one piece of the same size (two fourths, and three fourths), and different numbers of pieces of different sizes (one fifth and six tenths).

6. Using their fraction slips, students fill in a chart, indicating whether different numbers of tenths, sixths, fifths, and the like, are zero, close to zero, one, close to one, or one half. Students look for patterns in the chart ("close to one is the first number close to the second number") and compare two thirds with five tenths, nine tenths with four eights, and three sixths with one fourth.

7. Finally, students relate terms to symbols—two thirds = 2/3; ten eighths = 10/8. Using models and real problems, students partition, study figures, and write fractions for the particular parts.

"The Metric Mall." Not all subject-matter units are ordered in a simple-to-complex sequence. The self-instructional unit "The Metric Mall" was developed for third-, fourth-, and fifth-grade students and features a number of learning centers "stores," which offer problem-solving activities involving measurement. For example, at the "Map a Mall" administrative center, students are assigned such tasks as these:

▼ finding an escaped pet by using a map: The lizard went 3 cm north, 8 cm west, 7 cm south, and 9 cm northwest. Track the lizard. Where is he now?"

▼ determining the length of awning needed to cover a storefront

▼ calculating distances between stores and the lengths of ribbons needed for opening ceremonies

At the kitchen store, students find four sections:

1. A recipe corner stocked with ingredients for recipes in metric units to use with appropriate measuring bowls, cups, and spoons
2. The supply section with beans, rice, seeds, cereal, and candy (which students use in estimating the weight of each unit and determining the difference between active and estimated amounts)
3. A volume section (where students estimate and determine the capacity of an eyedropper, tea cup, bowls, and a tub)
4. A salad section (set up with scales and bins full of salad items the students use in comparing sizes, shapes, and weights)

Similar measuring activities are found at other centers of the mall—the soda fountain, hobby shop, pet store, jewelry store, post office, and Metric Olympic Store (Fay & Tsairdes, 1989).

Inquiry Units

Inquiry units can take the form of social projects in which students make a difference in the real world, or try to answer questions that they themselves generate from classroom materials.

Foxfire Projects.   More than 2,000 teachers following Foxfire principles are developing social projects of inquiry as mentioned in Chapter 3. The Foxfire network of teachers sprang from the experiences of Eliot Wigginton whose English classes for more than 20 years examined the culture, traditions, and history of their Appalachian community and then documented and published what they found in issues of *Foxfire Magazine.* Among the Foxfire community's principles are those stating that students should solve real problems or create real products that the community values and applauds. If, for example, students research national and world issues like change in climatic patterns, prejudice, or AIDS, students must "bring them home" by identifying local attitudes about the issues as well as illustrating their findings and showing the implications of these issues for their local communities.

All the work that the Foxfire teachers and students do flows from student desire—students choose, design, revise, execute, reflect, and evaluate their projects. Problems that arise during the project are solved by the class itself. Every student in the room is included and needed in the project, and all students are expected to operate on the edge of their confidence, not doing what they already know how to do. There must be an audience beyond the teacher for student work—another individual, small group, or the community. This audience, in turn, must affirm that the work is important, needed, and worth doing. Students indicate to the teacher the ways they will prove at the end of the project that they have mastered the objectives the project is designed to serve. They also say what they would like to know about the subject of inquiry and what they will be able to do at the end of the project that they cannot do at the beginning. Students are helped to monitor their own progress and develop their

▼ ▼

ACTIVITY 9–2 CONSTRUCTING
A CONCEPTUAL MAP FOR
A SUBJECT-MATTER UNIT

Conceptual mapping is a technique to show the relation of ideas that might be introduced in a unit. The map may be considered as tentative. Later, you might want to revise the map by adding other ideas and showing different relationships. The map can be used to assess and activate student background knowledge, to establish an advance organizer for learning, as well as to guide instructional planning.

There is no single correct way to order any subject matter, so feel free to express your own framework of ideas.

1. Select a subject-matter topic.
2. List general ideas about the topic—concepts, principles, processes, examples, analogies, facts—content that might be introduced in teaching the unit.
3. Choose an organizational pattern for showing relationships. There are many patterns from which to choose, including the following:
   a. Hierarchal: Place most inclusive generalizations, abstractions, or concepts at the top and the specific examples at the bottom of the map.
   b. Compare-and-contrast: Show how new concepts contrast with familiar ones or compare the attributes of two or more ideas.
   c. Problem solving: Show how the different concepts and facts relate to a specific problem.
   d. Cause-and-effect: Show the factors that affect or influence a condition.
4. Draw the map as an outline, diagram, schematic drawing, or chart indicating the content and relationships.

▲ ▲

own remediation plans. The progress of each student is the concern of every student in the room (Wigginton, 1989).

Hands On, Foxfire's journal for teachers, carries accounts by teachers as they apply the principles. For example, Amy Rodger's second-grade class voted down her original suggestion for a project and instead decided to make a half-hour videotape about environmental pollution in the county. The finished tape included four short plays written and performed, a song, and interviews with community residents and managers of the landfill. The tape won a state environmental award (Wigginton, 1989).

Barbara Lewis, a teacher in Jackson Elementary School in Salt Lake, has promoted social projects at her school and among teachers throughout the nation (Lewis, 1991). Sixth-grade students in Lewis's class discovered a hazardous waste site near their school. Students began their inquiry with the question: "How can we find out whether our water supply is contaminated?" The students' initial efforts to answer the question by contacting the health department were fruitless, and their efforts to interest residents in the possible dangers of hazardous wastes brought only "I don't care" responses. Nevertheless, the students sought more information about sites that had exploded and created toxic clouds. They also visited the local site where they were told there were no problems. But the children were unconvinced. After further reading about hazardous wastes, the students invited environmental specialists to their classroom. Armed with new information, the students formed a new solution, calling on a national environmental hotline to ask for help. They also wrote to the Environmental Protection Agency's regional office, called the local power company who owned the site, and asked TV, radio stations, and newspapers to cover the story. The students visited the mayor and secured his support. Under public pressure, personnel of the Environmental Protection Agency tested the site and found that harmful substances had polluted the soil and the ground water, threatening over 477,000 people.

The students mailed letters to business and environmental groups asking for donations for a clean-up. They also raised about $2700 for their contribution to the task. However, a state law impeded the use of funds for this purpose. So the stage was set for further inquiry and action. The new question became "How to change the law?" After reading about the national Superfund, which is for cleaning up abandoned toxic waste sites, the students wrote a resolution proposing a state Superfund. Legislators turned the resolution into a bill, and the students lobbied for it. They testified before a committee and spoke to the state senate. They also passed out flyers to all the legislators trimmed in red crayon. As the bill was passed, one lawmaker said, "No one has more effectively lobbied us than those young kids—and they didn't even have to buy us dinner."

"In Search of Our Mothers' Gardens."　　As an inquiry unit in literature, a junior high English class sought answers to such questions as:

▼　What is the state of mind that is most favorable to the act of creation?

▼　What are the circumstances that obstruct or silence that state of mind?

▼　Why have so many women (in history, literature, life) been silenced? (Donovan & Walsh, 1991).

The resulting unit, "Silence," drew upon several biographers and autobiographers. Students were awakened to the way culture constructed gender and silenced women as they read Virginia Woolf's *A Room of One's Own*. This text also helped students see the importance of each student's own life story and indicated the service students could do by taking themselves seriously in recording the memories of their own mothers and grandmothers, memories that otherwise might be lost.

In their reading of Carolyn Heilbron's *Writing a Woman's Life*, students learned how many women have been deprived of narratives by which they might have assumed control over their own lives. Alice Walker's *In Search of*

▼ ── ▼

ACTIVITY 9–3   SELECTING
IDEAS FOR A PROJECT

There are two commonly used approaches to selecting ideas for projects. One approach is to choose a topic that would be taught in your course and then look for or create with students a project around the topic. Another approach is to start with an idea for a project and then see how the content of the course can be related to the project.

Ideas for projects can be drawn from a range of categories: environmental (wildlife, conservation of resources); economics (consumer information, employment, technology, community development); health and safety (public health, disaster preparedness); communication (media, public opinion); interpersonal relations (family, recreation, racism); international-intercultural relations (immigration, student exchange).

1. List possible ideas for projects that will deal with any aspect of a real existing situation, condition, or issue of importance to the community.
2. Suggest some ways students might take action in one or more possible projects (for example, produce and disseminate an educational video related to an issue).
3. Indicate others that might be involved in the project and state possible sources for first-hand information.

▲ ── ▲

Our Mother's Gardens taught students what it meant for a black woman to be an artist in their great-grandmothers' time and how biography reclaims silences, allowing women of the past to continue their presences among us.

After reading these and other biographies, the students knew that they must become their mothers and grandmothers' biographers. The writing of a biography of a female relative or friend became an independent project in the class. Students chose someone they could research through interviews, diaries, letters, photographs, scrapbooks, genealogies, and other records. First, they wrote a preliminary description of the person with a brief explanation of why they chose that person and the sources available. Then they completed an initial 5–7 page biography (which was later rewritten using the course material as a context), and finally they gave a 2–3 page explanation of how the course material influenced the revision.

One student wrote her mother's biography, a less tragic version of Ibsen's *Doll House*. Several students echoed Walker's sentences, "In search of my mother's garden, I found my own" and "Why hasn't the world realized that we can learn from them and in the process discover our own selves?" A representative comment is this: "I gained an incredible respect for and knowledge of my grandmother. Even though I believe it would be easier to write a fairy tale account of her life, I feel strongly about her silence and want her voice to be heard" (Donovan & Walsh, 1991).

Henriques' Learner-Generated Units.   In view of current dissatisfaction with elementary science programs that rely on textbooks, it may be that units such as those of Androla Henriques (1990) give a glimpse of the future science curriculum. Henriques is not interested in encyclopedic presentation of scientific facts, nor in giving out well-organized information, nor in having students carry out guided experiments to confirm present conclusions. Instead, her units encourage students to find problems, make hypotheses, and carry out their own experiments. The goal of the unit is construction of knowledge by students.

The teacher has three things to do in Henriques' curriculum:

1. *Assemble a wide variety of objects that might be related to a theme.* Possible physical science themes are "water," "weight," "mixing and mixtures," and "motion." The objects assembled for the unit "mixing and mixtures" might include liquids (water, oil, vinegar, methylated spirits), powders (flour, sugar, salt, sodium bicarbonate, dyes), and grains (lentils, wheat, and others) In addition, newspaper, waxed paper, rags, cottonwood, straws, plastic spoons, and immersion coils for heating water might be provided.

2. *Observe children as they freely interact with the material.* The teacher makes notes of the problems students encounter as they attempt to do things with the material. The teacher also interviews children during the free activity sessions, asking: "What are you doing?" "Can you explain that to me again?" or "Tell me more." The teacher refrains from giving information and explanations. Children's responses are analyzed to reveal the mental activity in which they are engaging.

3. *Conduct synthesis sessions with children where children focus on problems encountered in the free sessions.* In the synthesis sessions, children discuss difficulties, confront points of view, question assertions, and propose other activities. New experiments may be designed by the whole class and entrusted to one or two groups of children to carry out.

In interpreting the child's activity during both the free spontaneous sessions and the synthesis sessions, the teacher identifies

▼   activities where the child focuses on acting upon objects, trying to get a certain result, and trying to understand how something works

▼   activities through which the child seeks to single out the factors that have contributed to a particular result, considering steps taken and the role different objects played in getting the results

▼   activities that are experimental, where the child wants to reproduce a result, planning a sequence of logical steps for an experiment that will support an assertion that the child believes to be true

THE ORGANIZING CENTER AS A VEHICLE FOR LEARNING: MORE THAN MEETS THE EYE

Much has been made of the theme, the topic, and the problem as bases for organizing instructional units. In the language of curriculum, these focal points are called organizing centers or instructional foci. Generally, if you ask students what they are studying, they reply by naming the center. Teachers, however, know that these centers are chiefly vehicles for the intellectual and emotional development of learners. Although the study of a noteworthy event, work of art, problem, or other phenomenon is valuable in its own right, it is of more worth when it leads to the construction of concepts, attitudes, skills, and concerns of educational importance.

Different organizing centers can serve the same educational goals. Teachers have much to do in influencing the kind of development that occurs as learners pursue the immediate focus of their study. Young children may believe they are learning to build bird houses, but the teacher may view the activity as an opportunity to form new concepts and skills in measurement, motor dexterity, or to learn how to use tools of construction. Another teacher may see the activity as a way to build the learner's self-confidence or to foster a concern about wildlife.

Although organizing centers should be broad enough so that students can find an area of personal interest, they shouldn't be so broad that the study becomes unmanageable or meaningless. Nevertheless, in the hands of a good teacher, nearly any center can lead to powerful ideas from science, math, social studies, psychology, English, and more. Further, the activities carried out under the rubric of the center can contribute to long-term educational goals.

The term *organizing element* refers to the content (ideas, concepts, skills, values) that are likely to be developed as students engage in activities related to a center. These content elements are generally reiterated or extended throughout other units and courses, culminating in what is sought in long-term goals. Common goals related to literacy and numeracy, plus dispositions such as creativity and persistence can be met through the study of most centers, provided that the activities associated with the study give opportunity for learners to engage in situations where these values apply. The fact that widely shared educational goals can be pursued through most organizing centers allows teachers and students to choose centers that are responsive to local and personal concerns. Units with widely diverse centers—"Saving our Tidepools," "The Hopi," "Cartoons," "The Hollywood Western," "The One Room School," "Informing Immigrants," "What Work Will There Be In Our Town in the Year 2000?," "How Do Frogs Survive?"—can all involve observing and analyzing data, critical thinking, problem solving, and foster both individual initiative and group cooperation.

Activities can integrate the arts, science, math, and social studies. The activities in some units call for imaginary solutions, such as simulations, mock trials, straw votes, and the building of model communities. The units of other teachers will feature academic solutions to real problems, and the activities will involve real experiences where students make use of the information they obtain to bring about civic improvement and quality of life in the community.

CURRICULUM'S REFLECTION OF TEACHER WORLD VIEWS

Sandra Wilde has shown how five female teachers differ in their response to the theme of gender stereotyping and careers (Wilde, 1990). The five teachers developed activities that had the same aims of exploring the destructiveness of limiting one's choices on the basis of gender, emphasizing the contributions of women and minorities, and exploring nontraditional careers for women.

▼ Judy Miller developed a first-grade unit, "What People Do All Day," that began with a discussion of what the children themselves did all day and then shifted to what their parents did all day. Next, the children addressed the questions: "Are there any jobs that can be performed only by members of one gender or another?" and "Imagine you are adults and can do any kind of work you want, what would you choose?" The children's responses showed that their perceptions had been shaped by traditional gender roles, the media, and people they know. Next, the students talked about the role of money in one own's career and life, and the teacher helped them develop realistic ideas about salaries. Subsequent lessons focused on the children's own lives and those of their families, explored their visions of the future, encouraged a nonsexist stance and knowledge of financial realities. A series of speakers—male and female—discussed their daily activities. In brief, the unit reflected Miller's community-based view of teaching and her determination to help children begin to see choices in their lives even at a young age.

▼ Linda Richardson developed a historical unit on pioneer life in which she emphasized women's history and students becoming aware that life was more difficult in the past than it is today. Students imagined they were living in the forest long ago and discussed how they would survive. Male and female roles were considered, and the teacher made no attempt to disguise the fact that tasks in pioneer families were often allocated by gender. The difficulty of women's work in churning the butter and doing laundry in a stream and the like was highlighted. Related activities, such as baking bread and making quilts, also conveyed the idea that life was not always easy and the importance of valuing everyone's work. This teacher wanted students to understand the importance of hard work and determination in achieving one's goals.

▼ Carmen Torres developed second-grade activities that would make students aware that women's achievements and their career choices should not be limited by gender. Among these activities was a visit by the female chief of police of a neighboring town. The general thrust of the visit was to counteract stereotypes and to show that women can combine their professional and personal lives. Later, a field trip to visit the police and fire stations drew attention to achievement across gender and ethnic lines. In addition to incorporating local role models, Torres drew examples from the larger culture, including the astronaut Sally Ride. As a result of this activity, students were left with a vision of highly visible careers, especially nontraditional careers for women. Little emphasis was given to what kinds of work would best suit the children as individuals or to appreciating the contributions of women in traditionally female occupations.

▼ Amanda Hidalgo developed activities for her fourth-grade class that addressed stereotypes that limit people on the basis of gender. One of her early activities called for students to pick three things they valued and would take to a desert island. Choices were charted revealing gender preferences. In a later activity, students explored their opinions. The class was encouraged to challenge stereotypes. Students also worked in mixed-gender groups, selecting example of biased pictures from magazines. Hidalgo addressed gender roles and careers by focusing on values, accepting and getting along with others.

▼ Connie Smith developed activities that would help children of both genders think about what is involved in being a responsible adult and family member. One activity in her unit was sewing simple dolls because she thinks that sewing is a valuable skill for everyone and that learning how would help boys feel that it is acceptable for them to sew. In other activities, students explored their feelings about marriage and children, and considered options other than those prevailing in the community as well as the importance of independence and personal goals. By focusing priority on adult family life, this teacher's unit aimed at helping students envision adult life when work would be another source of satisfaction and growth.

SUMMARY

Teachers create curriculum by planning and transferring these plans into challenging vehicles for learning. Systematic and detailed planning occurs more frequently in the preparation of instructional units than in course and daily lesson planning. Unit planning allows the teacher to create curriculum that is responsive to the local situation, individual students, and the teacher's own passion. Units differ in their flexibility. Some are fixed in purpose while others are designed to promote multiple outcomes. *Thematic units* have a broad focus, which allows for student participation in originating subthemes and alternative routes to common ends. *Subject-matter units* typically focus on prespecified topics and objectives, and the logic of the subject matter determines the organizational plan. *Inquiry units* have a central question but invite students to generate and pursue individually and in groups related tasks and subquestions.

Illustrations of each type of unit have been presented in this chapter. A distinction has been made between organizing centers or foci for study and organizing elements of content that are to be introduced through the activities of the study. The organizing elements consist of important subject matter, values, outlooks, processes, and the like that are related to curriculum goals. Organizing elements are the basis for coherence among instructional units, courses, and long-term goals. This chapter has shown the great variations among teachers in their interpretations of content and in the kinds of learning activities they provide even when they share common goals and the same curriculum theme.

QUESTIONS FOR DISCUSSION

1. Which metaphor best describes you as a unit planner:
    a. an explorer who searches with others to determine new places and routes?
    b. an architect who wants to build an edifice of knowledge?
    c. something else?
2. As students participate in planning and implementing a unit, should they also participate in discourse about the nature and purpose of education? Give your reasons.
3. What are the advantages and disadvantages of projects where students deal with real situations in the school or community as opposed to projects that treat imaginary or speculative situations?
4. How can a teacher best deal with student-initiated questions and activities that require an expertise the teacher does not have?

REFERENCES

Clark, C. M., & Peterson, P. L. (1986). Teachers' thought processes. In Merl Wittrock (Ed.), *Handbook of research in teaching* (3rd ed.), pp. 250–294. New York: Macmillan.

Donovan, M. A., & Walsh, M. (1991). In search of our mother's garden we found our own. *English Journal, 80*(4): 38–43.

Fay, N., & Tsairdes, C. (1989). Metric mall. *Arithmetic Teacher, 37*(1): 6–11.

Foxfire magazine. Rabun County, CA: Rabun County High School.

Henriques, A. (1990). Experiments in teaching. In E. Duckworth, J. Easley, D. Hawkins, & A. Henriques (Eds.), *Science education: A mind's on approach for the elementary years,* pp. 141–186. Hillsdale, NJ: Lawrence Erlbaum Associates.

Kohl, H. (1976). *On teaching.* New York: Schoeken Books.

Lewis, B. A. (1991). *The kids' guide to social action.* Minneapolis, MN: Free Spirit Publishing Co.

Meadows, D. (1990). *The Vietnam War: A four week instructional unit.* St. Louis: University of Missouri.

Payne, J., & Towsley, A. (1990). Implications for NCTM's standards for teaching fractions and percent. *Arithmetic Teacher, 37*(8): 23–26.

Wigginton, E. (1989). Foxfire grows up. *Harvard Educational Review, 59*(1): 24–49.

Wilde, S. (1990). Teacher autonomy and non-sexist curriculum: Case studies from two rural schools. *Curriculum Inquiry, 20*(1): 41–62.

GENERATING AND DESIGNING UNITS OF INSTRUCTION

This chapter begins by contrasting the published forms of instructional units with the actual order followed in generating and designing units. Procedures are given for designing themes, subthemes, and content; the planning of activities; and the securing of resources. Two approaches to designing subject-matter units are featured: the instructional systems approach and the problem-solving approach. Guidelines for the planning and implementing of inquiry units are elaborated on in connection with curriculum projects in both elementary and secondary school classrooms. Questions are raised, such as these: Should students choose the focus of their study? Should units deal with real events concerning the quality of life in the community or only with subject matter set out to be learned? How free are teachers and students to create knowledge that is not part of the official course of study? An activity that integrates the design factors of the instructional unit concludes the chapter.

Usually instructional units prepared as documents follow a particular form that outlines various components: title; statement of purpose; expected outcomes or objectives; rationale (reasons and philosophy) for the unit; outline of content (concepts, generalizations, problems, or issues); learning activities for beginning, carrying out, and culminating the unit; instructional materials for students and teacher use; and perhaps a statement of the means for evaluating the unit, including observations, self reports, products, and examinations.

The way units are generated does not follow the order in which the components appear on the form. One can start with any of several parts—evaluation, activity, content, materials, theme, questions, or objectives. Further, the unit plan may be regarded either as only a tentative map or possibilities to be redrawn by students, or as a plan to guide much of what will occur in the classroom.

Procedures for generating and designing units tend to be different when the unit is a thematic unit (as opposed to a subject-matter unit or an inquiry unit), although there is a current trend to create units that incorporate features from each. The sections to follow present procedures for developing components in the different types of units.

DESIGNING THEMATIC UNITS

Selecting a Theme and Generating Subthemes

Many teachers begin their design with a theme. There is an unlimited list of possible themes for a unit—phenomena, concepts, persons, events, places, or problems. Teachers narrow their choice to a theme of local importance, one relevant to the concerns of students and with potential for illuminating content related to the teacher's educational goals. A teacher is unlikely to suggest a theme if relevant materials and human resources are not readily available. Although the teacher may propose a theme, students should be encouraged to suggest in turn their own questions and concerns as possible themes or at least participate in brainstorming to identify possible subthemes for study.

Chapter 10 described Herbert Kohl's planning process, showing how his own values, concerns for student interests, and sense of educational purpose influenced his selection of a theme and how brainstorming by children of that theme created subthemes worthy of study. The theme and subthemes organized as a map suggest materials and activities. The map generally groups ideas together and may be arranged in a hierarchy, sequence, cause and effect, problem solution, or other organizational pattern. The language arts map suggested by the unit "Journeys," for example, lends itself to compare and contrast patterns (see Figure 10–1). This pattern is useful in helping students differentiate the schemata in different literary genres (Walmsley, 1990).

Selecting Content

The selection of content—values, processes, concepts, skills, generalizations, and forms of perception—should reflect the teacher's educational goals. Often these goals and the content they imply are similar to those set by state and local policy boards and promulgated through curricular frameworks and official

FIGURE 10–1
Language arts map

	Journeys			
	Factual Journeys		*Fictional Journeys*	
Symbolic journeys, e.g., Smith's visit to USSR	Children's own journeys	Journeys that challenge—personal endurance, adventure	Science fiction journey, e.g., *The Time Traveler*	Imaginary journeys, e.g., *Alice in Wonderland, Wizard of Oz*
	Journeys to improve technology, e.g., shuttle	Migration, e.g., birds, whales, butterflies		Realistic journey, e.g., Laura Ingalls Wilder stories

courses of study. Another source of content is found in the standards and other publications of professional organizations that represent the content fields. Teachers are asked to regard the content of these documents as representing the sinews or overarching ideas that are to be extended through the educational program—a formal curriculum rather than a cluster of topics.

In the "Journeys" unit, the teacher regarded the strategies for reading and writing in different genres as important curriculum content to be developed by learners throughout the unit. The notion of the writing process as prewriting, composing, revising, and editing was to be central in all activities related to the organizing centers or themes. Knowledge of reading as comprehending a complexity of literary styles and plots was also to be attained by students through the learning activities.

Planning Learning Opportunities

Three general principles guide the planning of learning activities:

1. There should be varied ways for students to engage in the content of the unit. Ideally, the content would be represented in visual and auditory qualities and expressed through movement and narration. Although the unit "Journeys" gave students opportunity to respond to a variety of types of literature and to express themselves in writing and discussing, the verbal mode dominated. Other teachers using the principle of variation might have included activities in drama, music, dance, painting, film, and the like in developing reading and writing; or have taken advantage of the wide choices in literature to help students find their connections to science, history, geography, and other subject areas.

2. The activities should be within the range of possibility for the students— consistent with their present attainments and predispositions. This principle, implying that students should have success in the activities, is met when teachers and peers provide the scaffolding (assistance, support, modeling) by which learners develop capacities for performing the activities independently. Also, the principle has a corollary: the activity should allow students to reach new levels of accomplishment.

3. The activities should be satisfying to the learners. Although learners differ in what they find satisfying, depending on age and prior experience, there are general features of satisfying activities, such as an opportunity to make choices; to interact with significant others; to combine thinking, feeling, and acting; and to confront novel and puzzling situations or events that can be resolved through problem solving.

Selecting Resources

The map for a thematic unit suggests many of the resources that will be needed. The map for "Journeys" identified appropriate fictional and nonfictional selections. Books, literature, poetry, magazines, newspapers, articles, extracts from larger works, documents, diaries, and official records were included (and the absence of films, videos, and other sources has been previously noted).

Teachers may feel constraints in their selection of resources—both human and material. Many teachers have a traditional orientation that favors an idealistic philosophy which holds that selection of resource persons, literature, art, and other cultural products be of recognized worth by a dominant class. Other teachers with a pragmatic philosophy are open, including representation for popular and diverse cultures, seeking resources that are representative of the lives of real people and that make a difference in the lives of students. The broad, unexpected areas of learning that are opened by thematic units are likely to exceed any teacher's knowledge. Accordingly, adult (teachers, parents, community persons) and student resources should be sought. A great strength of the thematic unit is that it is likely to draw on many community materials, records, collections, and sites.

Designing Subject-Matter Units

Two conflicting approaches exist to designing subject-matter units: the instructional systems approach and the problem solving approach. Those using the instructional systems approach assume the transmission of knowledge to learners. They focus on prespecified ends or objectives and the component parts making up these ends. The teacher as curriculum planner takes responsibility for determining both the ends and means of instruction. By contrast, those using the problem-solving approach assume that knowledge is created by students; therefore, they design units where students test their own ideas and hypotheses.

The Instructional Systems Approach.   The instructional systems approach is used to focus on the competencies of learners to perform in given situations at a prescribed level of achievement. Accordingly, the planning process begins at the end. The teacher starts by asking, "What is it that the learner must know and be able to do upon completion of the unit?" The teacher defines the kinds of situations and conditions to which the learner will be expected to respond and the criteria for acceptable responses. A sample of the performance test that will attest to success may be provided to clarify the target goal.

Next, the teacher makes a task analysis—a listing of the facts, concepts, generalizations, and skills thought to be necessary prerequisites to the final objective. The tasks are then ordered by some principle for sequencing (such as simple to complex). A concept map may be drawn to show what is to be learned and how it is to be ordered. Rules or principles for constructing the presentation of content and the interaction expected from learners as they complete the tasks are formulated. For example, one rule may state that the learner will be taught to identify instances of a concept, then to apply the concept in simple situations, and finally to apply the concept in the complex situation as defined in the domain specifications.

An excellent example of a subject-matter unit planned with a systems approach is "Measurement for Grades One and Two" by Susan Etheridge (Etheridge, 1986). Figure 10–2 shows the conceptual map used in this unit. The unit is based on the central questions: What is measurement? What do we measure? How do we measure and what are the units of measurement? Specific learning objectives are stated, and there are examples of the kinds of situations to be provided so that students can evidence attainment of the objective at the end of the unit. The unit is divided into the components of linear, weight, volume, and temperature measurement. Each component has objectives, materials, teaching strategy, and suggested activities. The sequencing of components is on the basis of easy (concrete) to more difficult (abstract) measurement.

The teaching strategy calls for introducing a topic and concept with a discussion of what the students already know about it, followed by definitions, examples and nonexamples of the concept, and modeling. Students, working in pairs and groups, have opportunity to practice the behavior called for in the objectives—estimating, measuring, comparing, and recording. In later lessons, they are given opportunities to solve the kinds of hypothetical measurement problems stated for the end of unit objectives.

The Problem-Solving Approach. Newer problem-solving units reflect three curricular perspectives:

1. the *academic perspective* and its concern that an authentic view of the subject matter and its methods be represented
2. the *utilitarian perspective* that holds that the unit should be relevant to everyday life
3. the *student-centered perspective* with its concern that the study trigger interests among students and prepare them for further learning

The problem-solving unit begins with an orientation showing the connection between a specific subject-matter domain and the context of everyday life— how the knowledge is helpful in using technology, making a consumer decision, or understanding a social or scientific issue. This relationship is cast as a central question that sets the scene for the unit. This question also functions as the basis for selecting the content and skills of the unit and gives rise to a variety of suitable student-generated activities.

The orientation is followed by direct teaching of basic information and skills necessary for pursuing the question. For example, in one science unit on weather change the central questions are these:

▼   Which factors determine the weather picture?

▼   How do these factors influence weather change?

▼   How can a reliable weather forecast be based on such information?

FIGURE 10–2
Conceptual map

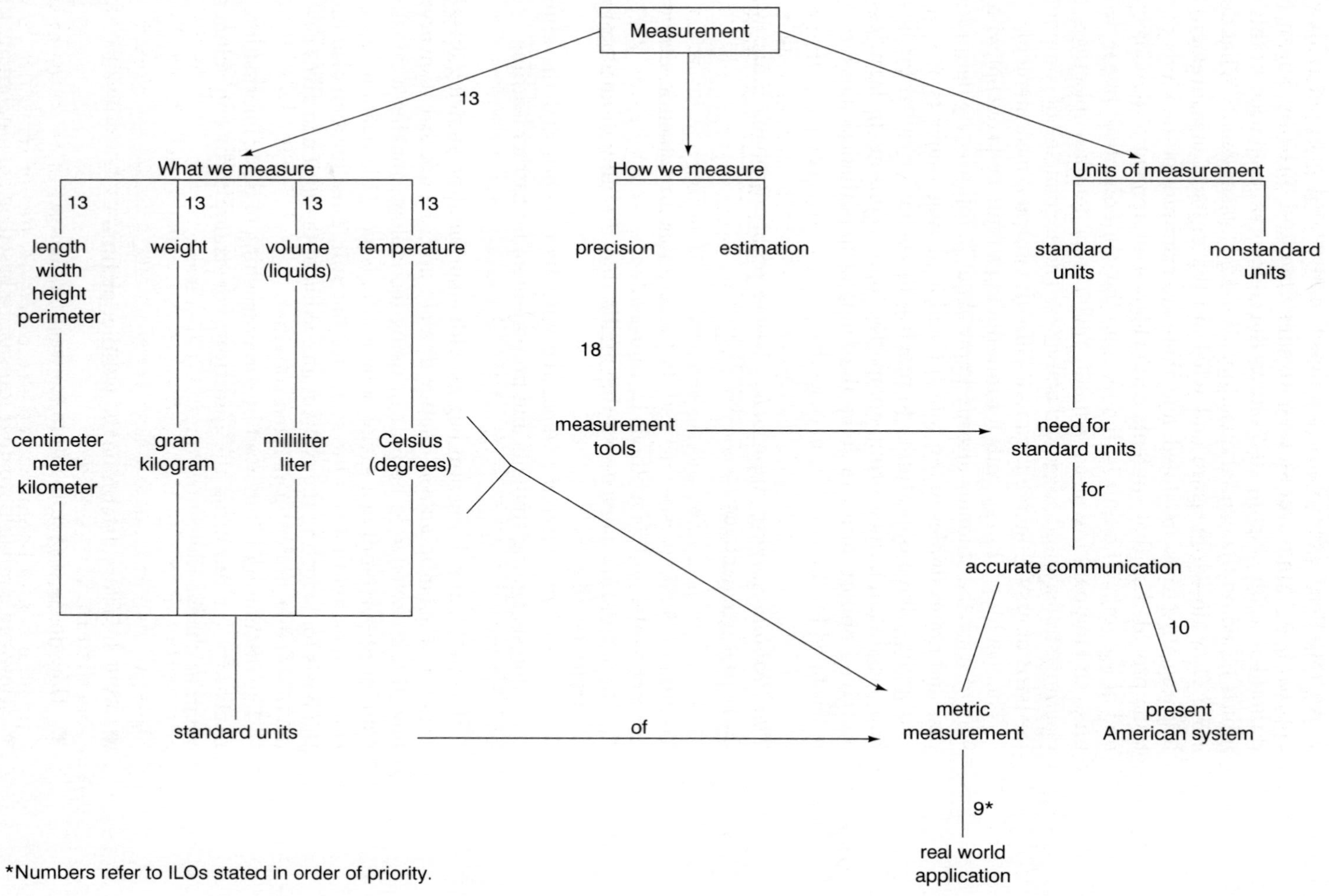

*Numbers refer to ILOs stated in order of priority.

In this unit, students are first taught methods for measuring temperature, air pressure, humidity, wind velocity, and direction, and then they learn how to interpret single weather charts and satellite photographs (Lijnse, Kortland, Eijkelot, Van Genderen, & Hooymayers, 1990). In addition, to access to common basic information, students work on different options in parallel groups. The essentials of all groups are required in subsequent phases of the unit. Hence, there is a reporting session for exchange of ideas among the various groups—those reporting on clouds and cloud formation, those responsible for information on precipitation, and those informed on fronts and high/flow pressure areas.

After students have the basic information and skills and the learning that takes place in studying the optional parts, they are ready to pose their own questions related to the central questions such as which method to use in forecasting, how to interpret forecasts, and what to expect from their reliability. In pursuing the answers to these questions, students engage in a variety of activities, some of which involve contacts with out-of-school sources. Although these activities allow for differences in interests, working styles, and capabilities, students are responsible for their own learning and for the learning of fellow students.

In trying to answer their own questions, students make and test their predictions (hypotheses), seek solutions for problems, test solutions, design their own procedures, and formulate new questions based on the outcomes. They also act as members of an academic community by discussing the assumptions underlying the activity and sharing predictions, procedures, and solutions. Problem-solving units encourage students to use their own backgrounds of experience in the activities, linking their views of the situation (and the world) to the views of a larger scientific community.

PROJECTS AS INQUIRY UNITS

Projects for both young and older learners offer opportunities for self-direction and personal involvement in learning, complementing formal instruction.

Projects for Young Learners

The inquiries of young children are likely to touch on a range of subject matters. In their description of projects for children ages 4–8, Lilian Katz and Sylvia Chard (1989) show how children investigate, record, and report their findings as they study real phenomena in their own environments. Projects are investigations, and the title of the project indicates the direction of effort—"How Houses are Built?" or "Who Measures What is in Our Town?"—unlike the titles of thematic units, which merely indicate subjects—"Houses" and "Measurement." The question form helps young children in their planning, giving focus to their investigations.

In projects, children actively negotiate the questions to be answered, the experiments to be conducted and other features of the effort. In the project "How Water Comes to Our House," children determine the data to be collected, such as where the water comes from; how it is treated, stored, and pumped to households; its uses, quantities used, its properties at different temperatures, and how the findings are to be reported. Children are encouraged to raise questions of personal interest and to take responsibility for the learning tasks.

Selecting an Issue or Topic.   Suitable issues or topics for possible projects by young children are those that:

▼   are partially familiar so that all of the children will be able to generate questions and some of the children will be able to serve as expert resource persons during the inquiry

▼   provide opportunity for students to apply and develop a range of subject matter and basic skills—reading, writing, measuring, drawing, mapping, making music

▼   give opportunity for children to collaborate and cooperate through such activities as model building, construction, dramatic play, making posters and graphs, creating diagrams, developing questions, interviewing, recording, and tallying surveys

▼   take advantage of local resources—sites, experts, and historical and currently critical events

Planning and Conducting the Project.   Projects are generally planned and conducted in three phases, after the teacher has selected the general issue or topic.

Phase 1: Getting Started.   The teacher encourages children to express their associations, knowledge and interest in the topic area. Children raise questions about the topic and begin to explore how these questions might be answered. Children are encouraged to take the initiative in exploring the topic, finding resources, and suggesting activities.

Planning in this phase includes identifying the information needed and means for collecting it. Children also decide about an audience for their work (parents, other students, or others) and begin to accept responsibility for the different tasks related to the undertaking.

Phase 2: Collecting Information.   When the children know what information they want from different sources and how this information will help answer their central questions, they prepare interview questions, observation forms, and consider the use of cameras, videos, and other equipment for data collection. Although secondary sources (texts, films, articles, reference works) are consulted, primary sources (interviews, field trips, and other first-hand experiences) are more characteristic of the project. The preparation of field trips includes adherence to school policy as well as clarifying the questions to be asked, people to be interviewed, observations to be made, and ways to record the data. Classroom rehearsal of the methodology is important.

After returning to the classroom, children discuss their findings. Conflicts in interpreting the data collected by different teams may require repeated visits to the site. As the work progresses, children give more attention to how they will present their findings to the intended audience.

Phase 3: Culminating the Project. In the primary grades, dramatic play using what the children have constructed is a common culmination. Children assume roles associated with the setting they have studied. Older children often present the findings to an audience through publications, panel discussions, displays, demonstrations, and other public presentations.

The culmination is an opportunity for children to review their work and to indicate what they know and can do now that they didn't know when they started. Culminations are also beginnings in that students indicate how they will use what they have learned in some new area of inquiry. A good study is known for the questions it generates.

Projects for Older Learners

Secondary school teachers think of projects as related to school subjects. They either select a subject-matter topic that is taught in the course and together with students create a project around a topic, or they start with an idea for a project and then see how the content of the course can be related to the project.

The projects involve students in taking appropriate action to improve, change, serve, or otherwise influence constructively some public matter. Students deal with real situations as opposed to imaginary or speculative ones and with issues that are significant to them.

In planning the project, teacher and students analyze what needs to be done, what can be done, and what the possible hurdles are. Students must be informed about the issues with which they propose to deal. In addition to general information from texts, essential information for a project is individualized in character. Usually students gain their information from local communities by consulting records, individuals, and organizations. When the students have worked out many of the details, they must get cooperation from school administrators and other adults with whom they may be working on the project. Steps to ensure community understanding is also a part of the planning process.

Students must be clear about the purpose of the project and weigh the difficulty of the concept and its likely demands on time and effort. There are variations for scheduling projects—a fixed block of time (such as a five-week project), a project where the class devotes one hour a week over an extended period of time, or a "seminar in the round" where students meet at a scheduled time to plan and review progress and to build connections between the project and their formal course work.

Some teachers prefer projects that draw on two subjects. For instance, in New Richmond, Wisconsin, a math teacher and a teacher of economics made it possible for students to conduct a study regarding a proposed community golf course. The study called for statistical application (math) and market research (economics). After the data was gathered and analyzed, the final products were videotaped documented statements that influenced a community's decision not

ACTIVITY 10–1   SELECTING CRITERIA FOR
USE IN DESIGNING ACTIVITIES FOR
INSTRUCTIONAL UNITS

Criteria are useful as heuristics. In making planning decisions in accordance with criteria, teachers take into account many more possibilities than when planning without stated criteria. The use of criteria will contribute to a more balanced and coherent curriculum plan. Whenever two or more people are to engage in curriculum planning and desire consistency in their plans, they should first agree on the criteria that will guide their efforts and then frequently check each others' work against these criteria.

What criteria would guide your curriculum development?

	Essential	Useful	Less Useful	Not Useful	Inappropriate
The activity should:					
1. Relate to large curriculum goals—critical thinking, problem solving, self confidence, or other valued ability and dispositions.					
2. Put students in touch with a powerful idea or form of perception.					
3. Be scaffolded so that students are not confused or frustrated.					
4. Challenge students so they will extend their present status.					
5. Allow for individualism so that those with different backgrounds and levels of development can contribute and progress.					
6. Fit within existing constraints of time, space, resources, and student characteristics.					
7. Provoke emotional and physical as well as intellectual responses.					
8. Offer multiple perspectives on a topic, issue, or problem.					

▼ ─── ▼

ACTIVITY 10–1 *continued*

1. Rank the following criteria as essential, useful, less useful, not useful, or inappropriate. Select the *five* most essential criteria that you would want to guide the planning of activities by a group of teachers.
2. Compare the criteria you rank as essential with what significant others (administrators, fellow teachers, students) consider essential. Try to account for differences through a discussion that will clarify the meaning of the statements, reveal possible consequences from applying the criteria, and identify reasons for the different views regarding what is essential.

▲ ─── ▲

	Essential	Useful	Less Useful	Not Useful	Inappropriate
9. Help students make connections to what they are learning in other subject fields.					
10. Contribute to the quality of life outside of school, (i.e., be real).					
11. Contribute to multiple goals and outcomes.					
12. Allow students to choose, design, revise, carry out, and evaluate the activity.					
13. Offer students many ways to construct knowledge—through movement, manipulation, visuals, not just through text and number.					
14. Conform to official mandates regarding the content to be taught.					
15. Give students opportunity to see how the activity fits within the bigger curriculum picture.					
16. Draw upon community resource people, sites, records, and other documents.					
17. Intergrate skills in larger natural tasks rather than in isolated skill exercises.					

▼ ——————————————————————————————————— ▼

ACTIVITY 10–2   CONSTRUCTING AN
INSTRUCTIONAL UNIT AS A DOCUMENT

As you know, there is no single procedure for designing units of instruction. Some teachers begin by thinking about the intended learners, content, or time frame. Often teachers are stimulated to plan by thinking about materials and activities. Still others commence with purposes and objectives. In this activity, it is suggested you consider all of these factors and more, but not necessarily in any particular order. Prior activities and illustrations and guidelines found in the chapter have suggested different types of units and techniques for designing them.

This activity is an opportunity to organize your unit planning as a document which can be presented to others. The format suggested is a common one. However, feel free to modify the form to suit your own purposes. Your unit may be a thematic, subject-matter, or inquiry type.

1.   Title for the unit.
2.   Make a statement identifying those for whom the unit is designed.
3.   Present a rationale or justification for this unit. How will the unit enrich the lives of the students? Contribute to educational goals and other values? Where does the unit fit into the overall curriculum?
4.   State the purposes, objectives, or possible outcomes to be achieved through this unit.
5.   Indicate the content in the unit. What are the overarching ideas, generalizations, central questions, concepts, processes, skills, perspectives, or other values that students might attain or construct through this unit? A cognitive map might be appropriate.
6.   Illustrate the nature of learning activities within the unit:
     a.   Describe the introductory activities that motivate and set the stage for initial inquiry. Indicate the degree of students' choice and ways for activating background knowledge.
     b.   Describe or illustrate implementing activities—tasks and ways for students to collect and analyze information related to the goals or "central questions" of the unit. You may wish to state the criteria you are using in planning learning activities or the principles which underlie your teaching strategies.
7.   Indicate possible resources for the unit. Include both primary sources (local resource persons, sites, materials) and secondary sources (texts, references).
8.   Indicate the ways you might evaluate the unit, including ways to collect evidence related to both intended and unintended outcomes—observations, self reports, products, and ways to interest and approach them.

▲ ——————————————————————————————————— ▲

to build the course (Beck, et al., 1991). The ideal in curriculum integration of two subjects is that students will advance in both.

SUMMARY

Units differ in their flexibility. Some are fixed in purpose; others are designed to promote multiple outcomes. *Thematic units* have a broad focus which allows student participation in organizing subthemes and alternate routes to common ends. *Subject-matter units* typically focus on prespecified topics and objectives, and the logic of the subject matter determines the organizational plan. *Inquiry units* have a central question but invite students to generate and pursue related tasks and subquestions, individually and in groups. Illustrations of each type of unit have been presented.

Unit planning rests on the distinction between the focal point or organizing center of the unit (theme, topic, problem, or central question) and the content (ideas, values, skills, concepts, perspectives, and the like) likely to be constructed by learners as they pursue the focus of their study. Teachers and students have wide latitude in what to propose as an organizing center and in choices for activities related to the center. Although the center or focus may be significant in its own right, it is chiefly a vehicle for engaging students in activities that will elicit content consistent with educational goals. The fact that there are widely diverse ways to help students create socially desired knowledge and preferences supports the practice of selecting foci and activities that respond to community, student, and teacher interests.

Although there is a recognized format for public presentation of the unit as a document, the process for creating the unit need not occur in any particular order. Resources, content, purpose, centers, activities, and the like are important design factors that are used when planning and implementing units. Guidelines for making decisions about these factors have been presented and different approaches to the planning of units have been illustrated. Variation in the procedures and the principles applied is accounted for by both the types of units and the value orientation of the teachers.

In considering units which integrate subject matters, we recognize the importance of trying to extend students' knowledge in several subjects rather than exploiting one field in the interest of another. Throughout the chapter, there has been an emphasis on the autonomy of the teacher and students in curriculum development without ignoring the problematic issue of the establishment of an appropriate relationship between the knowledge students construct through their experiences with an instructional unit and the official course of study or professional standards in a subject area.

QUESTIONS FOR DISCUSSION

1. Should knowledge constructed by students conform to what the state or district prescribes or should the students challenge these prescriptions? What is your position on this issue?

2. It is sometimes charged that instructional units tend to center on current and local interests and thus are tainted by "Presentism" and "Localism." Is the development of multiple perspectives and interest in other times and other places precluded by a focus on matters of immediate concern?

3. Children can learn mathematical measurement by engaging in the performing arts, building sets, plotting the path of a turtle using Logo, and many other ways. Educational goals in other areas can also be attained through varied experiences. What is the significance of this finding for teachers and policy makers?

4. In what circumstances might it be best to develop curriculum plans using the instructional systems approach with its focus on prespecified objectives, task analysis, and logical sequence of content?

5. The explosion of knowledge and the growing heterogeneity of individual subjects makes it difficult to identify essential content for organizational elements. Should we abandon the idea of curriculum coherence across units and courses?

6. What would you say to a teacher whose instructional unit plan is based on the idea that the curriculum should provide a break from everyday experience rather than build on it?

7. If curriculum is grounded in the events that students and teachers jointly construct in the classroom, can preplanning of units be anything more than setting the stage for learning?

REFERENCES

Beck, R. H., et al. (1991). Vocational and academic teachers work together. *Educational Leadership, 49*(2): 24–31.

Etheridge, S. M. (1986). Measurement for grades one and two. In G. S. Posner & N. Rudnitsky (Eds.), *Course design: A guide to curriculum development in teachers* (3rd ed.), pp. 172–188. New York: Longman.

Katz, L. G. (1989). *Engaging children's minds: The project approach*. New York: Ablex Publishing Co.

Katz, L. G., & Chard, S. C. (In press.) The project approach. In J. E. Johnson (Ed.), *Approach to early childhood education*, (2nd ed.). New York: Merrill/Macmillan Publishing Company.

Lijnse, P. L., Kortland, K., Eijkelot, H. M. C., Van Genderen, D., & Hooymayers, H. P. (1990). A thematic physics curriculum: A balance between contradictory curricular forces. *Science Education, 94*(1): 95–103.

Walmsley, S. A., & Walp, T. T. (1990). Interpreting literature and composing in the language arts curriculum, philosophy and practice. *The Elementary School Journal, 90*(3): 251–274.

Coda

▼ ─────────────────────────────────────── ▼

TEACHERS AND THE SUBSTANTIVE
ISSUES OF CURRICULUM

The curriculums of the teachers described in this text are linked by three substantive issues or questions that are fundamental to the curriculum field:

1. What should be the purposes, goals, or intents of the curriculum?
2. What activities or learning opportunities can best contribute to these purposes and also be of intrinsic worth?
3. How can the activities be arranged to extend and broaden learning?

None of the teachers discussed in this book gave the same answer to these questions. The orientations of these teachers, and of their students, to these questions depended on their interests and values. Further, these curricula are not directly comparable because they were created in response to widely different circumstances.

This is not to say that the curricula are equal in terms of generally accepted criteria. Major criteria for judging a curriculum are whether attention has been given to all three commonplaces or questions, not just one or two; whether the data used in deciding on answers are both comprehensive and valid; and whether the answer to each of the questions is consistent with the others.

The best curriculums do three things:

1. They address the wants and needs of learners, as described in Part 1.
2. They respond to social conditions (local, national, world) as shown in Part 2.
3. They draw on a wide range of resources of knowledge, including the academic fields, master practitioners of occupations, and the cultural capital of those living in a given community.

Parts 3 and 5 feature the use of such cultural resources, which take into account learners, society, and the intellectual heritage of cultures. Curricula that do this are considered to be better than those that overlook one or more of the sources.

The criterion that calls for consistency among goals, activities, and theory of learning is important in judging a curriculum. A corollary is that the development of a good curriculum requires considering alternative approaches to learn-

▲ ─────────────────────────────────────── ▲

ing activities and to curriculum organization. The models for initiating curriculum as found in Part 5 may assist in this regard.

Missing from this text is elaboration of the political and institutional constraints on teacher and student initiatives. Certainly, federal, state, district, and school curriculum policies influence classroom curricular choice. A teacher is more likely to teach mathematics when it is prescribed than to teach physical education. However, we have shown that the meanings generated in the mathematics class are likely to be far different from what officials have in mind. Indeed, the work of teachers as described in Part 4 of the text may be viewed as encouraging the warranted subversion of the official curriculum. Also, little attention has been given in this book to the professional organizations in setting curriculum standards and the way these standards establish a context for what teachers do. These omissions are deliberate. The rhetorical world of curriculum policy making and related efforts to centralize and to test curriculum have already been well publicized.

A final comment bears on the substantive issue of whether the curriculum should be a prescribed plan for learning. The concept of curriculum as an organizational plan began with the assumption of an orderly universe and the belief that curriculum could be organized to ensure that students could be systematically led to understand the parts that made up knowledge of that universe. Accordingly, curriculum was to put order into schooling and into learning. The notion of a prescribed curriculum that connects things for learners in a systematic progression is now challenged for many reasons: There is a problem of selecting from among multiple disciplines that purport to describe the world (more than 1,000 already existing and new ones being constructed); the varied interpretations of meaning and conflicting views regarding the nature of a given discipline by those who represent that discipline, and the personal knowledge and meanings that students construct as they relate their own background of experiences to the public knowledge taught in schools all make curriculum problematic rather than prescriptive.

The initiatives of the teachers selected for this text reflect a problematic view of curriculum, one that does not see curriculum as overly determined. Accordingly, the teachers seek rich and challenging opportunities in play, ideas, and the world from which students generate their own concerns, interests, questions, and passions, and perhaps, find their life-long directions. As they pursue their inquiries, students are expected to make their own continuities and to connect with subject matter and the world at large. As a counterpart to a cafeteria of school learning where one task follows another in discrete and often repetitive assignments, a curriculum of concern allows for more sustained focus on both the work of accomplished people or ideas of particular interest, or projects that unite students in a common pursuit. It enables teacher and students alike to concentrate effectively by engaging with a central problem and focusing on their goals.

As indicated in the classroom illustrations, most of the teachers help students keep their excitement for learning. Collaboration with peers in projects, discussing, explaining, considering alternatives, and drawing on a range of cultural perspectives help overcome the limitations of an individual's single view.

Students are also sustained by seeing their ideas in different contexts and by having opportunities to monitor the problem-solving strategies of those with more experience. The majority of the teachers put students in touch with the crafts and tools of disciplines that relate to their personal concerns and help them express themselves in appropriate ways so that their private ideas have the possibility of contributing to the lives of others.

SUBJECT INDEX

NAME INDEX